The Political Systems of
the Socialist States

By the same author

Kuba und der Weltkommunismus (1967)
Revolutionspartei und Politische Stabilität in México (1969)
Jugoslawien: Politik, Gesellschaft, Wirtschaft (1975)
Politisches Lexikon Europa, 2 vols. (1981)

The Political Systems of the Socialist States

An Introduction to Marxist-Leninist Regimes

Robert K. Furtak
Professor of Political Science
University of Landau

St. Martin's Press   New York

First published in the United States of America in 1986

Printed in Great Britain

ISBN 0-312-62527-8

Library of Congress Cataloging-in-Publication Data

Furtak, Robert K.
  The political systems of the socialist states.

  Bibliography: p.
  Includes index.
  1. Communist countries——Political and government.
2. Communist state. 3. People's democracies. I. Title.
JC474.F84   1986   320.9171'7   85-27623
ISBN 0-312-62527-8

Contents

LIST OF TABLES AND FIGURES

Tables

Figures

Preface

The intention underlying this textbook is to provide basic, up-to-date information on the political forces and institutions as well as the foreign policy of the socialist states. It is essentially descriptive; considerations of space forbade a discussion of political processes.

A survey presents the main characteristics of the political systems of the socialist states; peculiar features are elaborated in the chapters on the individual countries. These chapters proceed, in principle, on uniform lines. After briefly describing the constitutional foundations and basic features of the political system, they deal with the Marxist-Leninist parties, inclusive of their road to power and their position in regard to the Communist Party of the Soviet Union; the social organisations, including the so-called 'bloc parties'; and the state organs at central and local levels, including the judiciary. Deviations from this pattern exist in the chapters on those states which have a federative structure or show other special features, like Yugoslavia, because of its system of social self-management. Each chapter also deals with foreign policy not least because this field conspicuously reveals distinctive attitudes and distinctive behaviour of the socialist states, and, briefly, national defence. States which present historical, ideological and structural peculiarities and/or claim to possess model character are discussed in more detail than others.

Recommendations for further reading appended to the survey and to the chapters on the various countries should facilitate extended work on the political systems of the socialist states.

My thanks are particularly due to Mr Philip Woolley, MA

vii

(Oxon) and also to Mrs Karin Wörmer, who with much patience helped me to put the text into correct English. Errors in the content remain, of course, my own.

Stegen, Freiburg, July 1985   Robert K. Furtak

List of Abbreviations

ASEAN	Association of Southeast Asian Nations
BCP	Bulgarian Communist Party
BOAL	Basic organisation of associated labour (Yugoslavia)
CC	Central Committee
CDR	Committee for the Defence of the Revolution (Cuba)
CMEA	Council for Mutual Economic Assistance (also called Comecon)
CPC	Communist Party of China
	Communist Party of Cuba
	Communist Party of Czechoslovakia
	Central People's Committee (North Korea)
CPPCC	Chinese People's Political Consultative Conference
CPSU	Communist Party of the Soviet Union
CPV	Communist Party of Vietnam
CPY	Communist Party of Yugoslavia
CSCE	Conference on Security and Co-operation in Europe
DOSAAF	Dobrovolnoe Obshchestvo Sodeystviya Armii, Aviacii i Flotu (Voluntary Association for the Promotion of the Army, Air Force and Navy — USSR)
DPRK	Democratic People's Republic of Korea
DRV	Democratic Republic of Vietnam
EC	European Community
FEC	Federal Executive Council (Yugoslavia)
FRG	Federal Republic of Germany

FSUD	Front of Socialist Unity and Democracy (Rumania)
GDR	German Democratic Republic
GNA	Grand National Assembly (Rumania)
GPK	Great People's Khural (Mongolia)
HSWP	Hungarian Socialist Workers' Party
ICP	Indo-Chinese Communist Party
INF	Intermediate-range nuclear forces
KGB	Komitet Gosudarstvennoy Bezopasnosti (Committee for State Security — USSR)
LCY	League of Communists of Yugoslavia
LPF	Lao Patriotic Front
LPRP	Lao People's Revolutionary Party
MPR	Mongolian People's Republic
MPRP	Mongolian People's Revolutionary Party
M-26-7	Movimiento 26 de Julio (26 July Movement — Cuba)
NATO	North Atlantic Treaty Organisation
NLF	National Liberation Front (Vietnam)
NPC	National People's Congress (China)
OAL	Organisation of associated labour (Yugoslavia)
PDRL	People's Democratic Republic of Laos
PLA	Party of Labour of Albania
	People's Liberation Army (China)
PPF	Patriotic People's Front (Hungary)
PRC	People's Republic of China
PRON	Patriotyczny Ruch Odrodzenia Narodowego (Patriotic Movement of National Rebirth — Poland)
PSP	Popular Socialist Party (Cuba)
PUWP	Polish United Workers' Party
RCP	Rumanian Communist Party
RLG	Royal Lao Government
ROK	Republic of Korea (South Korea)
RSFSR	Russian Soviet Federal Socialist Republic
SAC	State Administration Council (North Korea)
SAWPY	Socialist Alliance of the Working People of Yugoslavia
SFRY	Socialist Federal Republic of Yugoslavia

SPA	Supreme People's Assembly (North Korea, Laos)
SRR	Socialist Republic of Rumania
SRV	Socialist Republic of Vietnam
SUPG	Socialist Unity Party of Germany
UNO	United Nations Organisation
USA	United States of America
USSR	Union of Soviet Socialist Republics
WPK	Workers' Party of Korea
WTO	Warsaw Treaty Organisation
YPA	Yugoslav People's Army

1 Introduction

This study deals with fifteen states which are ruled by political parties committed to the teachings of Marx, Engels and Lenin. They account for about a quarter of the world's territory and about a third of the world's population (Table 1:1). There are many more states, indeed, where the ruling party identifies itself with Marxism-Leninism and/or has proclaimed as its goal the establishment of socialism, such as Afghanistan, Angola, Congo (Brazzaville), Ethiopia, Mozambique, Nicaragua, South Yemen and others. If self-ascription were the defining criterion, the number of 'socialist' states would far exceed thirty. The considerable variation in the number of states qualified in relevant studies as 'socialist', 'communist' or 'Marxist-Leninist' demonstrates alone that self-ascription does not provide an objective basis for the classification of a regime.

So the only valid criteria, in determining the socialist character of a state, must be as follows: the possession of the monopoly of power by a political party which adheres to Marxism-Leninism and claims to be building socialism and/or communism; the elevation of Marxism-Leninism to the exclusive ideology of state and society; the predominance of public ownership of the means of production, and the centralised planning of the economy. Only the combination of these attributes constitutes a Marxist-Leninist regime, or a socialist state in the Marxist-Leninist sense. Both terms are equated here.

It is admittedly difficult, if not impossible, to draw a clear-cut line between socialist and non-socialist states, because the defining criteria fray at the edges and because the states which are commonly accepted as socialist display divergent features.

1

Table 1:1   *The socialist states*

State	Area (thousands of sq. miles)	Population mid-1982 (millions)	Communist Party membership c.1983
Socialist People's Republic of Albania	11	2.9	122,000
People's Republic of Bulgaria	43	8.9	825,876
People's Republic of China	3,704	1,008.2	40,000,000
Republic of Cuba	44	9.8	434,143
Czechoslovak Socialist Republic	49	15.4	1,600,000
German Democratic Republic	42	16.7	2,202,277
Hungarian People's Republic	36	10.7	852,000
Democratic People's Republic of Korea	47	18.7	3,000,000
People's Democratic Republic of Laos	91	3.6	35,000
Mongolian People's Republic	610	1.8	76,240
Polish People's Republic	122	36.2	2,327,349
Socialist Republic of Rumania	92	22.5	3,300,000
Union of Soviet Socialist Republics	8,621	270.0	18,331,000
Socialist Republic of Vietnam	126	57.0	1,727,784
Socialist Federal Republic of Yugoslavia	99	22.6	2,200,627
Total	13,737	1,505.0	77,034,000

Sources: World Bank, *World Development Report 1984* (New York, 1984) — area and population; Richard F. Staar (ed.), *Year-book on International Communist Affairs 1984: Parties and Revolutionary Movements* (Stanford, Cal., 1984) — Com-munist Party Membership (claim; for Laos estimate).

(Yugoslavia, for example, has no centrally planned economy.) Although the Communist Parties legitimise their rule in the same way, they show differences in the field of ideology, and the socialist states contain institutional and structural divergencies. Both these facts result from an increasingly discriminatory interpretation and application of the Marxist classics as determined by the mode of the communists' seizure of power, the social and cultural background of the party leaders, the political and socio-economic structure of a country and the system of values of the society inherited by the communists, the country's geographical location (its proximity to, or distance from, the Soviet Union), and the changing international environment.

In order to delimit the number of states for consideration in this study, I have employed a fourth criterion: the recognition of the socialist character of a state by the Soviet authorities. They call many communist-ruled countries states with a 'socialist orientation', obviously taking into account the ideological eclecticism of some parties which claim to be Marxist-Leninist, uncertainty about the further development of the regime or the fact that the Marxist-Leninist party has not yet consolidated its power. This last fact as well as the lack of a sufficient organisational base for exercising power seem to explain the present exclusion, for instance, of the People's Republic of Kampuchea from the 'socialist world system', even though its constitution of June 1981 declares that the state 'is gradually advancing towards socialism', and the Communist Party, whose membership is estimated at merely a few hundreds, is the leading political force.

Although the states dealt with are ruled by political parties which consider themselves communist and declare themselves to be striving ultimately for the establishment of communism, I have chosen to call them '*socialist*': first, because these parties have not yet realised a communist society as envisaged by Marx and Engels, so that the states rightly call themselves socialist, and, second, because in Marxist theory a 'communist state' is a contradiction in terms (as will become evident in the next chapter).

2 The Characteristics of Socialist Systems: A Survey

THE 'SOCIALIST STATE'

Marx and Engels viewed the state, in general, as a coercive force of the ruling class; in particular, the nineteenth-century capitalist state was seen as an instrument used by the bourgeoisie for the oppression and exploitation of the proletariat. They believed, therefore, that the abolition of the capitalist relations of production would do away with the class society and subsequently also with the rule of the proletariat as a class once it had seized power.[1] According to Engels, taking possession of the means of production in the name of society would be the last independent act of the state. The interference of a state power in social relations would become superfluous, and the government of persons would be replaced by the administration of things and the direction of the production processes — the state would *wither away*.[2] Lenin, too, argued that a 'particular repressive force' would become unnecessary as soon as the majority of the people exercised power, and that the proletarian state, whose activities would gradually decrease, would 'inevitably' wither away, even if this might take a long time.[3] However, contrary to the prediction of Marx, Engels and Lenin (before the October Revolution of 1917), in those countries where the owners of the means of production had been expropriated completely or to a large extent, a giant state machinery has evolved, which serves the Communist Party as an instrument for the domination of the people and the transformation of society.

When considering the states which may be defined as

4

socialist, the communists follow Marx and Lenin. Marx distinguished between the 'first' phase of the communist society, emerging from the capitalist one, and a second, 'higher' phase of the communist society. In the former stage the producer would receive according to his work, and this would create inequality. In the latter, however, characterised by the elimination of the division of labour as well as the difference between intellectual and manual work, and by affluence, each would receive 'according to his needs'.[4] Lenin called the first, 'lower' phase 'socialism', considering it as the transitional stage from capitalism to communism.[5]

According to Marx, in the period of transition from capitalism to the classless communist society 'the state can be nothing but the *revolutionary dictatorship of the proletariat*'.[6] In fact, the socialist states, except for the Soviet Union, consider themselves as dictatorships of the proletariat. At its Twenty-First Congress of 1959 the Communist Party of the Soviet Union (CPSU) declared that the USSR had entered the period of the 'comprehensive building of communist society', and in its Programme of 1961 it proclaimed the Soviet Union to be a 'socialist all-people's state'; that is, a state which is an instrument not of a class but of the whole people. Thus the Soviets departed from Marx, because the preconditions for communism were (and are) far from being realised in the USSR, so that they were rightly attacked by the Chinese. After Nikita Khrushchev, in October 1964, had been ousted from his position as first secretary of the Central Committee of the CPSU, the term 'all people's state' was for a while no longer used. Finally, however, it was embodied in the constitution of October 1977.

The constitutions of the other socialist states allocate all power to the 'working people', the 'working class and all working people' or simply to the 'people'. Only Albania, North Korea, and Vietnam clearly declare themselves to be a 'dictatorship of the proletariat'. The Chinese constitution says that the 'people' make up the dictatorship, apparently in view of the fact that about 80 per cent of the population are peasants; Yugoslavia's constitution states that the dictatorship of the proletariat has the specific form of a 'socialist self-management democracy'. Mongolia declares itself to be a socialist state 'in the form of a people's democracy'. Some socialist states have placed themselves in the transitional stage from the dictatorship of the proletariat to a people's state and call it the stage of a 'developed socialist society'. (The preamble of the Polish constitution speaks of the strengthening of the 'people's state'; the Czechoslovak constitution calls the state a 'people's organisation'.)

In the political sphere the socialist states show the following set of common features: (1) The permanent domination of state and society by one and the same political party, or in fact by a small, self-co-opting élite. The aforesaid allocations of power, therefore, are practically irrelevant, because the only real power rests with the Marxist-Leninist party, whatever stage of development the country might consider itself to have reached. (2) The acceptance of only one system of values, based on the teachings of Marx, Engels, Lenin and, in China, partially, Mao Zedong (Mao Tse-tung). It forms the binding ideology for social education and integration, and constitutes one, though not the sole, source for motivating and explaining political decisions. (3) Consequently, there is a lack of autonomous political or social sub-systems — except, to a limited extent, in Poland and Yugoslavia — because the entire political process and all media of communication are in the hands of the Marxist-Leninist party. (4) The organisation of the state — again, except for Yugoslavia — on the principle of democratic centralism (see pp. 8-9). This principle is supplemented by that of dual subordination, whereby the administrative organ at any given level of government is responsible and accountable to the administrative organ at the next higher level. This implies that the decision-making and administrative structure is strongly centralistic and hierarchical.

In the economic sphere the characteristics of the socialist states are public ownership of the means of production, and directive planning of economic processes. In Poland and Yugoslavia, however, agricultural land is predominantly in private ownership, and there is also a substantial private sector in trade, catering, and transport; moreover, in Yugoslavia foreign trade is not a monopoly of the state. Nevertheless, the socialist sector is to be considered prevailing in these two countries, too, when taking into account such indicators as its share in the national income and the number it employs. This is likewise true of Vietnam, which has not yet completed the introduction of socialist relations of production in its southern part, although probably not of Laos. Yet Yugoslavia definitely differs from the other socialist states in the lack of central, directive planning. Notwithstanding, it is socialist if the relations of production are considered to be the decisive criterion.[7] Marx and Engels considered the transfer of the means of production to the state only as a first step, by which the proletariat would abolish itself as a class and the state as a state. It is true that Marx advocated the regulation of production through planning in order to eliminate anarchic capitalist production, but he also said that the 'centralised government' must give way to the 'self-government of the producers'.[8] By introducing workers' self-management in socialised enterprises in June 1950, the Yugoslav communists created an institutional framework which would enable the producers to decide on the conditions and fruits of their work, although this right is in reality more or less formal and limited, due, among other reasons, to the effects of market forces. Anyway, Yugoslavia's 'market socialism', the combination of predominantly social property of the means of production with market mechanisms, offers the producers greater chances of participation than does the state-owned economy in the other communist-ruled states.

THE 'LEADING ROLE' OF THE MARXIST-LENINIST PARTY

There have been three different ways in which communists have achieved a monopoly of power. First, it has been achieved by the seizure of power by own efforts, either through the overthrow of a 'bourgeois' government (Russia) or as a result of a civil war and/or of a war with another state (Yugoslavia, China and Vietnam). Second, the takeover has been effected with the political and/or military aid of an existing socialist state: the Soviet Union in the case of the European states of Bulgaria, Czechoslovakia, the German Democratic Republic (GDR), Hungary, Poland and Rumania, and furthermore, Mongolia and North Korea; Yugoslavia in the case of Albania; and Vietnam in the case of Laos. Third, there is the special case of Cuba, where radical but ideologically drifting, revolutionaries with a bourgeois background took over power and did not accept Marxism-Leninism as the theoretical foundation of action until the political and socio-economic transformation of the country was already in full swing.

Once having achieved leadership in state and society, the Marxist-Leninist party will not relinquish it, nor can other political parties challenge it, because communists claim that their rule is legitimated by the historical mission of the proletariat. According to Marx and Engels, the working class is destined to consummate a predetermined development towards communism, and the communists, having the advantage over the mass of the proletariat of insight into the course of the proletarian movement, is called upon to lead it.[9] Lenin argued that the working class by itself develops only a trade-unionist consciousness and that in order to wage a real class-struggle it needs a vanguard organisation which should be composed mainly of professional revolutionaries.[10] Eventually, Stalin (with reference to Lenin) stressed that the dictatorship of the proletariat is 'essentially' the dictatorship of its vanguard,[11] and *de facto* the former was replaced by the latter.

The 'leading role' of the 'vanguard of the working class' — or, as only in the Soviet Union, the 'vanguard of the whole people' — with more or less emphasis, has been established in the constitutions of the socialist states. In this way the *de facto* situation ever since the establishment of communist rule has found its legalisation, too. The Yugoslav constitution, however, limits the leadership of the communists to 'guiding ideological and political action' for 'safeguarding and further developing the socialist revolution and socialist social relations of self-management' and to the 'strengthening of socialist social and democratic consciousness'.[12]

The realisation of the 'leading role' is ensured by the Leninist principle of democratic centralism, which underlies the organisation and the decision-making process of the Communist Party, and entails the following: (1) the election of all leading organs from the bottom to the top; (2) the accountability of party organs to the party organisations which have elected them and to higher organs in the party hierarchy; (3) the strict subordination of the minority to the majority; (4) the binding force of decisions made by higher organs on lower organs and all party members. Democratic centralism implies the adherence to the 'correct' political line, which is determined by those, who are just in power, and the prohibition — often violated, however, in the history of the Communist Parties — of factionalism. While adjusting to practical situations, the party must uphold ideological and organisational monolithic unity in order to be able to fulfil the 'mission of the working class'.

This unity does not, however, mean that differences of opinion are strictly prohibited. On the contrary, every party member has the right to express his opinion and to make suggestions or to criticise party policy within the party's organisations. But once a resolution has been passed, a party member may not act against it and may no longer express his deviating opinion. The Yugoslav communists stress the democratic component more strongly in as much as a party member is obliged to act according to the majority decision but is allowed to retain his personal view and may, if he disagrees with party policy, resign from the party.

For some socialist states with deep ethnic and cultural cleavages, the socialising function of the Communist Party is of great importance. The constant exercises in Marxist-Leninist attitudes and values, coupled with permanent and tight-knit controls, serve to reduce traditional values and beliefs. These are to be replaced by a new political culture based on the consensus on the foundations of a socialist order of society as defined by the party. Events in Czechoslovakia 1968, and in Poland 1980-81, however, have shown that the communists have so far not been entirely successful.

PARTY–STATE RELATIONSHIP

In order to perform their functions of leadership, direction and control in state and society efficiently, the ruling Communist Parties are organised in accordance with the administrative division of the state. (For an example, see Fig. 15:1 on pp. 222-3 which depicts the structure of party and state in the Soviet Union.) The state institutions put the party's decisions into effect: the representative bodies transfer party resolutions into constitutional and other law, and the administrative organs implement the laws. In fact, they carry out the resolutions and directives of the party's Central Committee, or rather those of the Political Bureau (or its functional equivalent) which is the *de facto* government, and of the Secretariat of the Central Committee. (The party congresses have a merely acclamatory function.) The following measures ensure the transfer of the party's will to the state organs and social organisations, and the control of its implementation:

(1)   The simultaneous holding of a party office and a government office by one person.

(2)   The system of *nomenklatura*.

(3)   The binding force of party resolutions and directives.

Supreme party and state functions can be merged in three different ways: first, between the party leader (the secretary general or the first secretary) and the head of government (chairman of the Council of Ministers) — at present in Cuba, Laos and Poland; second, between the party leader and the chairman of the permanent organ of the national assembly (the Presidium or its functional equivalent), who performs the functions of head of state — as at present in Albania, Bulgaria, Cuba, the GDR and Mongolia; and third, between the party leader and the individual head of state — as in Czechoslovakia, North Korea and Rumania. (In Yugoslavia these two offices were merged in the person of Tito.) In Cuba the party leader and head of state is concurrently head of government; in Czechoslovakia, North Korea and Rumania the head of state may chair the cabinet. In all these cases the power of state institutions derives less from the constitution than from the party leaders' membership of them. This is particularly true of the Presidium of the national assembly, which, in contrast to the Council of Ministers, does not have an administrative apparatus of its own.

The position of party leader and the offices of head of state or government are kept separate in China, Hungary, the Soviet Union (since March 1985), Vietnam and Yugoslavia. But even in these countries party and state offices are interwoven through membership in the Political Bureau or in the Central Committee of the Communist Party by heads of government and of state, the chairmen of the Presidia, and ministers. In Yugoslavia, where multiple holding of party and state offices is not permitted, the president of the Presidium of the Communist Party's Central Committee is an *ex officio* member of the State Presidium, which is the collective head of state. In addition there is a close personal liaison between party leadership and the armed forces, as for example in Albania, where the party leader, due to this position, is the commander-in-chief; or, in Cuba, North Korea and Rumania, where the party leader is at the same time head of state and by virtue of this office also commander-in-chief.

Institutionally, the party and the state, however, are kept apart in order to prevent the party from having to take responsibility for possible incorrect actions of the latter. Basically only Rumania has deviated from this principle by creating common organs of party and the state since 1972.

The *nomenklatura* is an important instrument by which the Communist Parties influence the appointment of personnel. This term applies to lists of the leading positions in the state administration, the judiciary, the foreign service, economic enterprises, the military and social organisations. Appointments to all of these positions require the approval of the Communist Party. Depending on the importance of the position or on the administrative or organisational level, these lists are kept either at the Secretariat of the Central Committee or at those of the local executive committees. Key positions may also be filled by experts without party membership, and the authorities, institutions and organisations in question can be heard. It is imperative, however, that the candidate for appointment be politically reliable and willing to realise the goals set by the party. When there are differences of opinion, the will of the party usually prevails.

The party's dominance, at all levels of state and social activity, is also assured by the binding force of party resolutions and directives of party on state organs, economic enterprises,

cultural institutions and social organisations. Direction and
control of the implementation are effected on the national
level by the Secretariat of the Central Committee and on the
local level by the executive committees, the primary party
organisations in places of work and of residence as well as by
the party groups in the various government authorities,
institutions and social organisations. The Secretariats of the
Central Committees usually have departments that run
parallel to important governmental departments. Local
executive committees, which direct and supervise the local
authorities and enterprises, are organised in a similar way.
They are supported by the primary organisations, party
committees and party groups, which transmit the party's
resolutions and directives, and supervise and report on their
implementation. When the party discerns irregularities or
abuses, it can effect the removal from office of whoever was
responsible. The party has the power to nominate the candidate for the assemblies of people's representatives and
controls the nomination procedure, and thus, finally, sees to
it that only system-liners receive a mandate.

'SOCIALIST DEMOCRACY'

The constitutions of most of the states under Communist
Party rule describe their political system as a 'socialist democracy'. Yugoslavia calls itself a 'socialist self-management
democratic community'; Mongolia a 'socialist state in the
form of a people's democracy'. Apart from the Communist
Party's monopoly of power, this form of democracy has the
following main features. First, all state power is constitutionally vested in the indivisible sovereignty of the people and is
united in the national representative body, which in formal
terms is the supreme organ of state power. Second, in support
of the Marxist theorem of a gradual withering away of the
state, there are abundant organisations and institutions for
the (channelled) participation of the citizens in matters of
state and society, without, however, giving them much actual
influence on decision-making. The participation, which is
based on the system of values as defined by the Communist

Party and accepts the leading role to which the party lays claim, takes place in the following ways:

(1) Through the exercise of the right to vote (election of the representative organs and of judges).

(2) Through the membership in social organisations and, with the exception of the Soviet Union, through the co-operation within the National Fronts and the like, which are umbrella organisations for political parties, social organisations and, sometimes, individuals for common activities; in addition — as a Yugoslav peculiarity — through the exercise of economic rights of participation in the form of workers' self-management.

(3) Through referenda, the discussion of bills and through co-operation in the committees of local representative assemblies.

(4) Through participation in the administration of justice as people's accessors and within the framework of social courts.

(5) Through the exercise of 'people's control' and by using the right to make suggestions for the improvement of the activities of the state organs, and the right to criticise them.

The 'Socialist Parliament'

According to the constitutions of the socialist states (except for Laos, which has not yet adopted a constitution) all state power resides within the representative bodies at each level of the state organisation. The executive and judicial branches of government are not part of an institutionalised system of separation of powers but are considered as merely auxiliary functional organs of the representative assemblies which exercise undivided, though only formal, power. That is why the constitutions do not regulate the relationship between the single branches of government in the manner of checks and balances.

Though conceived as 'parliament', the socialist representative assemblies are fundamentally different from the parliaments in liberal-democratic countries. Their theoretical foundation is the Paris Commune of 1871, which Marx had seen as the negation of bourgeois parliamentarism,[13] and they contain

elements of a councils' democracy. The national assemblies in
China, Cuba and Yugoslavia are not derived from general
elections but are elected by lower representative organs. This
is also the case in Hungary at the regional level (which is the
intermediary level in the state's structure), in China at province and district levels, in Cuba at the province level and in
Yugoslavia at the level of the republics and provinces. The
deputies or delegates are responsible to their electors or to
their electoral bodies, which may recall them on a motion of
the voters or of the National Front. Yet, in contrast to the
example set by the Paris Commune, the socialist mandate is
not an imperative mandate (except for Yugoslavia's Council
of Republics and Provinces). The deputies or delegates are
not bound by instructions from their electors or electoral
bodies but are primarily considered representatives of all-
national interests. Another feature of 'socialist parliamentarism' is that the national assemblies are not, as Marx has
assumed (permanent) working bodies.[14] They just convene
once or several times annually in plenary sessions which usually last only one day or a few days.

Exceptions to this rule can be found in Yugoslavia, whose
Federal Assembly and all other representative bodies are in
permanent session; in Poland, where the Sejm convenes for
sessions lasting two or three months; and in the GDR, whose
People's Chamber is in session from its first meeting after the
election to the end of the electoral term or its premature dissolution — but it, too, convenes only for single-day meetings,
four times a year on the average. If not specifically reserved
for the plenary session, the powers of the representative
assembly between sessions are exercised by its permanent
organ (the Presidium or the like), a hybrid organ of legislative
and executive power which acts as a 'substitute parliament',
apart from having certain powers of its own. In several
socialist countries it is also the collective head of state. Only
the Yugoslav assemblies (at the federal, republic and province
levels) and the People's Chamber of the GDR are not provided with an organ that deputises for or replaces them.

In spite of the supremacy of the Communist Party over the
state and the powers of the assemblies' permanent bodies as
well as of the governments, the national assemblies are not

just rubber-stamp parliaments which merely, without examination, pass into law the resolutions and directives from the party and the government. They are developing slowly into forums for discussion. This is particularly true of the Polish Sejm and the Yugoslav Federal Assembly as well as of the assemblies of the Yugoslav republics, where bills are also voted against. At times bills are thoroughly discussed and amended by the committees of the socialist parliaments, which often consult outside experts from the fields of science and economy.

The people have hardly any, or only a limited, influence on the composition of the parliaments. As a rule the candidates are nominated by the Communist Party, by 'satellite' parties — if existent — and by social organisations. In some countries the workers' collectives, meetings of voters, and in Hungary also individuals at the nomination meetings have the right to nominate candidates, who are put forward on a single list of the National Front or — as in the Soviet Union — on the single list of the 'bloc of communists and non-party people', under the auspices of the Communist Party. In this way a choice between several political alternatives becomes impossible. Seldom does the voter have the chance to choose between competing personalities. In many socialist countries, the number of candidates must or may exceed that of the deputies to be elected but only in Hungary and Poland multiple candidatures for one constituency seat are mandatory. Czechoslovakia and the Soviet Union, for example, have so far not made use of the possibility to nominate more candidates than seats available. Since the deletion of a candidate or a negative vote are considered to express non-confidence in the regime, which becomes apparent by the usually required use of the screened-off booth, only very few voters dare to act in this way. Consequently the candidates are as a rule elected with 98 per cent to almost 100 per cent of the valid votes.

It may seem that these non-competitive elections are irrelevant insofar as they do not influence the composition of the representative bodies. Their function is rather to integrate and to mobilise an ethnically, culturally, socially and religiously divided population and to rally it around the leadership of the party and the state. Furthermore, elections open a field for controlled political activity of the citizens and an opportunity for the party to present its achievements as well as its new goals. Finally, the organs of state power receive their constitutional legitimation through elections.

Social Organisations and Particular Interests

A special feature of all socialist states consists of the social organisations (especially the mass organisations), in which citizens are assembled according to occupation, age, sex or membership of a national minority in order to advance certain socio-political tasks. Among these organisations are the trade unions; the youth and women organisations; the associations of teachers, writers, journalists and those for similar professions; production and consumer co-operatives; sport clubs, as well as other associations which promote leisure, technical and scientific, or artistic activities. Political parties and, in some countries, the National Fronts are also regarded as social organisations.

The aim of the social organisations is not to articulate the special interest of certain professions or social strata — to the possible detriment of the society as a whole. Their main task is to fulfil those functions deemed necessary for the preservation and development of socialist systems such as the integration, political socialisation, mobilisation and social control of the citizens, and the transmission of the will of the Communist Parties to their members. In addition, based on the alleged fundamental consensus to build socialism and communism, the participation of social organisations in discussions and consultations about economic, social and cultural measures is being constantly increased, even though at times the party and state leadership may merely consider it opportune to sound out differences of opinion within the society in this way. Important social organisations, such as the trade unions, now and then have the right to initiate bills involving their fields of activity. In the GDR four social organisations occupy part of the seats in the People's Chamber.

Apart from the above, the social organisations do not have any institutionalised channels for promotion of their interests. On the other hand, it can be observed that their officials, when they hold important party and/or government offices, can

channel the special interests of the members of an organisation into the decision-making process. Social organisations
may also play a role in decision-making when they form the
power base of their leaders who at the same time hold high
party offices. In this way these functionaries can realise their
own interests, which may very well coincide with those of the
organisation.

A consideration of the aforesaid rights and possibilities
makes it clear that the social organisations are not always, and
in all socialist states, mere transmission belts for the will of the
Communist Party. Yet, on the whole, their possibilities of
articulating and realising the special interests of their members in the decision-making process are somewhat limited
because they are not autonomous and have to adapt to the
overall interests of society as determined by the party.

Professional groups have a greater chance to put through
particular professional and personal interests by offering
expertise in the course of the decision-making process. Due to
the 'scientific–technological revolution', high state officials,
managers of industrial enterprises, planning experts, the
military echelons and scientists have become indispensable
advisers and suppliers of information to the decision-making
organs of the party and the government. Their chance of being
heard lies in the fact that members of the top party and state
organs often identify themselves with one or other special
interest according to their own personal preferences.

Special interests may also be articulated by the religious
communities. This is above all true of the Catholic Church in
Poland. Its bargaining power is fairly strong because it is consolidated in the numerically large peasantry and has the ability
to mobilise a patriotic attitude.

In socialist states with a federal form of government
(Czechoslovakia, the Soviet Union, Yugoslavia) the territorial units may become the nuclei for particular interests, which
the parties of the federal units take up, formulate and advocate within the central party organs. In this way communists
have become the mouthpiece and agent for special interests
ranging from the protection of the national culture against the
tendencies of Russianisation, as for example in Latvia, to the
concrete material demands made by Slovak and Croatian

communists. The special interests of federal units may also
become a hotbed for ideological platforms, as can be observed
in Yugoslavia.

In Yugoslavia the pursuit of particular interests has actually
been institutionalised in the form of workers' self-management and territorial self-government. The Communist Party
has labelled this network of interests — organised, but not
competing with one another for power — 'pluralism of self-
management interests'.[15]

Bloc Parties and Political Dissent

Common to the political systems of socialist states is the fact
that an institutionalised, constitutional and responsible
opposition is lacking. In some socialist states, however, there
are other political parties besides the Communist Party.
Although they are regarded as an anachronism in a socialist
society in which the political and social unity of the people is
to be achieved, they are tolerated for historial and pragmatic
reasons. They developed during or after the Second World
War, or were licensed by the communists after their takeover,
and together with the Communist Parties they became junior
partners of an 'Anti-Fascist Democratic Bloc' or, as in China,
of the anti-Guomindang and anti-Japanese United Front.
These parties, which are usually called 'bloc parties' are
collective members of the National Fronts and the like —
which succeeded the 'blocs' — and within this framework they
create a loyal tie between the regime and those strata of society which traditionally reject or have reservations about the
communists, such as the peasants and the middle classes. But
on the grounds of a basic consensus about the unconditional-
ity of the fundamental features of the socialist political and
economic order and the leadership of the Communist Party,
the bloc parties may sometimes articulate special interests and
introduce alternative solutions as a corrective to political decisions.

Toleration of the minor parties does not mean that they
have the chance to oppose the Communist Party or to challenge its rule. Activities such as these would be interpreted as
a manifestation of class conflicts inherent in bourgeois
societies and would be irreconcilable with the *raison d'être* of

the Communist Party. Its position in the state is not determined by the electoral turnout but by its claim to lead the
working class in executing a historical mission according to
'objective laws' of the development of human society.[16]

The 'socialist multi-party systems' in Bulgaria, China,
Czechoslovakia, the GDR, North Korea, Poland and Vietnam are, therefore, not competitive party systems but
'hegemonic party systems'.[17] The non-communist parties cannot be compared to the partners in elections or government
coalitions in the 'Western' sense. A ruling Communist Party is
not dependent on compromises, because the nomination procedure and the electoral system guarantee the majority in the
representative assemblies to it alone or to the Communist
Party and its affiliated organisations (as is the case in the
GDR). The deputies from bloc parties may form separate
party groups within the parliaments, but apart from a few
exceptions, they do not vote independently.

Citizens whose opinions and goals deviate from the obligatory system of values and who question the Communist Party's
monopoly of power are not allowed to unite, or may only form
loose associations, and are often forced to work underground.
Inadmissible and criminalised are: oppositional activities
which openly aim at the change of the system; 'anti-systemic'
dissidence, which, though not subversive, is considered to be
'counter-revolutionary'; and 'fundamental' dissidence which
reveals itself in a behaviour deviant from basic communist values and priorities. Limited toleration is accorded merely to
'critical' dissidence, which presents deviating opinions with
regard to specific political issues.

THE 'SOCIALIST ECONOMY'

In accordance with the Marxist appeal to 'expropriate the
expropriators', in the socialist states all or at least the major
means of production (soil and waters, mineral resources,
industrial plants, means of transportation, banking, etc.) have
been socialised either, principally, in the form of state property (property of the 'whole people') or in the form of collective property (of agricultural, craftsmen's and trade co-opera-

tives). In Yugoslavia the non-private means of production are considered to be 'social' property. (There are different views of its nature, which cannot be discussed here.) In countries, where all land is state owned, it is leased to co-operatives for use. As a rule, but within limits, individuals have a right to the private use of farm plots, to raise livestock, and to engage in small handicraft, retail trade and services. Co-operative farmers are allowed to sell the produce of their plots on the free market; the same is permitted to the co-operative farms and individual farmers when they have fulfilled compulsory delivery quotas. This creates a 'second economy' which supplements the public sector.

Except for Yugoslavia, socialist economy is a 'command' economy. Economic activities are regulated by central planning in the form of annual plans and medium-term five-year plans. The individual enterprise, be it factory or state farm, is under the management of one man, the director, who, dependent upon the importance of an enterprise or a branch, is subordinate and responsible to local and central, or directly to central, administrative organs (ministries, agencies).

The plan-making process takes place in three stages. First, the central planning agency formulates the plan targets according to the guidelines of the top party organs and the results achieved in the previous planning year, and submits them to the enterprises (and industrial associations). Second, the enterprises taking into account these targets, draw up their production plan for the next year. In this phase the directors have a certain leeway; they tend to access the production capacities low and to indent for more resources that they need in order to increase the enterprise's chance to fulfil or even to overfulfil the plan targets. These individual plan drafts are aggregated and brought into line with the production programme by the branch ministries and finally by the central planning agency. Third, the planning agency draws up the general plan, submits it for approval to the central party organs and to the Council of Ministers (the government), which in turn presents it for adoption to the people's representative body. Once approved, the Council of Ministers assigns individual plan targets (concerning gross and net output, product assortment, investment, labour force, wage rates, wholesale and retail prices) to the branch ministries, and these pass them to the enterprises. Having the force of law the plan is compulsory on the ministries and enterprises, which are responsible for its implementation. Upon feedback of the results, the planning agency draws up the targets for the following year's plan.

In Yugoslavia the enterprises and market mechanisms to a great extent regulate the production and distribution of goods. Planning is indicative; that means that the state lays down general guidelines for the economic development which are legally binding only upon its organs, insofar as they are obliged to ensure the attainment of the economic goals by budgetary, foreign exchange and tariff policies. Market forces, however, do not develop entirely freely because of the system of 'social planning' via self-management and social compacts on production, investment, income distribution, and so on, between enterprises and organs of territorial self-government.

The economic policy of the socialist states aims to surmount economic backwardness in the shortest possible time; the aim of the USSR, in particular, has been to catch up with the industrialised capitalist countries. Industrialisation is supposed to create the economic basis for material abundance as a precondition for the construction of communism. Priority, therefore, is principally given to the growth of the capital goods industry at the expense of agriculture and the consumer goods industry. (But there are examples of a shifting of priority to the production of food and consumer goods at various times and in various degrees.)

The system of central planning and management usually faces four major problems: low productivity and low rationality in the allocation of resources; imbalance between supply and demand, which brings about a black market; neglect of the quality of goods, because production targets are predominantly specified in quantitative terms; and lack of innovative behaviour. Yugoslavia's 'market socialism' experiences high unemployment, high inflation and a negative balance of payment. Apart from these problems, the economies of advanced socialist states are confronted with increasing needs of the population, whose satisfaction is imperative in order to substantiate the pretension that socialism is superior to capitalism.

In order to surmount the shortcomings of their economy, socialist states have embarked on economic reforms 'within the system'; that is, while basically maintaining public ownership of the means of production and central planning. Measures aiming at the increase in labour productivity, the improvement of supply, the lowering of production costs and the raising of work motivation are: the limited admittance of market mechanisms (e.g. liberalisation of price formation for some products, inter-enterprise competition and contracting); the introduction of profit as success indicator and of the principle of the self-financing of the enterprises; the reduction of binding plan targets; partial reprivatisation of rural economy and the encouragement of private initiative in other sectors; the decentralisation of decision-making (concerning resource allocation, investment, labour force); the generation of new material incentives for the management and the employees to increase income (e.g. by profit-sharing); the concession of influence to workers' collectives or trade unions concerning the appointment of the enterprise directors. Major reforms have been launched in Hungary — as early as 1968 and again since late 1978 — as well as in China in 1978 and particularly since 1984. Minor changes are to be observed in Bulgaria, Cuba and Poland. In the Soviet Union a tentative economic reform is on the way. In addition to reforms, economic performance has been improved by joint ventures with capitalist firms.

'SOCIALIST LAW'

The conception of law (and justice) in socialist states does not entail the idea of permanently valid law but conceives law and justice to be bound by and dependent on society. Accordingly, law, as an element of what Marx called the superstructure (politics, religion, morals, etc.), on the one hand, reflects the socio-economic relations. On the other hand, it is an instrument of the ruling class — which in socialist states is theoretically the working class or the working people but actually the Marxist-Leninist party — for the consolidation of its power and for safeguarding the building of socialism and communism by the state and society. Law, therefore, is aimed directly at the creation of new social conditions and relations. This conception of the law has the following consequences:

(1)   Law is an instrument of the class struggle; it serves to enforce political decisions.

(2)   Law-making and the application of law are guided by respective political expediencies; in socialist states policy takes priority over the law.

(3)   Law does not primarily protect the individual but the collective entity. Individual rights are considered worthy of protection, but they are limited by collective social interests as defined by the Communist Party.

The instrumental character of law becomes evident from the socialist conception of the role of the constitution. The constitutions of the socialist states, too, lay down the norms for state and society, regulate the structure of the state as well as the appointment and powers of state organs, and bind their activities by law. But these provisions are in part misleading. Take, for instance, the national assemblies, which in all constitutions are characterised as the supreme organ of state power; in reality, however — except, to a certain extent, for Yugoslavia — they are the state organs with the least power. Furthermore, the constitutional norms have to be judged within the light of the constitutionally guaranteed political monopoly of the Marxist-Leninist party. Its leading role in state and society implies that it stands above the law. From this it follows, first, that the resolutions and directives of the party are not bound by law but rather themselves create law and, second, that all state organs have to fulfil the aims of the party regardless of the provisions of the constitution.

Apart from their legal function, socialist constitutions have a propagandistic and programmatic purpose. They reflect the level or stage achieved at any given time in the construction of socialism according to the Marxist base-superstructure theorem, and they proclaim the objectives for further development in state and society. Thus the constitutions form the legal framework for political and socio-economic transformations in the course of the construction and perfection of socialism. Accordingly, they are rewritten at every stage achieved in this process.

The socialist conception of law has special consequences for the position of and protection accorded to human and civil rights. The safeguarding of constitutionally guaranteed equal rights, socio-economic rights, individual rights of liberty and political rights depends on the more or less rigorous reservations and limits set by the general interests of society. In Yugoslavia the provisos are the principle of solidarity and the interests of society as laid down by the constitution. In Cuba the reservations have such far-reaching effect that the exercise of the rights of liberty is illegal and punishable when used in opposition to the existence and the goals of the state and the people's fundamental decision to build socialism and communism. Certain civil rights are bound by civil obligations as, for example, the right to work is correlated with the duty to work. In this way civil rights are reinterpreted as the obligation to participate in the realisation of the Communist Party's goals and are thus deprived of the quality of an individual right. However, some socialist states are at present paying more attention to civil rights than they did in the past.

The radical democratic concept that all state power is indivisible and only present in the representative assembly does not allow for the legal protection of human and civil rights by a really independent judiciary. In all socialist states judges are elected by the representative assemblies or by the citizens, and they are responsible and accountable to their electorate and are subject to recall.[18] Although judges are bound by the law when reaching a verdict, they have to consider the principle of 'party-mindedness' when interpreting and applying the laws. This means that they must let themselves be guided by the political goals to which the Communist Party has subordinated all legal norms.

Except for Yugoslavia, there are no constitutional or other supreme courts in the socialist states to control the conformity of laws and other legal acts with the constitution. (The establishment of constitutional courts envisaged in Czechoslovakia as early as 1968, and in Poland since 1982, has not yet become reality.) In accordance with the principle of the indivisibility of state power, the right to decide on the constitutionality of laws is vested in the representative assemblies or their Presidia or, as in Rumania and Hungary, in special organs set up by the representative bodies.

In all socialist states the Procuracy supervises the maintenance of 'socialist legality', which means the observance of the constitution, the laws and other norms by the state organs, social organisations and citizens, and their application according to the party line. The Procuracy is a centralised body and is responsible to the representative assemblies or their Presidia. It becomes active on its own initiative or on petition by a citizen who believes that his rights have been violated, and, usually, when obvious interests of the party do not stand in the way.

'PROLETARIAN AND SOCIALIST INTERNATIONALISM'

The constitutions of all socialist states contain declarations about the principles underlying their foreign policy and in this context, except for China, a profession of adherence to proletarian internationalism and/or socialist internationalism. But different ideas exist as to the content, interpretation, and application of internationalism.

During the early phase of the socialist movement (during the First and the Second International of 1864 and 1889), proletarian internationalism contained the idea of the fraternal solidarity of workers in their struggle to gain political power for their economical emancipation, and the idea of absolute equality among their parties and other organisations. During the Third (Communist) International, founded in Moscow in 1919, the idea of proletarian world revolution was postponed in favour of the Soviet national interest, which obliged all Communist Parties to give their altruistic support to Bolshevist Russia and the Soviet Union, respectively. The Communist Parties were not allowed to determine their policy on their own.

Since the Second World War, there has been added to this principle of solidarity that of socialist internationalism, which is applied to the relations of the socialist states among themselves and particularly to their relations with the Soviet

Union. In Stalin's days proletarian and socialist internationalism required Communist Parties and socialist states
to acknowledge the CPSU/USSR as the leading centre of the
communist world movement. Later the CPSU dropped this
claim officially but continued to demand solidarity, the
emulation of its model of socialism — tolerating slight deviations — and support for its foreign policy.

The Soviet military intervention in Czechoslovakia in
August 1968 and the so-called 'Brezhnev doctrine', with
which the intervention was justified, demonstrate particularly
well how internationalism has been regarded as a criterion for
conduct and activity in the interests of the Soviet Union. The
central theme of the 'Brezhnev doctrine' stipulates, first, that
the sovereignty of socialist states is limited — they may exercise it only to the extent not affecting the interests of the 'community of socialist states'; second, that socialist states have
only a restricted right of self-determination; and third, that
each Communist Party is responsible for its actions also with
regard to the other socialist countries and to the communist
world movement.[19] As during the time of the Stalin era and
of the Comintern, 'solidarity with the Soviet Union and the
support of the Soviet Union in the international arena' was
declared to be the 'fundamental component' of proletarian
and socialist internationalism.[20]

The principle of proletarian internationalism was reworded
at the Conference of (twenty-nine) European Communist
Parties in East Berlin in June 1976. In the joint declaration
they promised to develop 'their internationalist, comradely,
voluntary co-operation and solidarity on the basis of the great
ideas of Marx, Engels and Lenin, strictly observing equality
of rights and independence...non-interference into internal
affairs, the right to choose freely different roads in the struggle
for progressive social transformations and for socialism'.[21]
Apparently, for tactical considerations, in order not to dismay
those parties which insist on autonomy from the CPSU and
are in a position to maintain it, the CPSU recognises the
equality of all Communist Parties and abstains from overt
hegemonist pretensions. But, in fact, it continues to apply the
principle of internationalism according to the Leninist-
Stalinist conception insofar as it expects the Communist Par-

ties, particularly those in the WTO and/or CMEA member countries, to subordinate their domestic and foreign policies to the interests of the USSR, condemning any manifestations of nationalism.[22]

The constitutions of such states under Soviet hegemony as Czechoslovakia, the GDR and Hungary consider their respective countries as a 'solid link', an 'inseparable part' or as a 'part' of the socialist world system under the leadership of the Soviet Union. Bulgaria and also Cuba see their membership within the socialist world community as the prerequisite for independence and the development of socialism. The constitutions of Mongolia, Vietnam, Albania and North Korea recognise the principle of proletarian internationalism; the communists in the two latter countries, however, view it as a principle of equality among Communist Parties and refuse to subordinate themselves to the CPSU. Yugoslavia and Rumania declare their commitment to socialist internationalism but reject the Soviet interpretation of it. These states want the principle to be understood as the equality of relations on the basis of the principle of peaceful coexistence, which denies the right of interference in the internal affairs of a country in order, for example, to uphold jointly the socialist order. China only applies the principle of peaceful coexistence in its relations to other socialist states.

Thus, the Soviet interpretation of proletarian and socialist internationalism is accepted only by the states within the Soviet sphere of power — except for Rumania — or by those states which, like Cuba, Laos and Vietnam, feel obliged to practise internationalist solidarity towards the Soviet Union for the sake of its extensive aid. Within its sphere of power the Soviet Union determines to what extent foreign relations may serve the interests of the individual state, and whether a 'national' form of socialism, which deviates in content and methods from the Soviet model, may be realised without obstruction or sanction.

NOTES

1.   'Manifest der Kommunistischen Partei' ['The Communist Manifesto',
     1848], in Karl Marx and Friedrich Engels, *Werke* [Works] — hereafter
     MEW — vol. 4 (East Berlin, 1972), pp. 459–93, pp. 464ff. and 482.
2.   'Anti-Dühring' (1877-78), in *MEW*, vol. 20 (East Berlin, 1973),
     pp. 16–303, p. 262.
3.   'Gosudarstvo i revolyutsiya' ['State and Revolution', 1917], in
     Vladimir I. Lenin, *Polnoe Sobranie Sochineniy* [Complete Collection
     of Works], 5th edn. — hereafter *PSS* — vol. 33 (Moscow, 1962),
     pp. 1–120, pp. 42 and 96.
4.   'Kritik des Gothaer Programms' ['Critique of the Gotha Programme'
     (of the Socialist Workers' Party of Germany), 1875], in *MEW*, vol. 19
     (East Berlin, 1973), pp. 15–32, p. 21.
5.   'Gosudarstvo i revolyutsiya', *op. cit.*, pp. 91ff.
6.   'Kritik des Gothaer Programms', *op. cit.*, p.28.
7.   Marx, *ibid.*, p. 22; however, as against to Engels, 'Anti-Dühring',
     op. cit., p. 138.
8.   'Manifest der Kommunistischen Partei', *op. cit.*, p. 482, and 'Anti-
     Dühring', *op. cit.*, p. 261; Marx 'Der Bürgerkrieg in Frankreich' ['The
     Civil War in France', 1871], in *MEW*, vol. 17 (East Berlin, 1973),
     pp. 339 and 343.
9.   'Die heilige Familie' ['The Holy Family', 1845], in *MEW*, vol. 2 (East
     Berlin, 1972), pp. 6–223, p. 38, and 'Manifest der Kommunistischen
     Partei', *op. cit.*, p. 474.
10. 'Chto delat?' ['What is to be Done?', 1902], in *PSS*, vol. 6 (Moscow,
     1963), pp. 1–192, pp. 53ff. and 111ff.
11. 'K voprosam Leninizma' ['On Questions of Leninism', 1926], in Yosif
     V. Stalin, *Sochineniya* [Works], vol. 8 (Moscow, 1950), pp. 13–90,
     pp. 37–9.
12. Chapter 8 of the Introduction to the Constitution of February 1974.
13. 'Der Bürgerkrieg in Frankreich', *op. cit.*, pp. 339–40.
14. *Ibid.*, p. 339.
15. Edvard Kardelj, *Pravci razvoja političkog sistema socijalističkog
     samoupravljanja* [Directions of Development of the Political System
     of Socialist Self-Management] (Belgrade, 1977), pp. 80ff.
16. *Grundlagen des Marxismus-Leninismus* [The Foundations of
     Marxism-Leninism], 8th edn. (East Berlin, 1964), pp. 635 and 9.
17. Giovanni Sartori, *Parties and Party Systems: A Framework of
     Analysis*, vol. 1 (Cambridge, 1976), p. 230.
18. 'Der Bürgerkrieg in Frankreich', *op. cit.*, p. 339.
19. S. Kovalyov, in *Pravda* (Moscow), 26 September 1968, and
     L. Brezhnev at the Fifth Congress of the Polish communists, in
     Pravda, 13 November 1968.
20. A. Sovyetov, in *International Affairs* (Moscow), 1968, no. 11, p. 9.
21. *Pravda* (Moscow), 1 July 1976.
22. O. Vladimirov, in *Pravda* (Moscow), 21 June 1985.

FURTHER READING

(1) Marxism-Leninism (apart from the works of Marx, Engels, Lenin and Mao Zedong):

Kernig, C.D. (ed.), *Marxism, Communism, and Western Society: A Comparative Encyclopedia* (New York: Herder and Herder, 1972–73)

Kołakowski, Leszek, *Main Currents of Marxism: Its Rise, Growth, and Dissolution*, 3 vols. (Oxford: Clarendon Press, 1978)

Leonhard, Wolfgang, *Three Faces of Marxism: The Political Concepts of Soviet Ideology, Maoism, and Humanist Marxism* (New York: Holt, Rinehart and Winston, 1974)

(2) Constitutions and Party Statutes:

Simons, William B. (ed.), *The Constitutions of the Communist World* (Alphen aan den Rijn, The Netherlands, and Germantown, Md.: Sijthoff and Noordhoff, 1980)

—— and Stephen White (eds.), *The Party Statutes of the Communist World* (The Hague: Martinus Nijhoff, 1984)

Triska, Jan F. (ed.) *Constitutions of the Communist Party-States* (Stanford, Cal.: The Hoover Institution on War, Revolution and Peace, Stanford University, 1968)

(3) General Surveys:

Staar, Richard F., *Communist Regimes in Eastern Europe*, 4th edn. (Stanford, Cal.: Hoover Institution Press, 1982)

Szajkowski, Bogdan (ed.), *Marxist Governments: A World Survey*, 3 vols. (London: Macmillan, 1981)

(4) Single Issues (in theoretical, historical, and comparative perspective):

Adelman, Jonathan R. (ed.), *Communist Armies in Politics* (Boulder, Colo.: Westview Press, 1982)

—— (ed.), *Terror and Communist Politics: The Role of the Secret Police in Communist States* (Boulder, Colo.: Westview Press, 1984)

Beck, Carl *et al.*, *Comparative Communist Political Leadership* (New York: McKay, 1973)

Bertsch, Gary K., *Power and Policy in Communist Systems* (New York: Wiley, 1978)

Beyme, Klaus von: *Economics and Politics within Socialist Systems: A Comparative and Developmental Approach* (New York: Praeger, 1982)

Brown, Archie and Jack Gray (eds.), *Political Culture and Political Change in Communist States*, 2nd edn. (London: Macmillan, 1979)

Brus, Włodzimierz, *Socialist Ownership and Political Systems* (London and Boston: Routledge and Kegan Paul, 1975)

Brzezinski, Zbigniew K., *The Soviet Bloc: Unity and Conflict*, rev. edn. (Cambridge, Mass.: Harvard University Press, 1967)

Cohen, Lenard J. and Jane P. Shapiro (eds.), *Communist Systems in Comparative Perspective* (Garden City, N.Y.: Anchor Press, 1974)

Connor, Walter D., *Socialism, Politics, and Equality: Hierarchy and Change in Eastern Europe and the USSR* (New York: Columbia University Press, 1979)

—— and Zvi Y. Gitelman, *Public Opinion in European Socialist Systems* (New York: Praeger, 1977)

Djilas, Milovan, *The New Class: An Analysis of the Communist System* (London: Thames and Hudson, 1957)

Fejtö, François, *A History of the People's Democracies: Eastern Europe since Stalin* (Harmondsworth: Penguin, 1974)

Fischer-Galati, Stephen (ed.), *The Communist Parties of Eastern Europe* (New York: Columbia University Press, 1979)

—— (ed.), *Eastern Europe in the 1980s* (London: Croom Helm, 1981)

Fleron, Frederick J. (ed.), *Communist Studies and the Social Sciences: Essays on Methodology and Empirical Theory* (Chicago: Rand McNally, 1969)

Friedrich, Carl J. and Zbigniew K. Brzezinski, *Totalitarian Dictatorship and Autocracy,* 2nd edn. (Cambridge, Mass.: Harvard University Press, 1965)

Gripp, Richard C., *The Political System of Communism* (New York: Dodd, Mead and Co., 1973)

Gyorgy, Andrew and James A. Kuhlman (eds.), *Innovation in Communist Systems* (Boulder, Colo.: Westview Press, 1978)

Hammond, Thomas T. and Robert Farrell (eds.), *The Anatomy of Communist Takeovers* (New Haven, Conn., and London: Yale University Press, 1975)

Harding, Neil (ed.), *The State in Socialist Society* (London: Macmillan, 1984)

Harman, Chris, *Bureaucracy and Revolution in Eastern Europe* (London: Pluto Press, 1974)

Hazard, John N., *Communists and Their Law: A Search for the Common Core of the Legal Systems of the Marxian Socialist States* (Chicago: University of Chicago Press, 1969)

Hegedüs, András, *The Structure of Socialist Society* (London: Constable, 1977)

Herspring, Dale R. and Ivan Völgyes (eds.), *Civil–Military Relations in Communist Systems* (Boulder, Colo.: Westview Press, 1978)

Hirszowicz, Maria, *The Bureaucratic Leviathan: A Study in the Sociology of Communism* (New York: New York University Press, 1980)

Holmes, Leslie (ed.), *The Withering away of the State? Party and State under Communism* (London and Beverly Hills, Cal.: Sage Publications, 1981)

Ionescu, Ghiţa, *Comparative Communist Politics* (London: Macmillan, 1972)

Janos, Andrew C. (ed.), *Authoritarian Politics in Communist Europe: Uniformity and Diversity in One-Party States* (Berkeley, Cal.: Institute of International Studies, University of California, 1976)

Johnson, Chalmers A. (ed.), *Change in Communist Systems* (Stanford, Cal.: Stanford University Press, 1970)

Kanet, Roger E. (ed.), *The Behavioral Revolution and Communist Studies* (New York: Free Press, 1971)

Kuhlman, James A. (ed.), *The Foreign Policies of Eastern Europe: Domestic and International Determinants* (Leyden: Sijthoff, 1978)

Lane, David S., *The Socialist Industrial State: Towards a Political Sociology of State Socialism* (London: Allen and Unwin, 1976)

—— *The End of Social Inequality? Class, Status and Power under State Socialism* (London: Allen and Unwin, 1982)

Marcuse, Herbert, *Soviet Marxism: A Critical Analysis* (Harmondsworth: Penguin, 1971)

Mesa-Lago, Carmelo and Carl Beck (eds.), *Comparative Socialist Systems: Essays on Politics and Economics* (Pittsburgh: Center for International Studies, University of Pittsburgh, 1975)

Nelson, Daniel N. (ed.), *Local Politics in Communist Countries* (Lexington, Ky.: University Press of Kentucky, 1980)

—— and Stephen White (eds.), *Communist Legislatures in Comparative Perspective* (London: Macmillan, 1982)

Pravda, Alex, 'Elections in Communist Party States', in Guy Hermet *et al.* (eds.), *Elections without Choice* (London and New York: Macmillan, 1978), pp. 169–95

Rakowska-Harmstone, Teresa (ed.), *Perspectives for Change in Communist Societies* (Boulder, Colo.: Westview Press, 1979)

Rigby, Thomas H. and Ferenc Fehér (eds.), *Political Legitimation in Communist States* (London: Macmillan, 1982)

Rush, Myron, *How Communist States Change Their Rulers* (Ithaca, NY: Cornell University Press, 1974)

Schulz, Donald E. and Jan S. Adams (eds.), *Political Participation in Communist Systems* (New York and Oxford: Pergamon Press, 1981)

Seroka, Jim and Maurice D. Simon (eds.), *Developed Socialism in the Soviet Bloc: Political Theory and Political Reality* (Boulder, Colo.: Westview Press, 1982)

Seton-Watson, Hugh, *The Pattern of Communist Revolution: A Historical Analysis*, rev. edn. (London: Methuen, 1960); American edn.: *From Lenin to Khrushchev* (New York: Praeger, 1960)

Shakhnazarov, Georgii Kh., *Socialist Democracy: Aspects of Theory* (Moscow: Progress Publishers, 1974)

Shapiro, Jane P. and Peter J. Potichnyj (eds.), *Change and Adaptation in Soviet and East European Politics* (New York: Praeger, 1976)

Šik, Ota, *The Communist Power System* (New York: Praeger, 1981)

Sodaro, Michael J. and Sharon L. Wolchik (eds.), *Foreign and Domestic Policy in Eastern Europe in the 1980s* (New York: St Martin's Press, 1983)

Szajkowski, Bogdan, *The Establishment of Marxist Regimes* (London: Butterworths, 1982)

Tökés, Rudolf L. (ed.), *Opposition in Eastern Europe* (London: Macmillan, 1979)

Triska, Jan F. and Paul M. Cocks (eds.), *Political Development in Eastern Europe* (New York: Praeger, 1977)

Völgyes, Ivan (ed.), *Political Socialization in Eastern Europe: A Comparative Framework* (New York: Praeger, 1975)

Whetten, Lawrence L. (ed.), *The Present State of Communist Internationalism* (Lexington, Mass.: Lexington Books, 1983)

White, Stephen *et al.*, *Communist Political Systems: An Introduction* (London: Macmillan, 1982)

White, Stephen *et al.*, Communist Political Systems: An Introduction (London: Macmillan, 1982)

(5) Useful for Understanding Socialist Systems:

McCrea, Barbara P. *et al.*, *The Soviet and East European Political Dictionary* (Santa Barbara, Cal.: ABC-Clio Information Services, 1984)

(6) Current Information on, and Analyses of, Recent Events in Socialist States:

Annual publications: The *Europa Yearbook* (London) and the *Yearbook on International Communist Affairs: Parties and Revolutionary Movements* (Stanford, Cal.)

Periodicals: *Problems of Communism* (Washington, DC); *Review of Socialist Law* (Alphen aan den Rijn, The Netherlands); *Soviet Studies* (Glasgow); *Studies in Comparative Communism* (Guildford, Surrey); *Survey* (London), *The China Quarterly* (London).

3   Socialist People's Republic of Albania

BASIC FEATURES

In its constitution of 28 December 1976[1] Albania describes
itself as a 'state of the dictatorship of the proletariat' (article
2), Marxism-Leninism is elevated to the 'dominant ideology'
(article 3) and the class struggle is regarded as the instrument
for transforming a society which to a large extent is still
attached to traditional customs and values. The leadership of
state and society is exclusively in the hands of the Marxist-
Leninist party. The representative organs — the People's
Assembly and people's councils — as well as all other state
organs, are obliged to observe in their activities the principle
of the 'mass line'. This means that they have to keep in close
contact with the citizens, but ultimately this principle implies
the strict observance of the party's directives. Every single
citizen, all state organs and all social institutions are subject to
a tight network of reciprocal controls.

The preamble to the constitution declares that Albania has
entered the stage of the 'comprehensive construction of the
socialist society'. The social development is marked by the
gradual reduction of differences between town and country
and between manual and mental work. This is effected by
minimising the differences of income in the various sectors of
employment and between workers and management, by sending administrative and judicial personnel to work in the production process and by the gradual nationalisation of collective farms. The construction of socialism is to be realised —
harbouring the partisan myth — as completely as possible by
relying on one's own forces. The granting of concessions to

33

foreigners, the share of foreign capital in economic enterprises as well as the acceptance of loans from bourgeois and 'revisionist' countries are prohibited by the constitution. In 1967 Albania was declared an 'atheist state'; it is the only socialist state that forbids all religious organisation and activities by the population, the majority of which belonged to Islam (either Sunni or Bektashi) and others to the Orthodox or Roman Catholic Church.

THE COMMUNIST TAKEOVER

The Albanian communists came to power through a victorious struggle against first Italian and later German occupation. They were assisted by Yugoslav partisans but did not get any help from the Soviet Union. They fostered the formation of the Anti-Fascist National Liberation Movement in September 1942, which joined together communist and non-communist resistance groups. In October 1944 the Anti-Fascist National Liberation Council, dominated by the communists, constituted itself as the Provisional Democratic Government of Albania under the chairmanship of Enver Hoxha. By the end of November 1944, when the German troops had left Albania, the country was under the control of the communists; the rival non-communist National Front was eliminated. During the elections to the Constituent Assembly in December 1945 the single list of the Democratic Front which emanated from the (purged) National Liberation Movement, gained about 93 per cent of the votes. On 11 January 1946 the monarchy was abolished, and Albania was proclaimed a people's republic. The constitution ('Statute') promulgated on 14 March 1945 was based largely on the constitutions of the Soviet Union and Yugoslavia. The latter had temporarily stationed troops in Albania and its Communist Party dominated its Albanian counterpart. Since July 1950 the communists have become, constitutionally too, the leading force in the country.

THE MARXIST-LENINIST PARTY

After several futile attempts in the 1920s the Albanian Communist Party was founded in the underground with Yugoslav assistance in November 1941. At the First Congress in November 1948 it assumed the name Party of Labour of Albania (PLA). It adheres not only to the doctrines of Marx, of Engels, and Lenin but also to those of Stalin. In 1983 it claimed about 122,000 full members, which is approximately 5 per cent of the total population.[2]

About 2,000 primary organisations in factories, offices, institutions, towns and villages form the basis of the party pyramid. Most party members still lack sufficient school education. Local party officials — who are steeped in the tradition of their clans — tend to strengthen their positions of power. Severe criticism, however, from the party grass roots is to put an end to this. According to the Statute, the Party Congress is the supreme organ, meeting every four to five years. Between the Party Congresses this position is held by the Central Committee (CC). *De facto* all power is concentrated in the Political Bureau and the Secretariat of the CC, with Ramiz Alia at the top as First Secretary of the CC. Since 1941, until his death in April 1985, Enver Hoxha had succeeded in retaining this position by repeatedly purging the party and state apparatus as well as the armed forces and had led the party in a totalitarian Stalinist manner. The close connection between state and party organs is safeguarded by the membership of the Chairman of the Council of Ministers and the nominal head of state in the Political Bureau.

After breaking away from the CPSU in 1961 and after becoming detached from the Communist Party of China, a development which culminated in the renunciation of the teachings of Mao Zedong (Mao Tse-tung) in 1978, the PLA has pursued an entirely independent line within the communist world movement. Claiming to be the only party which is constructing 'genuine' Marxism and which embodies the 'pure' doctrine, the PLA is struggling against 'modern revisionism' (as in the Soviet conception of the 'all-people's state', or the Chinese policy of modernisation with capitalist aid and material incentives, or Yugoslav self-management socialism, or the Eurocommunists' renunciation of the dictatorship of the proletariat) and against 'imperialism' and 'hegemonialism' (of the Soviet Union as revealed in the doctrine of the 'limited sovereignty' of socialist states).

SOCIAL ORGANISATIONS

Social organisations are the Trade Union Federation of Albania, the Union of Labour Youth of Albania, the Women's Union of Albania; sport organisations, as well as cultural, scientific and technical organisations. They are subject to the PLA and united in the Democratic Front which is an instrument for the political control of the population.

The organisations especially serve to mobilise the citizens for the aims of the PLA, to implant the beliefs and attitudes of Marxism-Leninism (as interpreted by the Albanian communists) into the population and to strengthen the readiness for defence. The trade unions ensure the fulfilment of the economic plans and of work norms, the increase of productivity, the improvement of work discipline and the raising of educational standards — whereby moral incentives are to precede material incentives. In all this they are supported by the Councils of Workers' Control.

CENTRAL GOVERNMENT

The legislature is embedded in the People's Assembly, which consists of 250 members. They are elected for a term of four years and in constituencies with an equal number of inhabitants by universal, equal, direct and secret ballot. Citizens become entitled to vote and to be elected at the age of eighteen. The candidates are nominated by social organisations and become elected when they receive the absolute majority of votes in one-man constituencies for the single ticket of the Democratic Front, which practically polls 100 per cent of the votes. In the constitution the People's Assembly is designed as the 'supreme organ of state power, the bearer of the sovereignty of the people and of the state, and the sole legis-

lative organ' (article 66). In this capacity — but always in
accordance with the general line of the PLA and party directives — the People's Assembly defines the 'main course' of
domestic and foreign policy. It approves and amends the constitution as well as laws, decides on the constitutionality of
laws and interprets them, approves the economic plan and the
state budget, and ratifies and denounces international treaties
of 'particular importance' (article 67). Within its creative
function the People's Assembly, *inter alia*, elects, appoints
and dismisses its Presidium and the Council of Ministers,
which are formally responsible and accountable to it. Standing committees deliberate on bills, which can be initiated by a
single deputy, the Presidium or the Council of Ministers, and
control the activity of the state organs.

The People's Assembly only meets twice a year in full
session. Between the sessions part of its duties are performed
by the Presidium, whose members are elected by the People's
Assembly the vice-chairmen of the Council of Ministers, and
which during the next session of the Assembly have to be presented only for formal approval. It controls the implementation of laws, appoints and dismisses on behalf of the People's
Assembly the viice-chairmen of the Council of Ministers, and
ministers (on the recommendation of the chairman of the
Council of Ministers), members of the Supreme Court and
the deputies of the procurator general. Furthermore, the
Presidium concludes, ratifies and denounces international
treaties as far as this is not within the powers of the People's
Assembly; it directs and controls the work of the people's
councils, may dissolve them and proclaim a new election. It
abrogates illegal acts of the Council of Ministers, the people's
councils and of their executive committees. The Presidium is
formally responsible and accountable to the People's Assembly. Its chairman, at present Ramiz Alia, is nominal head of
state.

The Council of Ministers is the supreme executive and
administrative organ. It is formed by the People's Assembly,
as a rule from among the deputies. It is responsible for the
conduct of domestic and foreign policy, the conclusion of
international agreements, the composing of the draft of the
economic plan and of the state budget as well as for their

implementation. It directs and supervises the ministries and the local administrative organs, annuls illegal acts of ministers and suspends the application of illegal or irregular decisions of the people's councils. On the basis of laws, decrees, directives and recommendations, the ministers direct and supervise the economic, social and cultural institutions under them. They suspend illegal decisions of the executive committees of the people's councils and present them to the Council of Ministers, which decides upon their abrogation.

The implementation of the duties of the Council of Ministers is controlled by its Presidium, consisting of the chairman of the Council of Ministers — from 1954 until his alleged suicide or 'liquidation' in 1981, Mehmet Shehu, and since the beginning of 1982, Adil Çarçani — and his deputies. The ministers are responsible individually for their respective department as well as collectively for the activities of the Council of Ministers.

LOCAL GOVERNMENT

Albania is administratively divided into twenty-six districts and these, in turn, into towns and combined villages. The latter two are subdivided into urban districts and villages. The local organs of state power are the people's councils, which are elected for a term of three years. They are responsible for the economic, socio-cultural, judicial and security matters in their respective territorial administrative units, reconciling local interests with the broader interests of the whole state. The members of the people's councils are obliged to keep in close contact with their electors and to render account to them about their activities. They have the right to control the observance of socialist legality in state organs, enterprises and agricultural co-operatives. They in turn are rigidly controlled from above; apart from the rights of the Presidium of the People's Assembly in respect of the people's councils mentioned above, the people's councils too, on a higher level, supervise the activities of lower-level councils, may repeal their illegal acts, dissolve them and order the election of new councils.

The executive committees elected by the people's councils are not only their executive organ, but between the sessions they also administer the powers not exclusively reserved for the people's councils. According to the principle of dual sub-ordination, an executive committee is subject to the control by the people's council of the same and the executive commit-tee of the next higher administrative level. The latter may abrogate illegal acts of the lower executive committee and sus-pend those of a lower people's council.

ADMINISTRATION OF JUSTICE

The organs of justice comprise the Supreme Court, the district courts and the village and town district courts. The village and town district courts, consisting of an auxiliary judge and two 'social activists', decide on minor cases. District courts, con-sisting of judges and auxiliary judges, are courts of appeal for the village and town district courts, and are the courts of juris-diction for all criminal matters except capital crimes. The jurisdiction of the Supreme Court covers all capital crimes, and it directs and controls all subordinate courts. Trials often take place in the rural work centres, thus enabling citizens to take part and thus have them educated, because many still have a very traditional understanding of the law.

The judges of the Supreme Court are elected by the People's Assembly or by its Presidium; all other judges are elected by the people's councils. They are responsible to those organs, as well as to the Workers' Control. The judges are required to make their decisions according to the party line; that is, to interpret the law accordingly. Their independence is restricted to the reaching of a verdict. On annulment of a verdict they are obliged to exert self-criticism. The Ministry of Justice was abolished in 1966.

The supervision of the strict observance of the law by all central and local state organs, economic enterprises, institu-tions, social organisations, officials and citizens is the respon-sibility of the Procurator's Office. This consists of the pro-curator general and his deputies, who are appointed and dis-missed by the People's Assembly or by its Presidium, as well

as of the district procurators who are appointed and dismissed
by the latter. Furthermore, there are people's procurators in
villages, town districts, enterprises, and various institutions,
who are elected by the citizens. Being considered as an instrument of the dictatorship of the proletariat, the Procurator's
Office has to orientate all its activity in accordance with the
directives of the Communist Party and to ensure that the laws
are applied in accordance with the party line. It is entitled to
demand the annulment or amendment of illegal acts of state
organs, and so on, and should they not comply with the
request within the period stipulated, it has the right to suspend
the application of these acts. Furthermore, it has the duty to
accept and examine complaints addressed to it by individual
citizens. The procurator general is obliged to draw the attention of the People's Assembly and its Presidium to laws and
decrees which are unconstitutional, and the attention of the
Council of Ministers to ordinances and decisions which are
illegal. The procurators are accountable to the public and
obliged to exercise self-criticism. Criticism of the regime and
religious activity are severely punishable offences.

FOREIGN POLICY

Albanian foreign policy can be divided into four phases. Until
June 1948 it was orientated towards the interests of Yugoslavia: both countries were united by a customs union, their
economic plans were coordinated, the Albanian armed forces
were controlled by Yugoslav advisers. Yugoslavia's exclusion
from the Cominform in 1948 gave Albania the opportunity to
get rid of this domination, but it became politically, economically and militarily dependent on the Soviet Union. The latter
gave economic aid to Albania, but within the CMEA, which
Albania joined in 1949, it only wanted to give Albania the
status of a supplier of raw materials. In May 1955 Albania was
one of the founding members of the WTO.

Because of the 'de-Stalinisation' pursued by Krushchev, the
resulting normalisation of Soviet–Yugoslav relations in June
1955/June 1956 and the domestic and foreign policy of the
Soviet leaders which the Albanian Communists considered to

be 'revisionist', Albania found itself in increasing opposition to the Soviet Union. During the Communist World Conference of November 1960 in Moscow, Enver Hoxha violently attacked the Soviet leadership and left the conference early. In April 1961 the Soviet Union stopped its economic aid, in June 1961 it left its Albanian naval bases. In October 1961, at the Twenty-Second Congress of the CPSU, Krushchev sharply attacked the PLA, which had not been invited to this Congress; in December 1961 the USSR broke off diplomatic relations with Albania. In September 1968 Albania cancelled its membership in the WTO; furthermore it ceased all co-operation within the CMEA.

Due to the common struggle against Soviet and Yugoslav 'revisionism', Albania established close political and ideological ties with China, from which it received economic and technical aid and whose Cultural Revolution it partially copied. Yet in 1969, when China began step by step to give up its self-chosen isolation in international affairs, first signs of alienation between China and Albania were visible. After the rapprochement between China and the USA in 1971–72, differences deepened; after Mao's death in September 1976 the Albanians sided with the 'Gang of Four', and after the normalisation of the Sino-Yugoslav relations, the Sino-Albanian relations deteriorated further. In July 1977 the Albanians condemned the Chinese 'three worlds' theory' (see pp. 76-7), because it denied international class struggle. (In the Albanian view there are only two worlds: the socialist and the non-socialist.) One year later the Chinese government announced the stopping of economic and military aid and the withdrawal of Chinese experts. According to Albanian opinion, China has also become revisionist. As Albania had made it its duty to fight revisionism, the break with China has not lessened tensions with the Soviet Union.

The relations with Yugoslavia improved somewhat after the Soviet intervention in Czechoslovakia; in February 1971 both countries again exchanged ambassadors. However, the Yugoslav policy towards the Albanians living in the neighbouring Yugoslav Autonomous Province of Kosovo — they are claimed as part of the Albanian nation — still seriously impairs mutual relations. In 1981 they were subject to new tensions because of severe measures taken by Yugoslavia against Kosovo-Albanians following the revolt which was attributed also to Albanian activities by the Yugoslavs.

On the basis of the constitutional adherence to the principle of peaceful coexistence (apart from the commitment to proletarian internationalism), Albania has improved, and is strengthening, its relations with some capitalist countries. In 1971 it established relations with Greece, after the latter had officially given up its claim on Northern Epirus; it established and maintains fairly good relations with Italy, the Scandinavian and Benelux countries, France, Switzerland, Austria and Turkey. There are no diplomatic relations so far with Great Britain because of the British government's refusal to return the crown jewels, nor with the USA, nor with the Federal Republic of Germany, from which Albania demands the payment of reparations. Albania was the only European country which did not participate in the CSCE. Although Albania is a member of the UNO and actually maintains diplomatic relations with about one hundred states, it does not in fact take part in world politics because of its maniacal fear of dependence and of 'class enemies' such as the bourgeoisie, revisionists, imperialists and 'social imperialists'.

NATIONAL DEFENCE

The armed forces consist of the People's Army of about 40,000 soldiers, in addition to 5,000 security troops and a frontier guard of 7,500.[3] The People's Army is under the supreme command of the first secretary of the CC of the PLA who is also chairman of the Defence Council which directs, organises and mobilises all forces for the national defence. The constitution prohibits the establishment of foreign bases, the stationing of foreign troops on Albanian territory and capitulation.

NOTES

1. English text in William B. Simons (ed.), *The Constitutions of the Communist World* (Alphen aan den Rijn, the Netherlands, and Germantown, Md., 1980), pp. 8-31.
2. Richard F. Staar (ed.), *Yearbook on International Communist Affairs 1984: Parties and Revolutionary Movements* (Stanford, Cal., 1984), p. 293.
3. The International Institute for Strategic Studies, London, *The Military Balance 1984–1985* (Oxford, 1984), p. 51.

FURTHER READING

Griffith, William E., *Albania and the Sino-Soviet Rift* (Cambridge, Mass.: MIT Press, 1963)

Lendvai, Paul, *Eagles in Cobwebs: Nationalism and Communism in the Balkans* (London: Macdonald, 1970)

Marmullaku, Ramadan, *Albania and the Albanians* (London: C. Hurst, 1975)

Pano, Nicholas C., *The People's Republic of Albania* (Baltimore, Md.: Johns Hopkins Press, 1968)

Prifti, Peter R., *Socialist Albania since 1944: Domestic and Foreign Developments* (Cambridge, Mass.: MIT Press, 1978)

—— 'The Labour Party of Albania', in Stephen Fischer-Galati (ed.), *The Communist Parties of Eastern Europe* (New York: Columbia University Press, 1979), pp. 5-48

4   People's Republic of Bulgaria

BASIC FEATURES

According to the constitution passed by the National Assembly on 8 May 1971[1] and adopted by a referendum on 16 May 1971, Bulgaria defines itself as 'a socialist state of the working people from town and village, headed by the working class' (article 1). The constitution proclaims the construction of 'a developed socialist society' and establishes, likewise in article 1, the leading role of the Bulgarian Communist Party (BCP) in society and state, which, according to the Party Programme of 1971, is in the stage of transition from a state of the dictatorship of the proletariat to an all-people's state. Bulgaria has a (non-competitive) two-party system; apart from the BCP there is the Bulgarian National Peasants' Union. The fundamental principles of the political system according to article 5 are: national sovereignty, the unity of power, democratic centralism, socialist democratism and socialist internationalism.

THE COMMUNIST TAKEOVER

The course for the absolute rule of the communists was set on 9 September 1944, shortly after the Soviet Union had declared war on Bulgaria and Soviet troops had invaded the country. Power was assumed by a government of the Fatherland Front, which was a coalition of various anti-fascist forces — the left wings of the Agrarian Union and of the Social Democratic Party as well as the Zveno-group — and was dominated by the BCP. By taking over the Ministry of the Interior and the

Ministry of Justice, the communists gained key positions for their struggle against oppositional (pro-German and/or anti-communist) political groupings. The bureaucracy and the army were purged of bourgeois elements. On the basis of a referendum the monarchy was abolished on 15 September 1946 and Bulgaria was proclaimed a 'people's republic'.

At the manipulated elections to the National Assembly on 27 October 1946 the Fatherland Front received 78 per cent of the votes. Georgi Dimitrov — secretary general of the Comintern from 1935 to 1943 — became prime minister. In December 1947 Bulgaria received a constitution very similar to that of the Soviet Union. In it the 'anti-fascist' stage of government was superseded by the stage of the 'people's democratic state', a variant of 'the dictatorship of the proletariat', which is marked by the transition from a capitalist to a socialist society. The coalition partners were either eliminated (Zveno) or merged with the BCP (Social Democrats) or, by being made formally to participate in the government, were forced into the role of 'transmission belts' for the communists (Agrarian Union). Oppositional politicians and 'national' communists coming from the resistance movement were taken to court by those communists who had returned from exile in Moscow and had gained the upper hand within the party. The leader of the Agrarians, Nikola Petkov, and the leader of the 'national' faction of the BCP, Traicho Kostov, were executed.

THE MARXIST-LENINIST PARTY

The BCP emerged from the Bulgarian Social Democratic Party, founded in 1891 and also called the Bulgarian Social Democratic Workers' Party, which, in 1903, split into a 'broad' and a 'narrow' (radical) faction. In 1919 the latter became the Bulgarian Communist Party. In 1983 it claimed 826,000 members, embracing nearly 10 per cent of the population.[2] Applicants for party membership do not have to complete a candidate status but need only the recommendation from three party members. During the last thirty years the relative proportions of peasants and industrial workers in the party membership have been reversed.

The organisational foundation of the BCP are the primary organisations which are formed in production and service enterprises, agricultural co-operatives, administrative, educational, cultural and scientific institutions, villages and residential areas as well as in units of the armed forces. Above the basic level, the organisation of the party parallels the administrative structure of the state. Its national organs are the Congress, which convenes every five years, the Central Committee (CC) with the Political Bureau and the Secretariat both elected by it. Since 1954 Todor Zhivkov has been the first secretary of the party.

Within the communist world movement the BCP unconditionally supports the CPSU. It has always sharply criticised any 'left' and 'right' deviation from the Soviet ideological and political line, for instance, that of the CP of China during the Cultural Revolution and that of the Eurocommunists.

THE BLOC PARTY AND SOCIAL ORGANISATIONS

The second party, the Bulgarian National Peasants' Union, emerged from the Agrarian Party founded in 1899. In 1981 it filed about 120,000 members, of which 80 per cent are collective farm peasants and agricultural workers.[3] Thus, basically, this party is supposed to mobilise the rural elements, still quite strong in Bulgaria, for the aims of the BCP. According to article 1 of the constitution, both parties act in 'close fraternal co-operation'. The Peasants' Union has its representatives in the National Assembly, the Council of State, the Council of Ministers, as well as in the organs of local government.

Because the BCP claims to represent the interest of the whole society, the organised representation of particular interests apart from those of the peasants is very restricted. Social organisations like the trade unions, the Central Union of Co-operatives, the Dimitrov Communist Youth League and the National Peace Committee are primarily in charge of executing the decisions made by the BCP. The trade unions have to watch over the fulfilment of the economic plans, to organise socialist emulation and to stimulate the use of new technological know-how in the production process; in addition, they look after the social welfare of their members. Like some other social organisations the trade unions have the right of legislative initiative on matters of immediate concern to them. Individual interests are more easily articulated informally and realised within the BCP because it is not a monolithic unit but has various groupings. In part, these groupings date back to the split between 'national' and 'Moscow orientated' communists before the takeover, and partly they result from different conceptions of the economic and politico-cultural course to take.

In order to achieve 'socialist democracy', mass and other social organisations are to take over more and more government tasks. The passing on of such tasks is effected by the National Assembly. Cultural affairs are managed by the Committee for Culture, which, however, was set up by a resolution of the CC of the BCP. Its members are the associations of writers, journalists, artists, composers, actors, and so on. Representatives of supreme party and state organs, who no doubt are also members, control and thus ultimately limit the freedom of cultural life, but the Committee as well as the corresponding councils for culture on the local level are nevertheless supposed to contribute to the 'de-etatisation' of social activities.

The goal of the BCP and the social organisations is to integrate the population into a 'Bulgarian socialist nation' and to assimilate the national minorities, of which the Turks are the by far strongest. The BCP tries to obtain more support from the peasants because, in spite of a high rate of industrialisation, agriculture is still the economic mainstay of Bulgaria.

The social organisations are united corporately, single citizens individually, in the Fatherland Front. With about 4.4 million members in 1982,[4] it is the most comprehensive organisation to mobilise the citizenry for the realisation of the 'developed socialist society'. Among its tasks are the nomination of candidates for the elections to the people's representative bodies, the conduct of elections, the initiation of the recall of people's representatives, of referenda and of the discussion of bills, and the setting up of social courts.

CENTRAL GOVERNMENT

According to the constitution, the National Assembly is the supreme representative organ. Its 400 members are elected every 5 years in constituencies with an equal number of inhabitants. Citizens have the right to vote and to be elected as deputies from the age of eighteen. Candidates may be nominated either by one-fifth of the electors of a constituency or by the parties and mass organisations. Citizens and organisations may nominate candidates jointly within the Fatherland Front. If the latter is the case and that is the rule, no further candidate may be nominated. Although legally the nomination of several candidates is permissible, there is virtually only one candidate for each mandate. Thus nomination practically means a sure election. The candidates are drawn up on a single list of the Fatherland Front; one-fourth of the mandates is allocated to the satellite party. At the elections of June 1981, 99.93 per cent of the votes were cast for the list of the Fatherland Front; 271 deputies are members of the BCP, 99 of the Peasants' Union, 30 are not party-affiliated (among them, however, are members of the Youth League). The deputies are responsible and accountable to the electors and may be recalled. A recall may be demanded by one-third of the electors of a constituency or by the organisation which nominated the deputy; this may not, however, be effected merely on account of local interests.

The National Assembly meets for sessions at least three times a year. According to the constitution it, among others, is vested with the following powers: legislation, the direction of domestic and foreign policy, the adoption of the socio-economic plans and of the state budget; the declaration of war and the conclusion of peace, the ratification and denunciation of international treaties; the election and the removal of members of the Council of State, of the Council of Ministers, of the Supreme Court and of the chief procurator; the definition of the responsibilities of the Council of State, of the Council of Ministers, of the people's councils, of the courts and of the Procurator's Office; the control of the state organs and of the observance of the constitution and the laws, and the establishment of the formal and material constitutionality of laws. The plenum is assisted by standing and interim committees which are responsible and accountable to it.

Important powers of the National Assembly are, however, to a large extent exercised by its permanent organ, the Council of State. It consists of the chairman, vice-chairmen, the secretary and members who are elected by the National Assembly from its midst. Formally responsible and accountable to the Assembly, the Council of State embodies the unity of the legislative and executive powers. Between the sessions of the National Assembly it is in charge of the direction of domestic and foreign policy. Legislation lies practically in its hands as it issues decrees on 'matters of principle' (article 94 of the constitution) and may supplement or amend existing laws by decree; it merely has to present the decrees to the National Assembly for approval at its next session. It appoints and removes from office individual members of the Council of Ministers upon recommendation of this organ's chairman, which, just as the appointment of the commander-in-chief of the armed forces, only requires the formal approval of the National Assembly.

Among the original powers of the Council of State is the right to initiate laws, to give a binding interpretation of laws and decrees, to repeal illegal or irregular acts of the Council of Ministers, of the people's councils and of the local administrative organs; to control the activity of the Council of Ministers as well as the heads of the ministries and of other central bodies; and to supervise the observance of laws and law-decrees.

As collective head of state, the Council of State represents Bulgaria in its foreign relations. The chairman of the Council of State stands out among his colleagues as he 'organises and directs' (article 96) the work of this body. In addition, this position has gained particular importance from the fact that the first secretary of the CC of the BCP, Todor Zhivkov, has been chairman of the Council of State since 1971. Constitutional powers and its personal composition thus make the Council of State the decisive organ of state power.

The Council of Ministers consists of the chairman – since July 1971 Stanko Todorov – the vice-chairmen, the ministers and the chairmen of state committees. In fact, decision-making, as far as the Council of Ministers is concerned, is concentrated in an inner core, the Bureau. The formation of the government by the National Assembly is actually confined to the confirmation of the decisions made by the *de facto* supreme party organs. The Council of Ministers is responsible for the implementation of domestic and foreign policy, for the drafting, execution and realisation of the national plans for socio-economic development and of the state budget and for the maintenance of public order and security. As the controlling organ, it repeals illegal acts of the ministers and of the local executive committees. The ministries are supervised by the committees of the National Assembly and especially by the Council of State.

LOCAL GOVERNMENT

Bulgaria has a centralised form of government. It is divided administratively into districts as well as into urban and rural communes; the capital, Sofia, is subdivided into city districts. Several communes are combined into larger settlement units in order to secure a more rational economic development and an improvement of the infrastructure.

The people's councils and their executive committees are charged with the local execution of national and local policies. The people's councils are elected for two and a half years. They are defined as organs of state power and as organs of the people's self-government – the latter function having been strengthened since 1971, particularly with regard to the local economy. The members of the people's councils have, on the one hand, to act according to the national interest and, on the other hand, to represent the interest of their electors. They have to report to their constituents at least once a year and may be recalled by them. The district people's councils meet at least four times a year and the commune and city district councils meet at least six times a year. In order to support their activity, standing commissions are formed which are also open to ordinary citizens. The commune councils have to present important matters to the citizens for a discussion or a referendum.

The work of the people's councils and of their organs is directed and coordinated by the Council of State; the work of their executive committees is directed and coordinated by the Council of Ministers. Due to the principle of dual subordination, the people's councils on a lower administrative level are controlled by the people's councils on the next higher administrative level. A superior people's council may repeal the illegal or irregular acts of an inferior people's council; the executive committee on a higher administrative level may suspend illegal or irregular acts of an inferior people's council and repeal such acts of the executive committee of that people's council. The People's Assembly and the Council of State exercise supreme control over the people's councils.

ADMINISTRATION OF JUSTICE

The judicial system is organised on three levels: Supreme Court, district courts and city district courts. The judges of the Supreme Court are elected by the National Assembly, those at the district courts by the corresponding people's councils and all other judges by the citizens, and may be recalled. The Supreme Court ensures a uniform application of laws and controls the activities of all courts, especially through the annulment of final verdicts. It is responsible and accountable to the National Assembly and, between its sessions, to the Council of State. The courts are required not only to apply the laws but also to adhere to the Programme and the resolutions of the BCP. Social courts, as organs of the administration of justice apart from the regular courts, decide on minor criminal offences as well as on pecuniary quarrels between citizens. The Fatherland Front is responsible for their organisation and direction.

The Procurator's Office consists of the chief procurator, who is elected by the National Assembly for five years and accountable to it and to the Council of State, as well as of the procurators of the districts and city districts appointed by him. The procurators, apart from criminal prosecution, are in charge of the adherence to laws by all state organs, social organisations, officials and citizens. Citizens who feel offended in their rights may make a petition to the procurators. The latter may demand the annulment of illegal measures and the restoration of former rights.

If not expressly excluded by law, citizens may appeal against administrative acts before a regular court, too, which may annul an administrative act it considers illegal. The higher administrative organ decides on the efficacy of an administrative act appealed against by a citizen.

Ministries, administrative bodies, people's councils and economic enterprises are furthermore controlled by the Committees of State and People's Control — joint organs of the BCP and the state co-operating with representatives from the mass organisations. They watch over adherence to the laws and other judicial acts as well as to party directives, and are accountable to the CC of the BCP.

FOREIGN POLICY

Bulgarian foreign policy follows the line of the Soviet Union and, within this limit, also that of its national interest. The indissoluble alliance, friendship and co-operation with the Soviet Union and adherence to the principles of socialist internationalism — in the sense of subordination of national interests to those of the Soviet Union — are constitutional norms. The fostering of especially close ties with the Soviet Union in regard to ideology, politics, the economy, the military and culture, is defined as 'convergence' and not only has historical roots — Bulgaria owes its statehood to the Russians who defeated the Turks in 1877-78 — but is also motivated by ambitious economic self-interest. Bulgaria considers the constitutionally fixed membership of the socialist world community as a guarantee of its independence. It accepts and supports the 'socialist division of labour' within the CMEA, fully approving the Soviet goals of integration.

Relations with neighbouring Yugoslavia have been at times more or less strained because of the 'Macedonian question'. On the grounds of the Peace Treaty of San Stefano in March 1878 Macedonia was annexed by the Principality of Bulgaria; however, at the subsequent Berlin Congress it was attached to the Osman Empire and then as a result of the Second Balkan War of 1913 it was divided between Bulgaria, Serbia and Greece. Whereas within the Yugoslav federation Macedonians have their own nationality and are organised in a republic of their own, Bulgaria regards the Macedonians living on its territory as Bulgarians and denies them the status of a national minority as demanded by Yugoslavia.

For many years Bulgaria's relations with Greece were encumbered by Bulgaria's refusal to pay reparations, and also because of its support of the communists during the Greek civil war (1946-1949). Mutual relations improved after diplomatic ties were established in 1964. Bulgaria is somewhat reserved towards the Greek initiative in favour of multilateral co-operation in the Balkans, although it took part in the Balkan Conference in Athens of January and February 1976. Instead, Bulgaria advocates increased bilateral co-operation, especially in the economic field, which, for example, resulted in the construction of a Bulgarian-Rumanian Danube power station. Following its policy of peace and good neighbourliness in the Balkans, Bulgaria also strives for the establishment in that region of a zone free of nuclear weapons and has apparently succeeded in preventing the USSR to station nuclear missiles on its territory.

NATIONAL DEFENCE

Bulgaria is a founding member of the WTO. Its regular armed forces comprise 147,000 soldiers: army, 105,000; navy, 8,500; air force, 33,800; furthermore, Bulgaria keeps 15,000 border troops, 7,500 security troops and a people's militia of about 150,000.[5] Military-technical instruction and field-instruction serve as premilitary training for sixteen to eighteen-year-old pupils. The organisation of national defence is in the hands of the State Defence Committee, whose members are appointed and dismissed by the Council of State.

NOTES

1. English text in William B. Simons (ed.), *The Constitutions of the Communist World*, (Alphen aan den Rijn, The Netherlands, and Germantown, Md., 1980), pp. 38–67.
2. Richard F. Staar (ed.), *Yearbook on International Communist Affairs 1984: Parties and Revolutionary Movements* (Stanford, Cal., 1984), p. 302.
3. *Zemedelsko Zname* (Sofia), 19 May 1981.
4. *Rabotnichesko Delo* (Sofia), 20 June 1982.
5. The International Institute for Strategic Studies, London, *The Military Balance 1984–1985* (Oxford, 1984), p. 24.

FURTHER READING

Brown, James F., *Bulgaria under Communist Rule* (London: Pall Mall, 1970)

Dellin, L.A.D. (ed.): *Bulgaria* (New York: Praeger, 1957)

—— 'The Communist Party of Bulgaria', in Stephen Fischer-Galati (ed.), *The Communist Parties of Eastern Europe* (New York: Columbia University Press, 1979), pp. 49-86

Lendvai, Paul, *Eagles in Cobwebs: Nationalism and Communism in the Balkans* (London: Macdonald, 1970)

Oren, Nissan, *Revolution Administered: Agrarianism and Communism in Bulgaria* (Baltimore, Md.: Johns Hopkins University Press, 1973)

5 People's Republic of China

BASIC FEATURES

The People's Republic of China (PRC) defines itself in its fourth constitution, adopted on 4 December 1982,[1] as 'a socialist state under the people's democratic dictatorship, led by the working class and based on the alliance of workers and peasants' (article 1). Apart from workers and peasants, however, the preamble of the constitution also assigns to the intellectuals an important role in the establishment of socialism. The people's 'democratic dictatorship' is declared in the preamble to be 'in essence' the 'dictatorship of the proletariat'; the exploiting classes are considered to be eliminated but class struggle must continue 'within certain limits' for a long time. 'All power' is said to belong to the people, which exercises it through the National People's Congress and the local people's congresses (article 2). The state organs practice the principle of democratic centralism.

In contrast to the constitution of 1978,[2] which in article 2 referred to the Communist Party of China (CPC) as 'the core of leadership of the whole Chinese people' and placed it above the state, the present constitution mentions the party's leadership only in the preamble. First, as one of the four Basic Principles — the other three are the adherence to the socialist road, the upholding of the people's democratic dictatorship and guidance by the principles of Marxism-Leninism and Mao Zedong (Mao Tse-tung*) Thought; second, in

---

* The familiar Hepburn romanisation is given in parenthesis for politicians who held office before the introduction of Pinyin romanisation (1979). This also applies to names of provinces, autonomous regions and cities.

connection with the Patriotic Unity Front. The constitution does not define the content of the party's leading role. This, however, can be gathered from the General Programme of the Party Statute of 1982, according to which this role consists in political, ideological and organisational leadership. The provision of article 56 of the constitution of 1978, which made it the cititzens' duty to support the leadership of the CPC, has been dropped.

At the present stage of development the PRC aims at the improvement of the institutions, the development of socialist democracy, the perfection of the legal system and particularly the modernisation of industry, agriculture, national defence and science and technology, which is given priority over the class struggle. In order to achieve these 'Four Modernisations' the Chinese party and state leadership, which admits that by adherence to the teachings of Marx and Engels not *all* present problems can be solved, employs unorthodox methods. This fact becomes apparent in the economic reforms, which include the transference of decision-making powers to the enterprises in order to stimulate competition, the use of market mechanisms, the protection and promotion of individual economy, the private use of (collectively owned) plots, the stressing of material working incentives and the strengthening of the profit motive in order to increase economic efficiency. With this aim in view, and in accordance with the constitution, the PRC encourages foreign investments and joint ventures, and even permits the establishment of purely foreign enterprises; privileged treatment has been provided for them in Special Economic Zones. Insofar as these zones are situated adjacent to Hong Kong, Macao and Taiwan, they are also supposed to develop some attraction for the citizens of these territories, which in the short or the long run the PRC is striving to incorporate.

The economic policy implies a renunciation of Mao's idea of an egalitarian society. In fact, the Chinese leaders have abandoned a good deal of the teachings of the former party chairman, who for his part had already adopted Marxism to the concrete necessities of the Chinese style of socialist revolution, though, on the other hand, by 'seeking truth in practice', they do exactly what Mao demanded.

The constitution establishes clear rules of institutional behaviour, and it grants extensive civic rights to citizens. In order to restore the citizens' trust in legality, heavily damaged during the Cultural Revolution, the constitution determines that all state organs, the armed forces, *all* political parties and social organisations, enterprises and institutions must abide by the constitution and the law, and provides for the independence of the judiciary, however little practical significance this may have in view of the priority of policy over the law.

THE COMMUNIST TAKEOVER

The takeover by the CPC resulted from the 'anti-feudal' civil war against the Guomindang government of Jiang Jieshi (Chiang Kai-shek) and the 'anti-imperialistic' struggle against the Japanese. The theoretical foundations of the communists were (1) Mao's Doctrine on New Democracy, according to which the CPC in its struggle for liberation from domestic and foreign oppression — the preliminary stage of the socialist revolution — should be based on an alliance of all patriotically minded classes: workers, peasants, the petty bourgeoisie and 'national bourgeoisie'; (2) Mao's conception of a coalition government composed of representatives of the CPC, the Guomindang (Kuomintang: National People's Party) and of people with no party affiliation, but leaving no doubt about the leading role of the communists.

After its foundation in July 1921, the then very weak CPC, on the instigation of the Comintern, co-operated for a few years with the Guomindang, which was founded by Sun Yixian (Sun Yat-sen) in 1912. After the break between both parties in 1927 and unsuccessful attempts to initiate revolts in towns, the communists, severely persecuted by Jiang Jieshi returned to the countryside according to Mao's conviction that the peasants should be the main driving force of the revolution. In 1931 they proclaimed a Chinese Soviet Republic in the province of Jiangxi (Kiangsi). Giving way to the strong military pressure of Jiang Jieshi and suffering heavy losses, Mao led his troops during the Long March from October 1934 until October 1935, into the province of

Shaanxi (Shensi), and established his headquarters in Yan'an (Yenan). In 1934 he was elected chairman of the CPC Central Committee.

After the beginning of the Sino-Japanese war in 1937, the CPC and the Guomindang government agreed to fight the invaders jointly. But there were no co-ordinated actions, the Guomindang troops continued to fight the communists, and by 1942 the anti-Japanese United Front had disintegrated. In the course of their operations, however, the communists succeeded in broadening their area of control. By splitting up large-scale land-holdings, they gained the sympathy of the poor peasants as well as that of some of the bourgeoisie because of their resolute defence against the Japanese. When the Japanese surrendered in 1945 the civil war erupted again. After US-General George C. Marshall's unsuccessful attempts in 1945 and 1946 to establish a coalition government between the Guomindang and the CPC, the communists started a broad offensive and defeated the demoralised armed forces of Jiang Jieshi, who departed to Taiwan with part of his troops and the administrative apparatus.

With the takeover by the communists, the national 'new democratic' revolution has emerged victorious. In September 1949, on the initiative and under the control of the communists, the Chinese People's Political Consultative Conference (CPPCC) convened. It was the representative body of the Unity Front, consisting of delegates of the CPC, non-communist parties willing to co-operate with the communists, mass organisations and the People's Liberation Army (PLA). It adopted a Common Programme, in which the developing new state was defined as a state of the people's democratic dictatorship, led by the working class, and established a central government under the chairmanship of Mao Zedong. On 1 October 1949 the People's Republic of China was proclaimed. The National Committee of the CPPCC acted as parliament until the election, in 1954, of the First National People's Congress, which on 20 September of that year passed the first constitution of the PRC; Mao Zedong became head of state and Zhou Enlai (Chou En-lai) premier.

THE GREAT LEAP FORWARD AND THE CULTURAL REVOLUTION

During the period between 1953 and 1957, the PRC closely followed the Soviet model of building socialism by central planning and by predominantly developing heavy industry at the cost of agriculture. The continuation of this economic policy, however, proved impracticable for lack of capital, of technology and of skilled workers, whereas at the same time the immense rural labour-force potential remained unexploited. Mao Zedong therefore decided that economic strategy should be based on the participation of the masses of rural people, the employment of unsophisticated technology, the development of small industries and decentralised economic planning. In 1958, and in the course of a policy labelled the Great Leap Forward (until 1960) the Chinese established the so-called people's communes. Regarded as germ cells of a communist society, they were simultaneously, first, agricultural and industrial economic units, which took responsibility for planning, production and distribution, were sub-divided into production brigades and production teams, and used all means of production collectively (including the plots which the peasants had until then exploited privately); second, they were institutions which administered social, educational, cultural and, through the people's militia, military affairs; third, a form of social organisation characterised by the severance of family bonds and militarisation of social life (dormitory living, communal mess hall). They were also supposed to overcome the differences between workers and peasants, town and countryside, manual work and brain work.

The Great Leap Forward policy was based on Mao's idea that priority should be given to the change in conditions of production through class-struggle, revolutionary actions of the mass of the people and the stimulation of their creative spontaneity. This developmental strategy, however, encountered opposition from prominent party and state leaders, who gathered around the former president of the PRC, Liu Shaoqi (Liu Shao-chi), and Deng Xiaoping (Teng Hsiao-ping), and advocated an economic policy which would lay stress on the development of productive forces (machines, capital and science) and on material incentives.

In 1966 the struggle between the 'two lines' resulted in the Great Proletarian Cultural Revolution. It was, politically, a struggle for power between these two factions; ideologically, it was an attempt to replace 'bourgeois' values and behaviour by collectivist values through a change in the state of mind of the masses. Theoretically, it was based on Mao's Doctrine on Contradictions (of 1937–57), in which he had distinguished 'antagonistic contradictions' (between the people and its enemies), which can only be resolved by force, and 'non-antagonistic contradictions' (within the people), which may be resolved by open discussion, persuasion and education. The Cultural Revolution was characterised by the Maoist faction as a struggle between antagonistic forces continuing to exist also in a socialist and even communist society. Mao, who, when the Standing Committee of the CPC's Political Bureau voted on a new campaign against critical intellectuals turned out to be in the minority, gained the upper hand with the help of the military, appealed to the masses to legitimate his position against the Liu faction and called for permanent revolution. The standard-bearers of this movement were the Red Guards of students and pupils, developing spontaneously and highly politicised, and later also the Red Rebels (young factory workers) who sided against bureaucracy, privileges and bourgeois ideas and behaviour, using means of physical and psychic terror, disregarding any authority but that of Mao. In 1967 the party and state apparatus was virtually dismantled and replaced by Revolutionary Committees, composed — according to the principle of the 'triple alliance' — by representatives of the Red Guards, purged CPC cadres and the PLA, which was the sole body to discipline the Red Guards and to restore order.

In 1969, when the CPC held its Ninth Congress and steps were taken to reconstruct its organisation, the violent phase of the Cultural Revolution ended. Officially it is considered to have ended in 1976 with the arrest of the 'Gang of Four' one month after Mao's death, on 9 September. This group of party and state leaders around Mao's widow Jiang Qing (Chiang Ching) was accused of having attempted to seize power by mobilising the masses against the modernising economic policy initiated in 1975 by the then premier and vice-premier, Zhou Enlai and Deng Xiaoping, respectively — a course which the 'Gang' denounced as a rightist deviation from Mao's teachings.

THE MARXIST-LENINIST PARTY

The CPC considers itself to be 'the vanguard of the Chinese working class, the faithful representative of the interests of *all the Chinese people* and the core of leadership of China's socialist cause'; its final goal is 'the realisation of a communist social system' (General Programme of the Party Statute of 1982).[3] In 1983 the party claimed a membership of over 40 million[4] — roughly 3.9 per cent of the total population and constitutes by far the strongest Communist Party in the world. 'Any Chinese worker, peasant, member of the armed forces, intellectual, or any other revolutionary' (article 1 of the Statute) having reached the age of eighteen may join the party on the recommendation of two party members. Full membership is achieved after one probationary year. Primary organisations are established at places of work and of residence, and furthermore in the units of the PLA. Above the basic level, the party is organised according to the administrative structure of the state, but the PLA has a party apparatus of its own, subordinate to the central party organs.

Formally, the supreme organs of the CPC are the National Party Congress, which according to the Statute convenes every five years, and the Central Committee (CC), which holds a session at least once a year. The Twelfth Party Congress of September 1982 elected a CC of 348 full and alternate members. Almost two-thirds of them were elected for the first time, and they are, essentially, close adherents of the pragmatic modernisation policy. Another effect of the new election of the CC has been its limited rejuvenation. Quite a number of the former members, among them opponents to the new course, have been relegated to the Central Advisory Commission, which is a sort of 'council of elders': its members must have been party members for at least forty years, must have rendered the party great service and enjoy a high reputation inside and outside the party.

The CC directs the whole party activity, but in view of its rare sessions it is replaced in exercising this task by the Political Bureau and its Standing Committee. The latter is really the leading and authoritative organ of the CPC. It consists of six members: the secretary general of the CC, Hu Yaobang, who directs the work of the CC Secretariat; the chairman of the CC Military Commission and of the Central Advisory Commission, Deng Xiaoping; the first secretary of the Central Discipline Inspection Commission, Chen Yun; the president of the republic, Li Xiannian; the premier, Zhao Ziyang; and Marshal Ye Jianying*. The office of 'chairman' of the party's CC, first occupied by Mao Zedong and after his death by Hua Guofeng (Hua Kuo-feng), has been abolished. Through the accumulation of party positions and his albeit not entirely unquestioned authority, Deng Xiaoping exerts decisive influence on the decision-making of the party.

In order to safeguard the attainment of the goal of 'socialist modernisation', the CPC exercises leadership on the basis of three principles. First, ideological and political unity: every party member is obliged to fight against factionism, sectarianism and scheming. When determining its ideological line, the party has to link theory with practice. Second, the observance of the 'mass line': according to this Maoist principle (of 1943), the party has to maintain close contact with the masses; it must study and sum up their (scattered) views, convert them into concrete, systematic ideas, explain these ideas to the masses until they embrace them as their own, mobilise the masses to take action and test the correctness of the ideas in action. Criticism and self-criticism must help to find the 'right' solution, counteract a possible isolation of the party from the masses and prevent misuse of positions. Third, democratic centralism, which underlies the organisation and decision-making of the party: on the one hand, this principle implies strict implementation of party resolutions and the subordination of the lower party organisations to the higher.

---

*In September 1985, in the course of a further rejuvenation of the leading party organs, the 88 year old Marshal, who has been an opponent of Deng's modernisation policy, was caused to retire.

On the other hand, a party member, on condition that he implements the majority resolutions, is granted the right to retain his opinion and to submit it to a higher party organisation for consideration. If a lower party organisation holds the view that a decision of a higher organisation does not sufficiently take into account the concrete conditions in its area, it may apply for a revision to this decision. If the higher organisation insists on its decision, the lower one has to implement it but may turn to the next higher organisation but one. Any kind of personality cult is forbidden.

All activities of the CPC must be carried out within the framework of the constitution and the law. The primary organisations are obliged to educate party cadres in the observance of the law, which, to be sure, embodies the party's will. The functions of the party and the state are, in principle, to be separated from each other The party committees may no longer issue directives to state organs, although it may be long before this demand is fulfilled. A 'rectification' campaign, which is now going on, aims at the purge of all party members unwilling to pursue the post-Maoist reform policy. The study of Mao Zedong Thought has been widely replaced by the study of the *Selected Works* of Deng Xiaoping.

The relationship of the CPC with the CPSU is characterised by differences of opinion, which particularly concern the 'right' interpretation and application of the teachings of Marx, Engels, Lenin and Stalin, and which are rooted in different traditions of thinking and specific revolutionary experience. The dissent first became apparent in 1956, when Krushchev initiated 'de-Stalinisation' in the USSR, and when he declared the concept of peaceful coexistence to be the guideline of Soviet foreign policy towards the capitalist states, especially the USA, denying the inevitability of wars between socialist and capitalist states. It increased because of the Great Leap Forward on the road to communism, which became manifest in the establishment of the people's communes and by means of which the Chinese communists repudiated the Soviet claim to set a binding example for the building of socialism and later of communism. A further reason for the deterioration of relations has been the thesis, also put forward by Krushchev, that the USSR has transformed itself from a state of the dictatorship of the proletariat into an 'all-people's state', and the CPSU from a class party into a party of the whole people, which the Chinese denounced as revisionist deviation. The polemics which the CPC commenced in April 1960, and which were at first indirect, resulted in the rejection of the CPSU's claim to leadership in the communist world movement, and the branding of the Soviet Union as a 'socio-imperialistic' power. In 1963 party relations were broken off. The CPC stresses the equality and independence of all Communist Parties and demands that no Communist Party interferes in the internal affairs of another.

BLOC PARTIES AND SOCIAL ORGANISATIONS

From the days of the anti-Guomindang Unity Front, there have been eight small so-called 'democratic parties': the Democratic Workers' and Peasants' Party (with engineers and doctors, among others, as members); the Revolutionary Committee of the Guomindang (consisting of opponents of Jiang Jieshi within the Guomindang); the China Democratic League (which, formed mainly by intellectuals, had sided with the CPC against the Guomindang); the Association for the Promotion of Democracy (founded in 1945 by teachers, artists and intellectuals); the National Democratic Construction Association (which was formed in 1945 by members of the urban bourgeoisie); the Jiusan Society (whose members are mainly scientists); the Taiwan Democratic Self-Government League (founded by the CPC in order to organise the resistance of mainland Taiwanese against the Guomindang); and Zhi Gong Dang (which is supposed to mobilise support for the PRC among overseas Chinese).

Mass and other social organisations are the All-China Federation of Trade Unions, the Communist Youth League, which is the up-and-coming organisation of the CPC, the All-China Students' Federation, the Young Pioneers, the All-China Democratic Women's Federation, the People's Militia; the All-China Federation of Returned Overseas

Chinese; peasants' associations; organisations with specialised tasks in the fields of economy, science, culture, social welfare and sports; religious associations (of the Buddhists, the Taoists, the Muslims, the Catholics and the Protestants).

During the Cultural Revolution the social organisations had been dissolved or stripped of their functions and had been replaced by the Red Guards and the Red Rebels. The 'democratic parties' had to cease their activities and the religious communities were firmly suppressed. At the beginning of the 1970s, parallel to and partially after the reconstruction of the CPC, the organisations were revived, resumed their former functions and were also entrusted with new tasks.

The trade unions must first of all contribute to the increase of economic output by educating the workers ideologically and in specialist fields. They must fight manifestations of bureaucracy, and foster labour morale. It is further their task to strive for an improvement of the living conditions of the workers. The right to strike, guaranteed by the 1978 constitution, which was conceived less as an instrument of the workers to pursue material demands than as a means of criticism — for example, of bureaucratic behaviour on the part of the management — has been abolished. Demands for the formation of autonomous trade-unions on the model of the Polish Solidarity (see pp. 190-1) have been suppressed.

The 'democratic parties' are expected to play an active role in the realisation of the modernisation policy. They closely co-operate with the CPC on the basis of programmes which fully reflect the goals of the communists, and have representatives at the National People's Congress and its Standing Committee. Many of their members are experts in the fields of economy and science, and their knowledge is therefore welcomed by the state organs as well as their international contacts. The CPPCC, the organisation of the Unity Front and the framework for the co-operation of these parties, national minorities, the associations of the religious communities and the returned overseas Chinese as well as other social organisations with the CPC, and under its guidance, was reactivated in 1978. The National Committee of the CPPCC, which has a limited consultative function in the policy-making process, meets in session simultaneously with the national representative body. Its chairman, succeeding Deng Xiaoping, is Mrs Deng Yingchao, a member of the CPC Political Bureau.

The religious communities may again develop their activities which, according to article 36 of the constitution, are protected by the state, as far as they are 'normal' and do not disrupt public order. Many temples, mosques and churches, devastated during the Cultural Revolution, have been opened and restored, and lamas, imams and priests have been allowed to resume their functions. Religious affairs, however, must not be subject to foreign domination. Consequently, the Chinese Catholic Church is independent of the Pope; the latter may not exert any influence on the nomination of bishops.

According to the 'mass line' principle, the social organisations are not only intended to transmit the CPC's decisions into the daily life of the citizens, but they are also conceived, like the people's representative organs and the urban neighbourhood and villagers' committees of the people's self-management as a source of opinion formation, a sounding-board of the party's work and an instrument for the mobilisation of the citizens for the party's goals. The organisations operate, to be sure, under the strict control of the CPC. 'Guiding groups' of the party within the leading bodies of these organisations see to the implementation of the CPC's policy.

DISSENT

The constitution guarantees the citizens freedom of speech, press, assembly and association, procession and demonstration. Political or social activities, however, may not damage the interests of the state or of society, which are always defined solely by the CPC.

There have been two major examples of manifestation of dissidence in the history of the PRC. First, that of 1957, when intellectuals and members of the 'democratic parties', encouraged by the party's slogan of May 1956 'Let flowers of many kinds blossom, diverse schools of thought contend', attacked the PRC's monopoly of power and demanded the formation of political institutions, characteristic of Western democracies. The party tolerated these counter-revolutionary views for only about four weeks. It curtailed the campaign, the intellectuals involved had to exercise self-criticism, and many of them were confined to labour camps for 're-education'. The second outburst of dissent occurred in autumn 1978, when citizens put up wall posters on the 'Democracy Wall' in Beijing (Peking), in which they criticised some aspects of the socialist order of state and society, the dictatorship of the proletariat and also infringements of human rights. Although the constitution of March 1978 guaranteed the right 'to write big-character posters' (article 45), the government suppressed this activity at the end of March 1979 by administrative means; the Human Rights League was prohibited.

CENTRAL GOVERNMENT

The people's supreme representative body is the National People's Congress (NPC). Its members are not elected by the citizens but by the people's congresses of the provinces, autonomous regions and municipalities directly under the central government, and by units of the armed forces. The candidates are mainly proposed by the CPC, but the other licensed parties, mass organisations and groupings of citizens also have the right of proposal. The number of candidates must exceed that of the deputies to be elected. The deputies are obliged to listen to and convey the opinions and demands of the people, and to maintain close contact with the units which elected them. They are subject to their control and may be recalled. Of the 2,978 deputies elected to the Sixth NPC in May 1983 26.6 per cent are supposed to be workers and peasants, 9.0 per cent members of the PLA, 23.5 per cent members of the intelligentsia, 21.4 per cent administrative cadres, 18.2 per cent representatives of the 'democratic parties' and non-party aligned 'patriotic' personalities, and 1.3 per cent Chinese returned from abroad. The national minorities, which according to the constitution are entitled to appropriate representation, hold 13.5 per cent of the seats.[5]

The NPC is elected for a five-year term, which may, however, be extended, and it should meet in sessions, which usually last about two weeks, at least once a year. (In the 1960s and 1970s there were deviations both from the term of office and the constitutionally fixed frequency of plenary sessions.) This fact and its size alone make the NPC unsuitable for efficient parliamentary work. The constitutional powers of the NPC include: the amendment of the constitution; the election of the president and the vice-president of the republic; the (formal) decision on the appointment of the premier (on the proposal of the president of the PRC — not on the nomination of the CC of the CPC as under the constitution of 1978) and of the other members of the government (upon recommendation by the premier); the approval of the plans for national economic and social development and of the state budget; decisions on questions of war and peace. Its legislative power is principally limited to the drawing up and the revision of 'basic laws' on the state structure, civil affairs and on criminal offences.

Legislation is predominantly exercised by the Standing Committee of the NPC, which must meet in session every other week, with the help of committees, such as the Nationalities' Committee, the Finance and Economic Committee, the Education, Science, Culture and Public Health Committee, and the Foreign Affairs Committee. These committees, under the direction of the Standing Committee, discuss and draw up bills and draft resolutions. Apart from exercising original legislative power, the Standing Committee acts as 'substitute parliament' and exercises the functions of a parliament presidium together with judicial functions. Between the sessions of the NPC it is entitled to enact partial supplements and amendments to laws enacted by the NPC, to approve partial adjustments of the development plan and of the state budget, to decide on the appointment of ministers and of other senior officials, and to decide on the proclamation of a state of war. The Standing Committee convenes ordinary and extraordinary sessions of the NPC, and it may extend the term of office of the NPC. Among the judicial functions are the supervision of the enforcement of the constitution and the interpretation of the constitution and the laws. Moreover, the Standing Committee is empowered to annul administrative regulations and decisions of the State Council and of the organs of local government at the province level which contravene the constitution and the laws. The Standing Committee is elected by the NPC and is responsible to it. It is composed of the chairman (at present Peng Zhen) and twenty vice-chairmen who may serve no more than two consecutive terms, the secretary general and 133 further members.

The present constitution provides again for an individual head of state. From 1954 to 1959 the office of the chairman of the People's Republic of China was held by Mao Zedong. He was succeeded by his rival Liu Shaoqi, who, accused of revisionist deviation during the Cultural Revolution, did not exercise the office after 1966 and was unconstitutionally dismissed from this post in 1968. Under the constitutions of 1975 and 1978 the functions of head of state were transferred to the Standing Committee of the NPC, which entrusted the performance of some of the responsibilities of head of state to its chairman. The command of the armed forces was exercised by the chairman of the CC of the CPC. The president of the republic, since June 1983, Li Xiannian, is elected by the NPC for a five years' term of office, may be re-elected only for one subsequent term and be recalled by the NPC. He is assisted by the vice-president of the PRC, at present the Mongol Ulanhu, who will succeed him, should the office of the president become vacant. The president represents the PRC internally and externally; he promulgates laws, appoints and dismisses the premier and the members of the government, proclaims martial law and a state of war, and ratifies and abrogates international treaties. But he does not command the armed forces. This function has been entrusted to the Central Military Commission, virtually to its chairman, at present Deng Xiaoping, who is elected by the NPC and is responsible for the work of this organ.

The State Council, which is the 'Central People's Government', is the executive organ of the NPC and of the Standing Committee, and the highest organ of state administration. It consists of the premier, at present Zhao Ziyang, who in 1980 succeeded Hua Guofeng, the vice-premiers, the state counsellors, the ministers, the chairmen of commissions, the chief auditor and the secretary general. The term of office of the State Council corresponds to that of the NPC; the tenure of the premier, his deputies and the state counsellors is limited to two consecutive terms; this is, ten years. The premier directs the work of the State Council and bears full responsibility for it. There are Ministries, *inter alia*, of Foreign Affairs, Defence, Foreign Trade, Finance, Public Security (police), State Security, Justice, Education, Culture and for the administration of numerous industrial branches. Commissions are responsible for such fields as reform of the economic system, planning, science, technology and industry for national defence, nationalities' affairs and family planning. Altogether the State Council has about sixty members. This size makes an inner cabinet, the Permanent Conference, necessary, a body which, comprising the premier, his deputies, the state counsellors and the secretary general (who at present is one of the vice-premiers), decides on day-to-day matters of state together with the Secretariat of the CC of the CPC.

The powers and functions of the State Council include: the administration of state affairs; the enactment of administrative rules and regulations; the submission of drafts to the NPC or its Standing Committee; the drawing up and implementation of the economic plan and the state budget; the unified direction of the work of local organs of state administration and the revision or annulment of inappropriate decisions issued by them; the administration of the affairs of the national minorities and the safeguarding of the equality of their rights; the protection of the rights and interests of overseas Chinese and of those returned home. A special body established by the State Council and under the direction of the premier has to audit the revenues and the expenditures of the departments under the State Council and of the local governments, of the state financial and monetary institutions and of the state enterprises.

LOCAL GOVERNMENT

Beneath the national level the PRC has a four-tier administrative system. The province level consists of twenty-one provinces, five autonomous regions and three municipalities directly under the central government (Beijing, Shanghai and Tianjin: Tientsin). The district level is made up of areas (special districts), cities under province jurisdiction (which are step by step replacing the former) and autonomous districts. The next administrative level comprises the counties, autonomous counties and towns, as well as the municipal districts, into which the municipalities and other large cities are subdivided. The lowest administrative level is formed by the rural communes (*xiang*) and nationality communes, small towns and sub-districts (in larger cities, towns and municipal districts); the people's communes, as far as they still exist, have lost their governmental competences and exercise merely economic functions.

The representative bodies of these administrative units, with the exception of the areas which are administered by special organs of the province government, and the (urban) sub-districts, are the people's congresses. Only the deputies of the people's congresses at the commune and county levels are, for a three-year term, directly elected by the citizens; the deputies of all the other people's congresses are elected, for a five-year term, indirectly by the people's congresses at the respective next lower administrative level. The deputies are supervised by their electoral units or by their voters, respectively, and they are subject to recall. The people's congresses at and above the county level elect standing committees. The executive organs are the people's governments, at the top of which are the governors (in the provinces), the chairmen of the autonomous administrative units, the mayors, and the heads of the counties, city districts and communes, who are elected and may be recalled by the corresponding people's congresses. The people's governments have replaced the Revolutionary Committees, which were introduced during the Cultural Revolution and which, besides administrative tasks, then also exercised functions of local party organs. When, after 1969, the party apparatus was re-established, the

Revolutionary Committees had to give up the party functions, but they continued to be the local government under the constitutions of 1975 and 1978, and until around the end of 1977 and the beginning of 1978 they were also in charge of factories.

The people's congresses are bound to ensure the observance and implementation of the constitution, the laws, and administrative rules and regulations. The standing committees supervise the work of the people's governments and are entitled to annul inappropriate decisions and orders of the people's governments at the same level and inappropriate resolutions of the people's congresses at the next lower level. The people's governments at and above the county level direct the work of the people's governments at lower levels and are empowered to annul inappropriate decisions. According to the principle of dual subordination a local people's government is responsible to the people's congress at the same administrative level as well as to the government at the next higher level. The heads of the local governments are individually responsible for their work. All people's governments work under the leadership of the State Council and are subordinate to it.

At the urban and rural places of residence operate residents' and villagers' committees which are considered as 'self-management organisations of the masses at the basis level' (article 111). They are elected and recalled by the citizens, who are organised in residents' groups comprising several households. These committees, in turn, establish mediation committees, committees for public security, public health and other public affairs, which mediate in civil disputes, watch over public order, are responsible for the maintenance of workshops, shops and sanitary stations, and contribute to family planning (by distribution of contraceptives). Thus they see to individual needs, give people a certain degree of social security but also help the state to control the conduct of the citizens.

SELF-GOVERNMENT OF THE NATIONAL MINORITIES

On the territory of the PRC there are fifty-five officially recognised minorities, which amount to 6.7 per cent of the total population. As far as they live in compact communities, the constitution grants them autonomy. The most important minorities inhabit areas which have the status of autonomous regions: the Zhuang (Guangxi: Kwangsi), the Tibetans (Xizang: Tibet), the Uighurs (Xinjiang: Sinkiang), the Mongols (Neimenggu: Inner Mongolia), and the Hui, who are Chinese Muslims (Ningxia: Ningsia). Autonomous districts and autonomous counties are granted to minor nationalities.

The people's congresses and people's governments in these areas are supposed to exercise not only state power but also self-government. The people's congresses are authorised to regulate affairs in accordance with local economic and cultural conditions. The 'regulations' which they may pass, however, need endorsement by the Standing Committee of the NPC or by the standing committee of the people's congress of the province or autonomous region to become effective. Self-government comprises administration in the fields of economic development, education, science, culture, public health and physical culture; the administration of finances, which implies the independent use of revenues allocated to the autonomous areas by the state; and the independent administration of local economic development, in accordance, however, with the state plans. The national minorities are granted the use of their language, and they have liberty to preserve their customs and habits, or to reform them. In performing their functions, the organs of self-government should employ the language or languages commonly used in the respective areas.

On the whole, however, the constitutional powers of self-government should not be taken at their face value. The CPC's policy towards the national minorities aims above all at their full integration into the Chinese state and their education in socialist values. The minorities hold a certain number of seats in the NPC — at present twice as many as their share in the local population. But the NPC is by no means a body of real decision-making.

The autonomous areas, which cover about one half of China's territory, are declared to be inalienable parts of the PRC, and manifestations of 'chauvinism' are strongly opposed. Any attempt at independence is suppressed by military force, as demonstrated between 1958 and 1959 when the Tibetans, who had been annexed by the PRC in 1951, revolted against Chinese rule. The compulsory or voluntary settling of Han Chinese in autonomous areas, particularly in Tibet and Xinjiang, on the one hand, and growing national consciousness, on the other have led to cultural conflicts; and the feeling of some nationalities that their territories are being regarded as producers of cheap raw materials have increased tensions. Due to a low educational level, the national minorities still lack their own cadres and they feel discriminated against when admission to a high school and tenure of an administrative position require knowledge of the Chinese language. The central government is constitutionally committed to give the national minorities financial, material and technical assistance in order to accelerate their economic and cultural development, and to help them train their own administrative cadres, specialists and skilled workers. Their autonomous development, however, will ultimately depend on the renunciation of all attempts at Sinianisation, on the overcoming of Han chauvinism, on the unhindered exercise of the minorities' religions (Islam and Buddhism), on giving them real chances to settle their affairs with the help of the central organs, but without too much interference, and on treating them virtually as the equals of the Han in all sectors of public life. As far as autonomous areas are in close contiguity with the Soviet Union, a good-will policy towards minorities is also in the interest of the security of the whole country.

Yet, after all, the PRC is a unitary state, organised on the principle of democratic centralism, which requires the absolute subordination of lower administrative units to higher ones.

ADMINISTRATION OF JUSTICE

Judicial organs comprise the Supreme People's Court, the people's courts in the local administrative units, military and other special people's courts. The Supreme People's Court, whose president is elected by the NPC and whose vice-presidents and judges are appointed by the NPC's Standing Committee, supervises the work of the local people's courts and is responsible to the NPC and to its Standing Committee. Local people's courts operate at and above the county level. Those at a higher level supervise those of a lower level, and they are responsible to the people's congresses, which have elected them. Minor civil disputes and misdemeanours are mostly settled by the local mediation committees, which through their activity to a large extent relieve the work of the courts.

In contrast to the practice which developed during the Cultural Revolution and was characterised by the 'mass line' principle gaining the upper hand over jurisdiction by professional judges, emphasis is now laid on the law as the guiding line of jurisdiction and on proper legal procedures. The provision of article 41 of the 1978 constitution, which required participation of the masses as accessors in the administration of justice and inclusion of the masses for discussion and suggestions 'with regard to major counter-revolutionary or criminal cases' has been omitted from the present constitution. The courts should exercise jurisdiction free from interference by administrative organs, social organisations or individuals. A series of measures — like the enactment of a new criminal code and a criminal procedural code, of a law on civil procedure, of a law on the organisation of the courts and procuracies, the restoration of the Ministry of Justice, the training of lawyers, the establishment of the right of the accused to defence — aim at creating more confidence in 'socialist legality'.

Arrests must be carried out by a public security organ and only with the approval or by decision of the procuracy or a court. Of particular significance, in view of the humiliating judicial arbitrariness which many Chinese experienced during the Cultural Revolution, is article 38, which declares the personal dignity of citizens inviolable and which prohibits insult, slander, false accusation or defamation of citizens. The constitution pays great attention to fundamental rights, handling them in a more detailed manner than previous constitutions. The limitations to their exercise is laid down in the general clause of article 1, which prohibits sabotage of the socialist system, and by article 51, which determines that citizens must not damage the interests of the state, of society and of the collective, nor infringe upon the lawful freedoms and rights of other citizens.

The preamble of the constitution calls upon the Chinese people to fight forces and elements which are hostile to the socialist system and seek to undermine it. The law, consequently, also serves the class-struggle which is expected to continue, 'within certain limits', for a long time to come. This implies the struggle against 'capitalist, feudal, and other decadent ideologies' and the suppression of 'counter-revolutionary activities' (articles 24 and 28). Increasing criminality is counteracted by admission to labour and re-education camps and by severe penalties, including the death penalty, which is intended to act as a deterrent.

The constitution grants citizens the right to lodge with the relevant state organ a complaint or a charge of violation of a law by state organs or state functionaries. The state organ concerned must deal with the complaint or charge by investigating the facts. Citizens who have suffered losses, by infringement upon their rights, are entitled to compensation. The overall supervision over the obedience to the law is entrusted to the Supreme People's Procuracy and to the local people's procuracies. The former is responsible to the NPC and its Standing Committee; the latter are responsible to the local people's congresses and to the people's procuracies at higher levels.

FOREIGN POLICY

The preamble of the constitution declares that Chinese foreign policy adheres to the principles of peaceful coexistence, serves the struggle against imperialism, hegemonism and colonialism, supports the developing countries in their struggle for independence and strives to safeguard world peace and to promote human progress. The ideological frame of reference for interpreting international relations is the 'three worlds' theory' introduced by Deng Xiaoping in April 1974 and based on Mao Zedong's teachings on contradictions. This theory rejects the class criterion and divides states up into the 'first world', which consists of the two 'imperialist' super-powers, the USA and the USSR, the latter of which the Chinese for a time regarded as even more dangerous than the former. The 'third world' is made up of the developing countries of Asia, Africa and Latin America, and the 'second world', in between, comprises the capitalist *and* socialist industrial states. Nevertheless, the PRC regards peaceful co-existence as a guiding principle of its foreign policy also with respect to the USA and the USSR. It should underlie China's relations with all states, independent of their social order; that is, the socialist ones as well. This implies the rejection of the principle of socialist internationalism, which according to the Soviets should govern relations between socialist states. The Chinese attitude corresponds with their view that international relations should develop on the basis of the strict equality of states.

The PRC's foreign policy may be divided into five phases. The first, lasting until 1957–58, was characterised by close relations with the Soviet Union on the basis of a pact of alliance and an economic agreement of 1950, and a policy of confrontation between the PRC and the USA. To this period belonged also the intervention in the Korean War and the participation in the Bandung Conference (1955), where the PRC established contacts with Third World countries. The second phase, beginning in 1958, was marked particularly by the emergence of tensions with the USSR: the Soviets withdrew their support for the Chinese nuclear programme, recalled their technicians, trade relations were loosened and the two Communist Parties accused each other of having betrayed Marxist-Leninist principles; in the Sino-Indian border war of 1962 the USSR remained neutral. A further feature of this period consisted in China's attempt to unite developing countries into an anti-imperialist front, at first against the USA, later against the USSR, too. The third phase began in 1966, when the PRC, preoccupied with the Cultural Revolution, severed relations with most countries (one of the exceptions was Albania). The confrontation with the Soviet Union, whose military intervention in Czechoslovakia aroused fears of 'penal action', increased, culminating in armed clashes at the Ussuri River in March 1969. (Apart from the ideological controversy, relations with the USSR are also burdened by quarrels about the common border established in the nineteenth century by 'unequal treaties'.)

When, in 1969, negotiations with the Soviet Union proved unsuccessful, the PRC sought a rapprochement with Japan and the USA. In this fourth phase of its foreign policy, beginning in 1971, the PRC exchanged its 'main enemy', the USA, for the USSR, and by extensive activities in foreign policy sought to surmount the isolation imposed by the USA and the USSR which had become apparent in the 1960s. In October 1971 the PRC was admitted to the UNO (replacing Taiwan). In 1972 it established diplomatic relations with Japan, and in August 1978 the two countries concluded a Treaty on Peace and Friendship. In February 1972 US-President Nixon paid a visit to the PRC and on this occasion both sides agreed that neither would strive for hegemony in the Asian-Pacific area but would both oppose hegemonial ambitions of other states (i.e. the Soviet Union). After prolonged negotiations, the PRC and the USA established diplomatic relations on 1 January 1979. In a joint communiqué the USA adopted the Chinese view that Taiwan is an integral part of the PRC, broke off diplomatic relations with Taiwan, recognised the government of the PRC as the sole legal Chinese government and annulled the security treaty with Taiwan. In April 1979 the Standing Committee of the NPC decided against prolonging the Sino-Soviet Treaty on Friendship and Mutual Assistance concluded in 1950 for a term of thirty years.

The PRC improved its relations with Western Europe, too, evincing keen interest in its unification. Because of the American refusal to sell arms to the PRC, Western Europe gained an important role for China as supplier of arms. In April 1978 the PRC signed a trade agreement with the EC. Relations with European socialist countries, as far as these are under Soviet hegemony, have been overshadowed by the Sino-Soviet conflict. Rumania alone has always maintained friendly relations with the PRC and has tried to mediate between the Soviets and the Chinese. Owing to common opposition to the hegemonial policy of the Soviet Union, Tito's visit to the PRC in August and September 1977 and Hua Guofeng's return visit in August 1978 resulted in a reconciliation with the Yugoslav communists, whom the Chinese had formerly accused of revisionism. This development, however, contributed to the break between the PRC and Albania.

Relations with the Third World were characterised less by attempts to revolutionise them than by endeavours to counteract Soviet influence. The unification of Vietnam and its close dependence on the Soviet Union aroused China's concern about a threat to its south-west border. The PRC, however, could neither prevent the domination of Laos by Vietnam nor the overthrow of the Pol Pot regime and the Vietnamese invasion of Kampuchea. Reprisals against Chinese living in Vietnam, Vietnamese behaviour towards Kampuchea and border disputes induced the PRC to 'reproach' Vietnam in a border war of four weeks in February 1979.

At the beginning of the 1980s the PRC dissociated itself from the 'strategic alliance' with the USA against the USSR, envisaged in the 1970s, and herewith introduced another phase of foreign policy. True to the supreme principle of its foreign policy to maintain and secure independence, it seeks a balanced position between the super-powers. This search has found its expression in a limited detachment from the USA, and in steps towards a rapprochement with the USSR. In autumn 1982 both sides initiated 'consultations' on the improvement of relations. The Soviets, however, refuse to comply with the Chinese preconditions for a normalisation of mutual relations, which consist of a demand for the reduction of Soviet armed forces in Mongolia and along the common border as well as of the SS-20 missiles stationed in the Asian part of the Soviet Union, and an end to the intervention in Afghanistan and the support for Vietnam's invasion of Kampuchea. The attitude of both countries is a product of their interest in security and consequently leaves them little scope for manoeuvre. The dialogue has therefore produced meagre results so far. Only in the fields of economic and cultural co-operation has some progress been made.

Chinese–US relations deteriorated towards the end of Carter's presidency and became even cooler when President Reagan showed signs of renewing official relations with Taiwan. Yet, although the Chinese consider the reunification of the island with the mainland as a primary, constitutionally fixed aim of their foreign policy and have not definitely bound themselves to regain Taiwan exclusively by peaceful means, the Reagan Administration has promised gradually to reduce the delivery of arms to the Taiwan government. This has paved the way for the establishment of a pragmatic relationship marked by common (but also conflicting) interests and a policy of reciprocal advantage, which became apparent during Reagan's visit to China in April 1984. Already in June 1983 the USA granted the PRC the status of a friendly, though not allied, country, a fact which enables the PRC to import 'dual' technology; that is, technology which may be used both for civil and military purposes. An agreement on co-operation in the peaceful exploitation of nuclear energy is another proof of close relations.

In the case of Hong Kong the Chinese have already registered a concrete success in their reunification policy. In October 1984 they and the British signed an agreement on the return of the islands and the New Territories (on the mainland) to the PRC in 1997, when the lease of the latter will expire. The agreement provides for fifty years of autonomy for Hong Kong under the central government, and for the maintenance of the present socio-economic system — which, by the way, the PRC also takes into consideration with regard to Taiwan.

In regard to Europe, the PRC continues to consider it as a 'strategic centre' in the East–West conflict and encourages the unification of Western Europe as a precondition before it can also become an independent military stronghold against the USSR and a decisive factor in a multi-polar world. China's economic co-operation with the EC should contribute to the realisation of its modernisation programme without it becoming too dependent on the USA. Like Japan, Western Europe should, in Chinese eyes, counterbalance the super-powers.

China's relationship with Third World countries is somewhat ambiguous. On the one hand, the PRC regards itself as a part of the Third World and, as such, advocates close South–South co-operation and a New International Economic Order. On the other hand, it is a member neither of the Non-Aligned Movement nor of the Group of 77, and its commitment to the cause of the Third World is rather theoretical. By increasing exports the PRC decreases possibilities of trade for developing countries and has reduced its development aid. In fact, it has abandoned its former policy of support to revolutionary movements. The only case of engagement in the struggle against foreign oppression is that of Kampuchea, where the Chinese are helping the anti-Vietnamese guerillas with arms.

On the whole, the PRC's foreign policy in the first half of the 1980s reflects its pre-eminent goal, the maintenance of world peace, which serves best its domestic policy of modernisation. Accordingly, the Chinese leaders have abandoned Mao's thesis of the inevitability of a third world war, but they are nevertheless well aware of the dangers to peace and are therefore increasing China's defence potential, the improvement of which forms one, albeit the last, of the four modernisation targets.

NATIONAL DEFENCE

The PRC's regular armed forces, the PLA, total about 4 million, of whom 3,160,000 serve in the army, 350,000 in the navy and 490,000 in the air force. In addition there are paramilitary forces of about 12 million, among them the security troops, which have been transferred from the control of the PLA to that of the Ministry of Public Security, and the militia of some 10 millions.[6] There is general compulsory military service for men between eighteen and twenty-two years of age, however, the number of persons belonging to the corresponding age-groups far exceeds the number of conscripts. Volunteers may serve eight to twelve more years and obtain a thorough training in the handling of modern arms. Besides defence tasks the

PLA also performs civil tasks. It runs its own enterprises in the fields of agriculture, industry, transport and the building and construction industry, by which it partly finances itself.

The present leaders, though not without opposition, have abandoned Mao's Doctrine of a People's War, according to which the decisive force to repel an attack should not be arms but manpower. They emphasise, instead, the re-equipment of the armed forces with a wide range of modern arms, manufactured by the Chinese themselves or imported from Western countries, combined with the professionalisation of the armed forces. Particular stress is laid on the further development of nuclear weapons. In 1964 the PRC tested its first atomic bomb, and in 1980 it launched its first intercontinental missile. It currently has at its disposal some intercontinental missiles and sixty intermediate-range and fifty medium-range missiles.[7]

Unlike in former times, when the PLA was an instrument of the party and an authority above the state which intervened in the power-struggle during the Cultural Revolution and in the succession struggle around the 'Gang of Four', it is at present considered to be an institution of the state without priority over the civil sector. This is stressed by the constitutional provision that the armed forces are under the direction of the Central Military Commission of the PRC. This regulation, however, does not in any way mean the withdrawal of the Communist Party from the command. In view of its leading position in the state, it is *de facto* the Military Commission of the CC, which decides on affairs concerning the armed forces. Anyhow, as long as both organs are constituted by the same persons and are chaired by Deng Xiaoping, which is at present the case, the question of which of them is the decisive one remains purely academic.

NOTES

1.   English text in *Review of Socialist Law* (Leyden, The Netherlands), IX (1983), pp. 183–206.
2.   English text in William B. Simons (ed.), *The Constitutions of the Communist World* (Alphen aan den Rijn, The Netherlands, and German-

town, Md., 1980), pp. 76–92.
3. English text in William B. Simons and Stephen White (eds.), *The Party Statutes of the Communist World* (The Hague, 1984), pp. 91–113 (my italics).
4. Richard F. Staar (ed.), *Yearbook on International Communist Affairs 1984: Parties and Revolutionary Movements* (Stanford, Cal., 1984), p. 209
5. *Beijing Review*, 31 May 1983.
6. The International Institute for Strategic Studies, London, *The Military Balance 1984-1985* (Oxford, 1984), pp. 92–3.
7. *Ibid.*, p. 91.

FURTHER READING

Camilleri, Joseph, *Chinese Foreign Policy: The Maoist Era and its Aftermath* (Seattle, WA: University of Washington Press, 1980)
Falkenheim, V.C., 'Democracy, Modernization, and Participatory Values in Post-Mao China', in Donald E. Schulz and Jan S. Adams (eds.), *Political Participation in Communist Systems* (New York and Oxford: Pergamon Press, 1971), pp. 254–73
Gardner, John, *Chinese Politics and the Succession to Mao* (New York: Holmes and Meier, 1982)
Goldman, Merle, *China's Intellectuals: Advise and Dissent* (Cambridge, Mass.: Harvard University Press, 1981)
Harrison, James P., *The Long March to Power: A History of the Chinese Communist Party, 1921–72* (London: Macmillan, 1973)
Lee, Hong Yung, *The Politics of the Chinese Cultural Revolution: A Case Study* (Berkeley, Cal.: University of California Press, 1978)
Liu, Alan P., *Political Culture and Group Conflict in Communist China* (Santa Barbara, Cal.: Clio Books, 1976)
Mehnert, Klaus, *Peking and Moscow* (London: Weidenfeld and Nicolson, 1963)
Moody, Peter R., *Opposition and Dissent in Contemporary China* (Stanford, Cal.: Hoover Institution Press, 1977)
Pye, Lucian W., *The Dynamics of Chinese Politics* (Cambridge, Mass.: Oelgeschlager, Gunn and Hain, 1981)
Saich, Tony, *China: Politics and Government* (London: Macmillan, 1981)
Schram, Stuart R., *The Political Thought of Mao Tse-tung*, rev. edn. (Harmondsworth: Penguin, 1969)
—— (ed.), *Authority, Participation and Cultural Change in China* (Cambridge: Cambridge University Press, 1973)
Schurmann, Herbert F., *Ideology and Organization in Communist China*, 2nd edn. (Berkeley, Cal.: University of California Press, 1968)
Segal, Gerald and William T. Tow (eds.), *Chinese Defence Policy* (London: Macmillian, 1984)
Snow, Edgar, *Red Star over China* (London: Gollancz, 1963)

Solomon, Richard H., *Mao's Revolution and the Chinese Political Culture* (Berkeley, Cal.: University of California Press, 1971)

Wei, Lin and Arnold Chao (eds.), *China's Economic Reforms* (Philadelphia: University of Pennsylvania Press, 1982)

Wilcox, Francis O. (ed.), *China and the Great Powers: Relations with the United States, the Soviet Union and Japan* (New York: Praeger, 1974)

Wilson, Richard, W. *et al.* (eds.), *Value Change in Chinese Society* (New York: Praeger, 1979)

Yin, John, *Government of Socialist China* (Lanham, Md.: University of America Press, 1984)

6 Republic of Cuba

BASIC FEATURES

The socialist character of the Republic of Cuba is established in article 1 of the constitution of 24 February 1976.[1] According to article 4 'all the power belongs to the working people', who exercise it through the assemblies of people's power and other state organs or directly. The 'highest leading force of society and of the state' (article 5) is the Communist Party of Cuba (CPC). The institutional structure, however, is superseded by a personal and paternalistic pattern of relations between the people and Fidel Castro, who is gifted with a charismatic form of leadership. Personifying the Latin-American type of the caudillo, Castro tries to obtain direct legitimacy from the people by entering into mental and verbal dialogue and demanding acclamation, so that in the political system of Cuba there are elements of plebiscitarian democracy. Furthermore, through the personal union of the head of state and the head of government, who is not, however, elected by the people, there are elements of a presidential system. Through the accumulation of these offices and the supreme command of the armed forces, the constitution allows for the outstanding personality of Fidel Castro. By holding these offices and the chairmanship of the party, all power effectively rests in his person.

THE CASTROIT TAKEOVER

Cuba differs from all other socialist states because its

socialism is not the result of the takeover by a Marxist-Leninist party. It is not the work of the Cuban communists, formerly organised in the Popular Socialist Party (PSP) but of intellectuals coming from the town and rural bourgeoisie and ideologically homeless. In commemoration of an unsuccessful attack against the Moncada barracks in Santiago de Cuba on 26 July 1953 they founded the 26 July Movement (M-26-7). The social basis of the rebellion was not formed by industrial workers, and poor peasants and tenants did not join the guerrilla movement until shortly before the victory, and only in scattered areas. Thus the rebellion was neither a proletarian nor a peasant revolution. Nor were the aims of the insurrection, as proclaimed by Castro, those of a proletarian revolution; they were rather an agricultural reform and the restoration of the liberal-democratic constitution of 1940, which in March 1952 had been suspended by General Fulgencio Batista. The Cubans organised in the M-26-7 and the guerrillas only had occasional contacts with the PSP. The latter's attitude towards the rebellion was restrained until the middle of 1958. After the victory of the rebellion, however, the PSP was the only party which was permitted to develop its activities freely and was sponsored by friendly forces within the M-26-7, especially by Castro's brother, Raúl.

At the beginning of 1959 the revolutionaries took power. The state apparatus was destroyed; political parties — except the PSP — were prohibited; elections, considered to be an attribute of a representative democracy, were done away with. Apart from the rebel army and its political branch — the M-26-7 — and the PSP only the Revolutionary Directorate, a student resistance movement, could maintain itself as a third, not very important, political force.

Only in the post-insurrectional phase, after the revolution had taken a socialist course, did the Castroit revolutionaries begin to use the Communist Party's theory of Marxism-Leninism to support the revolutionary changes determined by national and international conditions. On 1 December 1961 Castro declared himself a Marxist-Leninist in public. It is controversial whether he was a Marxist-Leninist before that — certainly he was not a member of the PSP. His speeches, manifestos and papers written before that date do not refer conclusively to a former identification with the Marxist-Leninist doctrine. Equally, the revolutionary movement led by Castro was hardly communist. There is no reason to doubt Castro's account that years later, particularly in view of the changes brought about by socialism, he brought his consciousness into line with reality. Cuba had in practice been socialist since the end of 1960 and was declared as such by him on 15 April 1961.

The same year saw the fusion between the PSP, on the one hand, and of the members of the M-26-7 and the Revolutionary Directorate loyally following Castro's course, on the other. Opponents, among them old-guard communists, were eliminated. The new party merging from this integration was named the United Party of the Socialist Revolution of Cuba. During its process of organisation additional members were chosen from among 'exemplary workers' according to a complicated selection procedure. At the beginning of October 1965 the United Party was renamed the CPC which, however, did not hold its First Congress until 1975.

At the beginning Cuban socialism showed a number of features which were different from the Soviet model. Resulting from the 'planning debate' (1962–65) and according to Ernesto (Ché) Guevara's conception of the creation of a 'new man', prominent features were the priority given to moral working incentives and the abolition of working norms and piece rates — and, until 1968, a relatively large degree of cultural freedom. Political institutions and the economic system did not become aligned to the Soviet model until the 1970s. At the end of 1976 state power was institutionalised by the establishment of a nation-wide system of representation, formed by organs of 'people's power'.

THE MARXIST-LENINIST PARTY

Recruitment into the CPC is effected mainly from the Union of Young Communists and also from workers proposed by the labour collectives, checked by party commissions and finally confirmed or rejected by the collectives. In July 1980 the CPC had about 434,000 full members and candidates

organised in 26,500 party cells.[2] Thus the originally fixed limit
of 60,000 has been repeatedly exceeded and since the First
Party Congress of December 1975 the number has more than
doubled; it amounts to about 4.5 per cent of the total population.

The organs of the CPC on the national level are as follows:
the Party Congress, the Central Committee (CC) elected by
the Party Congress, the Political Bureau and the Secretariat
with Fidel Castro as first and his brother Raúl as second secretary. The Secretariat of the CC and the Political Bureau is
dominated by close followers of Fidel or Raúl Castro from the
rebel army. Among the members of the CC there are quite a
number of officers of the Revolutionary Armed Forces and
the security forces, although their representation has declined
since 1975.

In the 1960s and at the beginning of the 1970s the CPC was a
weak organisation. It exercised its leading function in state
and society mainly through members who came from the rebel
movement and the armed forces, from where also the political
and administrative élite was recruited. Since the middle of the
1970s, however, the influence of the military in the party (as
well as state) apparatus has decreased in favour of civilian
personnel.

During the first years of the revolution the relations of the
Castroit movement and the CPC with the CPSU were not free
from differences of opinion and tensions in spite of massive
economic and military aid from the Soviet Union. Fidel Castro was not prepared to accept 'something like a church, a
religious doctrine, with a Rome, a Pope and an Ecumenical
Council'.[3] The decision in favour of the sino-guevarist conception of a 'new man' and of building up socialism and communism simultaneously provoked the CPSU ideologically.
Shortly before, and parallel with, bringing the political and
the economic system into line with that of the Soviet Union,
the Cuban leaders sided with the ideological position of the
CPSU and identified themselves completely with the Soviet
interpretation of proletarian-socialist internationalism.

SOCIAL ORGANISATIONS

The major social organisation is the Committees for the Defence of the Revolution (CDR) which filed about 5.3 million members in 1980,[4] that is, roughly 80 per cent of the population over fourteen. Another social mass organisation, with about 2.4 million members in 1980[5] is the Central Organisation of Cuban Trade Unions, whose main task since the reintroduction of working norms in September 1970 has been to stimulate and to control their execution as well as to organise 'socialist emulation' between workers' collectives. Further mass organisations are the Federation of Cuban Women, the Federation of University Students, the Federation of Secondary Education Students, the Union of Pioneers and the National Association of Small Farmers. The Union of Young Communists, just as the CPC, is considered to be a political organisation based on the principle of selection of its members.

All these organisations have a dual function. They represent, for instance by exercising the right of legislative initiative, special interests of certain groups of the population and professions in conformity, however, with the CPC's aim of establishing socialism and communism. They mobilise the citizens in support of the party and the government and assist both in their efforts to socialise values and attitudes according to the Marxist-Leninist conception of man and society and to maintain readiness for their defence. Their methods are indoctrination, productive work and paramilitary education. Special emphasis is put on the knowledge and consciousness of Latin-African heredity, on the tradition derived from the wars of independence against Spain, and on the duty to fight against 'imperialism' and 'neo-colonialism'. The social organisations are also responsible for organising mass meetings which serve as a medium of communication between Fidel Castro and the people.

In this regard the CDR are by far the most important organisation. They are a specifically Cuban institution as they were founded in September 1960 as auxiliary organs of the armed forces and the militia in order to repulse counter-revolutionary actions. When after 1961 these actions decreased, the function of the CDR changed. It shifted from tracking down real and/or alleged counter-revolutionaries to exposing black-market business, corruption, and so on. They also took over administrative tasks, especially in the sector of housing, health and distribution, and controlled the implementation of revolutionary measures. Some of these duties have in the meantime been handed over to local authorities, but the CDR have still kept their importance as the instrument to control and mobilise the masses. By implementing party directives as well as own initiatives the CDR are supposed to create a willingness of the Cuban people to take over social responsibility in the private and the production spheres, to understand the tasks and problems involved in creating the collective well-being of a housing block and the commune, and to participate in local decision-making processes within the limits and according to the aims set by the party and state organs.

CENTRAL GOVERNMENT

The National Assembly of People's Power is the supreme state organ, formally vested with far-reaching powers. Its 499 members are not elected directly by the citizens but by the commune assemblies predominantly from among their members for a five-year term. The candidates who must be at least eighteen years of age are selected by commissions composed of representatives from the mass organisations and chaired by a representative of a leading CPC organ. The number of candidates must exceed that of the seats.

The National Assembly convenes twice a year. It is authorised *inter alia* to amend the constitution (a total modification requires a referendum in addition), to approve laws (bills on special subjects may be presented to the people for prior discussion), to check the constitutionality of laws and all other general provisions, to approve the state budget, the economic and social plan, as well as the guidelines for domestic and foreign policy, to call for the holding of referenda and to supervise all other state organs.

The members of the National Assembly are bound to listen

to the grievances, suggestions and criticism of citizens, to explain the policy of the state to them, and are accountable to them for their activities. They may be recalled by their electors but they do not have an imperative mandate. A minimum number of 10,000 voters has the right of legislative initiative. The deputies have the right to address inquiries to the Council of State and the Council of Ministers as a whole and to individual members of these organs; all state organs as well as state-owned enterprises are obliged to support the deputies in their functions. The mandate is an honorary one; the deputees are granted leave from their place of work without pay and receive allowances equivalent to their salary.

The National Assembly elects from among its members a permanent organ: the Council of State which collectively represents the Cuban Republic in international affairs and implements the resolutions of the National Assembly. The Council of State is also vested with legislative and judicial powers: between the sessions of the National Assembly it issues law-decrees which, however — as the constitution establishes — can be annulled completely or in part by the Assembly. It has the power to give a definite interpretation of the laws and to instruct the courts and the public procurators. It also has to ratify or denounce international treaties, to carry out referenda and to call for a general mobilisation.

The chairman of the Council of State is both head of state and head of government as well as commander-in-chief of the Revolutionary Armed Forces. Holding the highest offices of the government he determines the policy guidelines. He not only supervises the ministries but is entitled to take over any ministry himself. In case of absence, illness or death the first vice-chairman, at present Fidel Castro's brother Raúl, deputises for him.

The Council of Ministers is the highest executive and administrative body. Its members are: the head of state as chairman, the first vice-chairman and vice-chairmen, who together make up the Executive Committee of the Council of Ministers and which in urgent cases may take actions for the whole body; the ministers, the chairman of the Central Planning Board, the chairmen of state committees, and of several state institutions (such as the Academy of Sciences) as well as the secretary. The ministers are heads of 'classic' and of special economic departments; there are state committees for science and technology, standards control, prices, social security and the National Bank. The secretary general of the Central Organisation of Trade Unions is entitled to take part in the sessions of the Council of Ministers or its Executive Committee. The members of the Council of Ministers are appointed and replaced on recommendation of the chairman of the Council of State and of the Council of Ministers by the National Assembly and between its sessions by the Council of State. Just as between the Political Bureau of the CPC and the Council of State, there is also a strong personal network between the Political Bureau and the Council of Ministers.

The functions of the Council of Ministers are, among others: the implementation of laws and resolutions of the National Assembly as well as of the legal decrees of the Council of State; the drafting of bills, of economic plans and of the national budget, and the ratification of international treaties. The Council of Ministers is responsible and accountable to the National Assembly.

LOCAL GOVERNMENT

Cuba is divided for administrative purposes into fourteen provinces, and 169 communes (municipalities) including the special area of the Isle of Pines, which is controlled directly by the central government. The criterion for the administrative structure is economic efficiency, to ensure a balanced development of industry and agriculture.

The 'superior local organs of state power' (article 101 of the constitution) are the province and commune assemblies, elected for a two-and-a-half-year term. Only the latter are elected directly by the citizens; the province assemblies, just as the National Assembly, are elected by the commune assemblies. The chairmen of the commune executive committees are, in virtue of their office, delegates to the corresponding province assemblies. Citizens are entitled to vote and be elected delegate at the age of sixteen. Candidates for the elections to the commune assemblies are nominated by the citizens in neighbourhood meetings and elected from multi-candidate lists. If none of the, at least two, candidates gains the absolute majority of votes cast, a second ballot is held between the two candidates who have received the most votes.

The delegates are an important channel of communication between the population and the local authorities but not free from party directives. They have to inform the assemblies about the opinions, needs, problems, and proposals of the people as well as to report to the latter on the measures adopted by the assemblies for solving the problems presented to them, and to inform the population about possible difficulties. They are not bound by the directives of their electors, but they are accountable to them for their performance in the assemblies.

The organs of people's power in the provinces and communes are organs for the administration of the economy with regard to the implementation of the plans for economic and social development. Under the policy of decentralising government they are responsible for the direction and control of all production and service industry enterprises, except those of national significance, and for the maintenance of health, cultural and educational services. It is furthermore their duty to maintain internal order, to protect socialist property, to defend the rights of the citizens and to strengthen the country's capacity for defence.

The executive committees of the province and commune assemblies, which are elected from among their members, direct and supervise administrative and economic activities in their territory; they are authorised to appoint and replace administrative officials and managers of local enterprises. According to the principle of dual subordination, the executive committees of the commune are responsible to the assemblies on the same level and to the executive organ on the higher level, and they have to report periodically to the commune assemblies as well as to the province executive committee. The local administrative departments are responsible to the corresponding assembly and its executive committee as well as to the superior organ of the corresponding administrative branch.

The National Assembly is authorised to modify or to repeal such resolutions or orders coming from the local organs of the people's power as violate either the constitution or other laws, decrees and resolutions enacted by organs on a higher level or are detrimental to 'the general interests of the nation' (article 73). The Council of State has the same authorisation with regard to the resolutions or provisions originating from local executive committees, and it may suspend such acts of the province and commune assemblies but is required to report this to the National Assembly.

ADMINISTRATION OF JUSTICE

The judicial organs are the People's Supreme Court as well as the people's courts in the provinces and communes. The courts are subject to the National Assembly and to the Council of State and are bound by its directives, a fact which signifies the unity of power vested in the National Assembly. The courts are composed of professional judges and lay judges with equal rights. The chairman and the judges of the local courts are elected by the representative assemblies and ' may be recalled. The courts are accountable to the assemblies. The Supreme Court has the right to propose laws and issues instructions in order to ensure a uniform interpretation and application of the law.

The system of justice has the primary function of protecting the socialist state. Individual rights are derived from the collectivistic conception of justice and law — all acts contravening the socialist order of the state, the economy and society are criminal acts. At the same time, such behaviour is considered counter-revolutionary. The constitution lists the following functions of the courts: the maintenance and strengthening of the economic, social and political system; the protection of socialist property and the personal property of the citizens; the protection of life, dignity, honour and family; the education of the citizens in loyalty to their home-country, to the socialist cause and to the standards of socialist life; the prevention/punishment of illegal acts and of anti-social conduct. The penal system consists of re-education, forced labour and indoctrination.

Fundamental rights such as the freedom of conscience, religion, speech, association and assembly are guaranteed by the constitution if they are not exercised 'contrary to the existence and goals of the socialist state' (article 61), but these rights cannot be claimed. There is no constitutional jurisdiction. Citizens can only address petitions and complaints to state organs, which are obliged to observe the legal norms according to the principle of socialist legality.

It is the duty of the General Procurator's Office to control adherence to the law and other legal regulations by state organs, economic enterprises, social institutions and citizens. The office is subject to the National Assembly and the Council of State. The procurator general is elected by the National Assembly and may be recalled by it; he has to follow the instructions of the Council of State and is accountable to the National Assembly.

FOREIGN POLICY

Geographically Cuba belongs to the Western hemisphere, neighbouring on the USA; historically and culturally it belongs to Latin America; by blood it feels related to Africa; as a developing country it is part of the Third World; due to its political and socio-economic order and its value system it is a socialist country. These factors determine the three areas of Cuban foreign policy: (1) the USA; (2) Latin America, the Caribbean and other countries of the Third World; (3) the Soviet Union and other member countries of the CMEA, which Cuba joined in July 1972. Distant relations are maintained with the People's Republic of China. Considering its size (a population of only about 10 million) and its economic potential, Cuba's foreign policy has an exceptionally wide scope of action.

The principles for action and conduct of dynamic Cuban foreign policy have been established in the constitution. In article 11 Cuba declares itself to be 'part of the socialist world community'; in article 12 it adopts 'the principles of proletarian internationalism and the combative solidarity of peoples' and maintains 'its internationalist right and duty' to help 'those under attack and the peoples who struggle for their liberation'. But it also declares its readiness to integrate itself into the 'large [Latin-American and Caribbean] community of nations' and to maintain 'friendly relations with those countries, which — although having a different political, social and economic system — respect its sovereignty, observe the rules of coexistence among states'.

In spite of a changing evaluation of the areas of action and the employment of varying means, Cuban foreign policy has shown a continuity of complementary aims for more than two decades: the struggle to safeguard its independence from the USA; the maintenance of military and economic aid from the Soviet Union while preserving a certain autonomy of action; the intensification of economic relations with West European countries in order to procure foreign currency and modern technology; the promotion of revolutions and the stabilisation of anti-Western regimes in Latin America, Africa and Asia through military, technical and administrative aid. For the latter field of action Cuba has profited from its revolutionary experience and its experience as a developing country. Although radicalism and the lack of willingness to compromise may be counter-productive to Cuba's ambition for leadership in the Third World, Cuba to a certain degree continues to serve as a model. It has demonstrated that it is possible to shake off dependence on the USA (albeit at the price of dependence on the USSR), achieve social redistribution and the satisfaction of basic needs — be it on a low level — in a developing country dependent on the export of a monoculture: sugar, in the case of Cuba.

The Soviet Union is Cuba's most important foreign partner. Cuban and Soviet interests coincide as far as a change of the international balance of power in favour of socialism is concerned, but Cuba as a protagonist of a South–South co-operation also pursues a policy of its own. In the 1960s Fidel Castro refused to become subject to the Soviet bloc's discipline. Cuban support of guerrilla actions in Latin America were not in accord with the Soviet policy of détente. Cuba did not join the Soviet policy of peaceful coexistence until the late 1960s and early 1970s.

This drastic change manifested itself, *inter alia*, in Cuba's willingness to improve its relations with the USA, which in order to retaliate for the nationalisation of North American property had broken off economic relations with Cuba in 1960 and diplomatic relations in 1961. In September 1977 both sides opened 'interest sections'. Yet, from the Cuban point of view, a complete normalisation of relations is hampered by the US trade embargo, the US presence in Guantánamo and anti-Cuban subversion. Together with the partial relaxation of US–Cuban tensions, the normalisation of relations with most Latin-American states began. In October 1975 Cuba was a founding member of the Latin American Economic System (SELA). But because of its activities in the Caribbean (Grenada) and in Central America (Nicaragua and El Salvador) some Latin American and Caribbean countries have again dissociated themselves from Cuba, and the Reagan Administration, which has reverted to the earlier US condition for the establishment of normal relations — the abrogation of Cuban military ties with the Society Union — has intensified the isolation of Cuba.

Fulfilling its 'internationalist duty'[6] Cuba has since the end of 1975 become involved militarily in Angola and Ethiopia, where the revolutionary and missionary enthusiasm of the Castroits, still surviving from the insurrectional phase of the Cuban Revolution, has found a new field of activity.

In the second half of the 1970s Cuba gained a leading position in the Non-Aligned Movement, which held its Sixth Summit Conference in Havana in 1979. The Cubans, however, did not succeed in establishing a unilateral pro-Soviet orientation of the movement. As a country economically and militarily dependent on the USSR and therefore committed to it, Cuba lost some of its prestige within the movement and encountered a conflict of loyalties when the USSR intervened in Afghanistan.

NATIONAL DEFENCE

Cuba's armed forces, equipped with modern Soviet weapons, in 1984 amounted to 153,000 — with 125,000 of them in the army, 12,000 in the navy and 16,000 in the air force.[7] Between 32,000 to 33,000 soldiers are estimated to be stationed abroad (roughly 19,000 in Angola and approximately 3,000 in Ethiopia).[8] The regular troops are assisted by paramilitary forces: 15,000 security troops; 3,500 frontier guards; the Youth Labour Army of 100,000; Civil Defence Force of 100,000; and the Territorial Militia of about 530,000 members.[9]

Paramilitary education and military service serve the strengthening of the revolutionary consciousness of the nation and its readiness to fight 'imperialism' everywhere in the world as well as to defend the country against the USA, whose attitude towards Cuba is felt as a permanent threat. The stationing of Soviet missiles produced the 'Cuban Crisis' in October 1962, which was settled by the removal of the missiles from the island, although the USA did not undertake never to intervene in Cuba. The Soviet Union has repeatedly assured the Cubans that they would protect their security, but has refrained from formalising the guarantee in a treaty and to admit Cuba to the WTO.

NOTES

1. English text in William B. Simons (ed.), *Constitutions of the Communist World* (Alphen aan den Rijn, the Netherlands, and Germantown, Md., 1980), pp. 100–34.
2. *II Congreso del Partido Comunista de Cuba: Documentos y Discursos* (Havana, 1981), pp. 104–5.
3. *Bohemia* (Havana), no. 41, 8 October 1965.
4. *II Congreso, op. cit.*, p. 92.
5. *Ibid.*, p. 80.
6. Fidel Castro — according to *Granma, Weekly Review* (Havana), 11 January 1976.
7. The International Institute for Strategic Studies, London, *The Military Balance 1984-1985* (Oxford, 1984), pp. 119–20.
8. *Ibid.*, p. 120.
9. *Ibid.*

FURTHER READING

Allison, Graham T., *Essence of Decision Making: Explaining the Cuban Missile Crisis* (Boston: Little Brown, 1971)

Bender, Lynn D., *The Politics of Hostility: Castro's Revolution and United States Policy* (Hato Rey, Puerto Rico: Inter American University Press, 1975)

Blasier, Cole and Carmelo Mesa-Lago (eds.), *Cuba in the World* (Pittsburgh, Pa.: University of Pittsburgh Press, 1979)

Domínguez, Jorge I., *Cuba: Order and Revolution* (Cambridge, Mass.: Harvard University Press, 1978)

—— (ed.), *Cuba: Internal and International Affairs* (Beverly Hills, Cal.: Sage Publications, 1982)

Draper, Theodore, *Castroism: Theory and Practice* (New York: Praeger, 1965)

Fagen, Richard R., *The Transformation of Political Culture in Cuba* (Stanford, Cal.: Stanford University Press, 1969)

Gonzalez, Edward, *Cuba under Castro: The Limits of Charisma* (Boston: Houghton Mifflin, 1974)

Huberman, Leo and Paul M. Sweezy, *Socialism in Cuba* (New York: Monthly Review Press, 1969)

Lambert, Francis, 'Cuba: Communist State or Personal Leadership' in Archie Brown and Jack Gray (eds.), *Political Culture and Political Change in Communist States*, 2nd edn. (London: Macmillan, 1979), pp. 231–52.

LeoGrande, William M., *Cuba's Policy in Africa, 1959–1980* (Berkeley, Cal.: University of California, Institute of East Asian Studies, 1980)

Lévesque, Jacques, *The USSR and the Cuban Revolution: Soviet Ideological and Strategic Perspectives, 1959-77* (New York: Praeger, 1978)

Mesa-Lago, Carmelo (ed.), *Revolutionary Change in Cuba* (Pittsburgh: University of Pittsburgh Press, 1971)

—— *The Economy of Socialist Cuba: A Two-Decade Appraisal* (Albuquerque, NM: University of New Mexico Press, 1981)

Suárez, Andrés, *Cuba, Castroism and Communism, 1959-1966,* (Cambridge, Mass.: MIT Press, 1967)

7 Czechoslovak Socialist Republic

BASIC FEATURES

Czechoslovakia defines itself as a socialist state in its constitution of 11 July 1960.[1] According to this constitution 'all power' is vested in the 'working people' (article 2). The 'leading force of society and the state' (article 4) is the Communist Party of Czechoslovakia (CPC). Its claim for leadership may not be questioned by the other four parties.

By the constitutional law of 27 October 1968,[2] on 1 January 1969 Czechoslovakia became a federal state of two nations with equal rights, the Czechs and the Slovaks. Accordingly, the federation consists of the Czech Socialist Republic and the Slovak Socialist Republic, which have their own constitutions and are considered to be sovereign states. By the amendment of the constitution of 20 December 1970, however, the powers of the federal government have been substantially strengthened. Moreover, independently of the constitutional regulation of the relationship between the federation and the republics, the effectiveness of the federal state structure is greatly restricted by the principle of democratic centralism, which determines the organisation and the decision-making of the CPC, but likewise of the whole state.

THE COMMUNIST TAKEOVER

The CPC, which in May 1921 held its constitutive Party Congress, was able to develop unhindered in Czechoslovakia, which between the wars was a liberal parliamentary democracy. In October 1938, after Czechoslovakia had been forced to cede the Sudetenland to the German Reich and President Eduard Beneš had resigned, the CPC was prohibited; the party leadership, with Klement Gottwald at the head, emigrated to Moscow.

In December 1943 Beneš, who had formed an exile government in London, negotiated with Gottwald in Moscow on the re-establishment of Czechoslovakia after the war. In renewed negotiations in March 1945 in Moscow too, both agreed on the formation of a 'government of the National Front of Czechs and Slovaks', which was established shortly afterwards with the Social Democrat Zdeněk Fierlinger as Prime Minister in Košice (Eastern Slovakia). It was based on a coalition of the Czech and Slovak section of the CPC, the Czechoslovak Social Democratic Party, Beneš's Czechoslovak National Socialist Party, the (Czech and Catholic) People's Party as well as the (Slovak) Democratic Party, which was founded by bourgeois groupings during the Slovak upheaval in September 1944. The communists took charge of eight of the twenty-five ministries, among them the key Ministry of the Interior (the police) and the Ministry of Information. National committees, strongly influenced by the communists, took over local government. In May 1945 the government moved to Prague, and Beneš again assumed the office of president of the republic.

The government programme, which the communists regarded as a programme for the transition to a socialist revolution, provided, *inter alia,* for state control of the monetary, credit and insurance system, the key industries and energy; furthermore, it provided for the confiscation of German and Hungarian property as well as that of collaborators. In October 1945 the mines, the iron and steel industry, banks, insurances, the chemical and pharmaceutical industries were nationalised, as well as enterprises of other branches from a certain size upwards.

In May 1946 elections to the constituent National Assembly were held. The communists polled 38 per cent of the votes and were assigned 114 seats. Together with the Social Democrats they held a narrow majority of the altogether 300 seats. Gottwald became prime minister.

In February 1948 the communists took over power without
the presence of Soviet troops, but not without at least indirect
Soviet influence. On 20 February 1948 a government crisis
broke out, when out of protest against communist infiltration
of the police apparatus twelve non-communist ministers
resigned. The threat of the trade unions, strongly influenced
by the communists, to call a general strike, and activities of
the armed workers' militia induced Beneš, fearing a civil war,
to accept the resignation of the ministers on 25 February and
to agree to the new composition of the cabinet as dictated by
Gottwald. Now half of its members were communists. They
occupied all important departments except — temporarily —
the Foreign Ministry. At the elections to the National Assembly in May 1948 nearly 90 per cent of the electorate voted for
the candidates of the unity list of the parties of the National
Front. On 7 June 1948 Beneš, who had refused to approve the
new constitution of 9 May 1948, proclaiming Czechoslovakia
a 'people's democracy', resigned, and Gottwald became his
successor. At the end of June 1948 the left wing of the Social
Democratic Party merged into the CPC and the remaining
parties were forced into line. The political system was reorganised on the Soviet model.

THE 1968 REFORM MOVEMENT

When, in January 1968, Alexander Dubček succeeded the
orthodox Antonín Novotný as first secretary of the Central
Committee of the CPC, the way had been paved for a democratisation of the political system. The new course soon
resulted in the formation of free public opinion (criticising the
Soviet Union), the reduction of the state security apparatus,
the stimulation of the role of the National Assembly, the continuation of the economic reform (aiming at decentralisation
of industrial decision-making and at the introduction of market mechanisms). In its Action Programme of 5 April 1968
and its draft Statute of 10 August 1968, the CPC showed a
readiness to democratise its organisation and its relationship
to state and society. It was apparently willing to tolerate political pluralism insofar as its leading role was not seriously

challenged. The Soviet leadership, however, declared this development to be 'counter-revolutionary' and a threat to the common interests of the countries of the 'socialist community'.

On 21 August 1968 Soviet troops intervened together with those of four other member states of the WTO. Dubček at first tried to continue the reform policy, albeit more cautiously, but in April 1969 he had to resign. He was replaced by Gustáv Husák, who step by step reversed all achievements of the 'Prague Spring' except the federalisation of the state. The party and state apparatus was thoroughly purged of reformists: the CPC lost almost one-third of its members — about 150,000 withdrew voluntarily, about 400,000 were excluded; hundreds of thousands of supporters of the reform movement were ousted from the representative organs, social organisations and state institutions, tens of thousands of them were banned from their profession, and repressive measures were taken against all critics of the 'normalisation'.

THE MARXIST-LENINIST PARTY

In 1983 the CPC numbered 1.6 million members, thus comprising about 10.3 per cent of the population.[3] Full membership has to be preceded by two probationary years. Primary organisations are established at work places, in settlements and in army units. They control, *inter alia,* the execution of party decisions in production, transport, trade as well as state-owned agricultural enterprises, and supervise fulfilment of the production plans by management.

The supreme organ is the Party Congress, meeting every five years, and in the interim the Central Committee (CC). The decisive organs, however, are the CC Presidium, consisting of full members and candidates, and the CC Secretariat, headed by the secretary general, at present Gustáv Husák.

The members of the CPC in the Slovak Socialist Republic form the Communist Party of Slovakia, which has central organs of its own, with the first secretary of the CC at the top. It has no autonomous status, however, but merely that of a regional organisation of the CPC. It has to orientate its activities towards the resolutions of the Party Congress and the CC of the CPC; the secretaries of the Slovak CC have to be confirmed by the supreme organs of the CPC. The party organisations in the Czech Socialist Republic are controlled directly by the national party organs, hence the CPC remained unaffected by the federalisation of the state.

After having eliminated reformist forces, the CPC is a particularly obsequious follower of the CPSU, criticising all opponents of the CPSU's claim to leadership in the communist world movement and every deviation whatsoever from the Soviet model of socialism.

BLOC PARTIES AND SOCIAL ORGANISATIONS

In the Czech lands there are two non-communist parties: the Czechoslovak People's Party, mobilising citizens with Christian-social ideas, especially in the countryside, and the Czechoslovak Socialist Party, recruiting its followers mainly from the urban middle class. During the 'Prague Spring' there had been efforts to make these parties, whose members doubled at that time, independent of the CPC within a competitive multi-party system. After the reform movement had failed they were again, however, brought into line with the CPC and are politically of no significance. In the Slovak lands this also applies to the Slovak Freedom Party and the Slovak Revival Party — the successor of the Democratic Party. All these parties support the socialist social order and unconditionally subordinate themselves to the CPC. They participate in elections within the framework of the National Front, which finances and controls them.

The largest social organisation is the Revolutionary Trade Union Movement. It comprises eighteen branch trade unions and is structured according to the principle of democratic centralism. It is the foremost duty of the trade unions to ensure the fulfilment of production goals. Although they have limited influence on the formation of working conditions and wages in the enterprises and a few social functions, they do not by any means defend the interests of the workers. Further social organisations are: the Socialist Youth Union (with young persons between fourteen and twenty-eight years) and the Pioneer Organisation, the Women's Union, the Co-operative Farmers' Association, the Association for Co-operation with the Army; there are also the professional associations — as for instance the Authors' Association, founded anew in December 1977 and, unlike its predecessor in the 1960s of no significance, the Composers' Association and the Visual Artists' Association. In addition, there are cultural associations of the national minorities (Hungarians, Poles, Ukrainians and Germans). Most of the social organisations have subdivisions in both the Czech and the Slovak republics.

Parties and social organisations are collectively united in the National Front of Czechs and Slovaks, which 'is the political expression of the union of the working people of the towns and countryside led by the Communist Party of Czechoslovakia' (article 6 of the constitution). Any political activity except in the National Front is suppressed.

RELIGIOUS COMMUNITIES

In Czechoslovakia there are eighteen religious communities approved by the state of which the Roman Catholic Church is by far the largest, particularly in the Slovak lands. The state assumed the material supply of the churches and thus also a strong control; the clergymen are paid by the state and may only practise with its consent. Catholic clergymen who are eager to stress their loyalty towards the regime are united in the organisation *Pacem in terris,* thus disobeying an order of the Pope of March 1982. The state policy towards the Catholic Church, aimed at controlling or suppressing its activities, has produced a kind of Catholic underground church which secretly educates and ordains priests. Priests who are hindered in the exercise of their functions take on other work, and are active as worker priests.

DISSENT

In the aftermath of the CSCE, critics of the regime, among them several former leading reform Communists, gathered around the 'Charter 77'. Its original approximately 250 signatories did not consider themselves as a political opposition. Instead, they were resolved to fight for respect for human rights as granted in the Czechoslovak constitution, the Final Act of the Helsinki Conference and the UN Covenant on Civil and Political Rights, also ratified by Czechoslovakia. Among the Chartists, whose number once exceeded 1,000 persons, were predominantly members of the intelligentsia but also clergymen and workers. The grouping has been severely weakened by emigration, or repressions such as loss of work or imprisonment. The same fate was suffered by members of the committee for the defence of victims of unlawful persecution.

CENTRAL GOVERNMENT

The supreme organ of state power is the Federal Assembly. It consists of two chambers of equal rights: the House of the People with 200 deputies elected over the whole state territory and the House of Nations with 150 deputies, seventy-five from each republic. Both chambers are elected directly for a five-year term. The active voting age is eighteen, the passive twenty-one years. The candidates are proposed by the parties and social organisations, nominated by the National Front and elected via single lists in one-member constituencies. The number of candidates may exceed that of mandates, but no use is made of this possibility. At the elections of June 1981 the candidates of the National Front polled nearly 100 per cent of the vote. About 60 to 70 per cent of the mandates are usually allocated to the CPC, the remaining to the bloc parties and to non-party candidates.

The Federal Assembly meets for two or three days twice a year. It is formally the sole legislative organ of the federation concerning matters which fall under the exclusive jurisdiction both of the federation and the republics, and it enacts basic legislation in matters falling within the competence of the republics when uniform regulation is a necessity. It has the right of initiating laws, discusses basic questions of domestic and foreign policy, decides on the medium-term economic plan and the federal state budget, and so on. The adoption of bills which, in fact, are initiated or agreed upon in advance by the supreme party bodies requires the simple majority of the deputies in each of the chambers. In order to avoid outvoting of the Slovaks by the Czechs or *vice versa* in the House of Nations, the deputies elected in the Czech republic and the deputies elected in the Slovak republic vote separately — *inter alia,* when the adoption of the economic plan and of the federal state budget is concerned. In such cases a decision is adopted only if the majority of each of both parts of the deputies have voted in favour of it. If the two houses cannot reach a concurrent decision, they may establish a conference committee, principally consisting of ten deputies of each House. If no agreement is reached on the federal state budget, these proceedings are obligatory. If both Houses do not reach agreement on the recommendation of the conference committee within five months of the first vote, the same bill may be introduced at the earliest after the lapse of one year following the rejection. The Federal Assembly may be dissolved if the proceedings to agree on a common text do not produce agreement.

Each House elects from among it deputies twenty members of the Presidium of the Federal Assembly on condition that ten members each from among the deputies of the House of Nations must have been elected in the Czech and in the Slovak republic. The Presidium is in charge of the work of the Federal Assembly and exercises its competences between its sessions — except for the election of the president of the republic, the adoption of constitutional laws, decisions on the federal state budget, a declaration of war and the passing of a vote of no confidence in the government. The Presidium issues law-decrees which require the approval of the Federal Assembly at its next session, otherwise they cease to have effect. The provisions concerning the prohibition of outvoting also apply to the taking of decisions of the Presidium.

The president of the republic is elected by the Federal

Assembly on proposal of the CC of the CPC and the CC of the National Front for a five-year term of office. The election requires a three-fifths majority of the deputies of the House of the People, as well as a three-fifths majority of the deputies of the House of Nations elected in the Czech republic and of those deputies of this House elected in the Slovak republic. The president represents the federation in foreign relations; he is commander-in-chief of the armed forces, proclaims a state of war, appoints and dismisses the chairman and the other members of the government, high state functionaries and generals. He has the right to attend cabinet meetings and to take the chair there. He is furthermore entitled to initiate bills, to attend the sessions of the Houses of the Federal Assembly and to dissolve it. If the office of the president of the republic becomes vacant or the president is unable to exercise his functions, they are performed by the government, which may entrust its chairman with some of the powers of the president. Since May 1975 the office of the president has been held by the secretary general of the CC of the CPS, Gustáv Husák, who succeeded General Ludvík Svoboda.

The federal government consists of the chairman, vice-chairmen — two of them being the chairmen of the governments of the republics — ministers and heads of some other central authorities. The chairman and his deputies form the Presidium of the government. Government decisions are taken by a simple majority of its members, hence outvoting is possible. Equal representation of Czechs and Slovaks in the government is no longer practised so rigorously as in the first years after the federalisation of the state.

The federal government, which is accountable to the Federal Assembly, is the supreme executive organ of the Czechoslovak federation in the fields of its exclusive competence and in matters of joint federal–republican jurisdiction. Accordingly, there are Ministries of Foreign Affairs, National Defence, Foreign Trade, Technical Development and Investment, Fuel and Power, Transport, Telecommunications, Domestic Affairs, Finance, Labour and Social Policy, Agriculture and Food-Supply, and for the direction of some key industries. Further members of the federal government are the chairmen of the State Planning Committee, of the Federal Price Board and of the Committee of People's Control of the Czechoslovak Socialist Republic. The members of the government are entitled, and obliged on demand, to take part in the meetings of the chambers of the Federal Assembly, their commissions and the Presidium. At the request of at least one-fifth of the deputies of each chamber, the Federal Assembly may express a vote of no confidence in the government.

According to the principle of 'co-operative federalism', the federal organs are supposed to consult the organs of the republics on matters in which the federation has the exclusive jurisdiction; for example, in the field of foreign policy. They are not obliged, however, to take into account the points of view of the republics. In sectors which fall within the jurisdiction of the republics the federal government has the right to consider questions of principle of importance to the whole society and to co-ordinate their solution in order to secure a uniform state policy throughout the federation.

REPUBLIC GOVERNMENT

The organs of people's representation are the Czech National Council, consisting of 200 members, and the Slovak National Council, consisting of 150 members. (Of the deputies of the latter elected in 1981 130 are Slovaks, 16 are Hungarians, 3 are Ukrainians, and 1 is Czech.) Like the Federal Assembly, each National Council elects a Presidium which exercises a good deal of its functions when it is not in session. The Preidium takes urgent measures requiring the enactment of a law in the form of law-decrees which must be approved at the next session of the National Council; otherwise they become null and void.

To the legislative competence of the republics belong all matters which are not under the exclusive jurisdiction of the federation (e.g. matters of culture, education, public health and justice), insofar as the uniformity of the legal order does not require fundamental federal legislation; to it also belong matters which are under the joint jurisdiction of the federation and the republics (e.g. in the fields of economy, social policy and state security) and which the republics may regulate insofar as they are not regulated fully by federal legislation. The National Councils may introduce bills in the Federal Assembly, which have to be coordinated in joint commissions. The provisions of the constitutional law on the Czechoslovak Federation concerning the division of jurisdiction are rather complicated, and their application could cause problems, if democratic centralism did not result in a finally uniform policy in both republics and thus in the federation as a whole.

Each republic has its own government. Its members — the chairman, vice-chairmen and ministers — are appointed and dismissed by the Presidium of the National Council. The governments are responsible to the National Councils, which may express lack of confidence in them. They implement the laws of the National Councils as well as those of the Federal Assembly, if the implementation is incumbent upon them, and they direct and control the activity of the local organs of state power and state administration. The federal government is entitled to suspend or repeal a measure of a republic government if it is contrary to measures taken by it.

LOCAL GOVERNMENT

The republics are administratively subdivided into regions, districts and communes, the capitals Prague and Bratislava being treated as equal to the regions, and four other large cities being treated as equal to the districts.

The territorial-administrative units are governed by national committees, whose members are elected by the citizens for a five-year term, accountable to them and subject to recall. Each national committee elects from among its members a council which is its executive organ and accountable to it and establishes commissions and other auxiliary organs of administration. In accordance with the principles of democratic centralism and dual subordination, a council is subordinate both to the national committee of the same and to the council of the next higher administrative level or to the republic government. The executive organ next higher in the hierarchy may repeal incorrect decisions. A legal act or decision adopted at the plenary session of a national committee contravening a law or decisions of a higher state organ may be annulled by the next higher national committee, the National Council or the government.

The national committees administer such public sectors as services, transport, housing, road-building, culture, education, health, and protection of the environment. Their scope of activity, however, is rather limited because the financial means granted them out of the budget of the republics are insufficient. Through citizens' committees, elected for five years in public meetings, citizens may articulate their needs and make proposals for the regulation of local affairs; their influence on decision-making, however, is very restricted.

ADMINISTRATION OF JUSTICE

Justice is administered by the Supreme Court of the Czechoslovak Socialist Republic, the Supreme Court of the Czech republic, the Supreme Court of the Slovak republic, regional and district courts as well as military courts. The Supreme Court of the federation supervises the jurisdiction of the Supreme Courts of the republics, and the legality of the decisions of all courts, and ensures the uniformity of jurisdiction by giving its opinion concerning the interpretation of the laws and by deciding on complaints of violation of law, challenging judgments of the Supreme Courts of the republics and military courts. The judges of the Supreme Court of the federation are elected for a ten-year term by the Federal Assembly; the judges of the Supreme Courts of the republics and professional judges of regional and district courts are elected by the respective national councils. Lay judges of regional and district courts are elected by the national committees for a four-year term of office. All judges are subject to recall.

The constitutional law of October 1968 provided for the establishment of the Constitutional Court of the Czechoslovak Socialist Republic and of constitutional courts in the republics. The Constitutional Court of the federation shall decide on the conformity of laws and other generally binding legal regulations of the organs of the federation and the republics with the constitution; it shall settle conflicts of competence between organs of the federation and the republics and protect the rights and freedoms guaranteed by the constitution against infringements by decisions of federal organs, insofar as the law does not grant other judicial protection. The constitutional courts have not, however, become a reality.

Nor is there administrative jurisdiction. Citizens who claim that their legally guaranteed rights have been violated by a measure of an administrative organ may only appeal to the organ which has taken the measure, or to the higher organ. A judicial examination of decisions of administrative organs is possible only in a few cases. Furthermore, citizens may lodge a complaint with committees of people's control, which were established in enterprises in 1971, with the national committees, the governments of the republics and the federal government. Guided by the directives of the CPC, these committees have wide authority to control the activity and the observance of the laws and other legal regulations by all organs of state and economic administration except the courts, the procuracy and the organs of state security.

The control of the legality of the activity of administrative organs, courts, economic and other organisations, and citizens is also vested in the Procuracy, which consequently is not only an organ for preferring charges. The procurators are also entitled to intervene in civil actions if they consider this necessary in order to protect social and individual rights. The Procuracy, being a highly centralised authority, is headed by the procurator general of the Czechoslovak Socialist Republic, who is appointed and recalled by the president of the republic and accountable to the Federal Assembly.

FOREIGN POLICY

Czechoslovak foreign policy is entirely orientated towards the interests of the Soviet Union. Fraternal solidarity with the USSR and membership in the socialist world system of which Czechoslovakia constitutes a 'solid link' are laid down in the preamble to the constitution. The basis for the close ties with the Soviet Union was already contained in the Treaty on Friendship and Mutual Assistance of December 1943, when, however, the Czechoslovaks were also guided by security interests, which Great Britain and France had not considered in 1938–39. The chance to orientate itself towards the West, which had been offered in July 1947 by the invitation to take part in the Marshall Plan, proved illusory. The Czechoslovak government had first agreed to join this programme of economic aid, but then, upon Soviet pressure, had to decline.

After the communist takeover Czechoslovakia was quickly integrated into the East European network of bilateral pacts of friendship and mutual assistance. In 1955 it became a foundation-member of the WTO, for which it possesses a significant strategic position and is an important supplier of arms. Nor had its active co-operation in the WTO been questioned in 1968, when the former General Prchlík advocated a change of command structure to the Soviet Union's disadvantage. On 21 August 1968 Czechoslovakia was occupied by troops of the WTO — except those of Rumania. The Soviet Union justified the invasion first by the request for help by some Czechoslovak party and state functionaries, later by the need to save socialism (more precisely, what the Soviet leaders mean by socialism). Czechoslovakia denounced it before the UN Security Council as a violation of its sovereignty and as interference in internal affairs. In October 1968 the stationing of Soviet armed forces was legalised by a treaty. On renewal of the Czechoslovak–Soviet Treaty on Friendship and Mutual Assistance in May 1970, Czechoslovakia recognised the so-called 'Brezhnev doctrine' by committing itself to the common protection of the socialist order. It furthermore accepted the duty of giving military support to the USSR if any country should attack it, thereby including e.g. the People's Republic of China. This is in contrast to the WTO, which limits the obligation to mutual aid to the event of an attack on one of its members in Europe.

In the CMEA, of which Czechoslovakia had also been a founding member, it supports — in full accordance with the Soviet Union — increased integration; for example, by coordination of the economic plans. Within the framework of 'socialist division of labour' Czechoslovakia produces high-quality finished products, above all machines, and whole factory plants especially for the Soviet Union on which it is wholly dependent for its oil and to a large extent for the supply of iron ore. Furthermore, it is obliged to grant economic and technical aid to developing countries, particularly to those with a 'socialist orientation', and it delivers arms into crisis areas within the Soviet sphere of interest.

The normalisation of relations with the Federal Republic of Germany failed for many years because of the Czechoslovak claim to declare the Munich Agreement of 1938 retrospectively null and void. It was not until December 1973 that both states agreed to establish diplomatic relations.

Because of the lack of popular support the regime is totally dependent on the Soviet Union. Consequently, it unconditionally supports Soviet foreign policy and, at present, proves to be the Soviet Union's most reliable ally within the WTO. Czechoslovakia condemns severely any attempt of other WTO countries to pursue a foreign policy towards the West or China which is not entirely in line with Soviet interests, as well as any tendency in domestic policy which is not in full accordance with the Soviet model of socialism.

NATIONAL DEFENCE

Czechoslovakia maintains armed forces totalling roughly 207,000 soldiers — 148,000 in the army and 59,000 in the air force. Furthermore, it maintains 11,000 border troops and the People's Militia of about 120,000.[4] The Association for Co-operation with the Army is in charge of the paramilitary training of the population. Responsibility for the country's defence lies with the State Defence Council. Its members are appointed and recalled by the president of the republic, who is entitled to participate in, and chair its meetings.

NOTES

1. English text in William B. Simons (ed.), *The Constitutions of the Communist World* (Alphen aan den Rijn, The Netherlands, and Germantown, Md., 1980), pp. 140–58.
2. English text, *ibid,*. pp. 582–624.
3. Richard F. Starr (ed.), *Yearbook on International Communist Affairs 1984: Parties and Revolutionary Movements* (Stanford, Cal., 1984), p. 312.
4. The International Institute for Strategic Studies, London, *The Military Balance 1984–1985* (Oxford, 1984), pp. 24–5.

FURTHER READING

Brown, Archie and Gordon Wightman, 'Czechoslovakia: Revival and Retreat', in Archie Brown and Jack Gray (eds.), *Political Culture and Political Change in Communist States,* 2nd edn. (London: Macmillan, 1979), pp. 159–96
Golan, Galia, *Reform Rule in Czechoslovakia: The Dubček Era 1968–1969* (Cambridge: Cambridge University Press, 1973)
Kusin, Vladimir V., *The Intellectual Origins of the Prague Spring: The Development of Reformist Ideas in Czechoslovakia, 1965–1967* (Cambridge: Cambridge University Press, 1971)
—— *Political Grouping in the Czechoslovak Reform Movement* (London: Macmillan 1972)
—— *From Dubček to Charter 77: A Study of 'Normalization' in Czechoslovakia, 1968–1978* (Edinburgh: Q Press, 1978)
Mlynář, Zdeněk, *Nightfrost in Prague: The End of Human Socialism* (New York: Karz Publishers, 1980)
Oxley, Andrew, Alex Pravda and Andrew Ritchie, *Czechoslovakia: The Party and the People* (London: Allen Lane, 1973)
Paul, David W., *Czechoslovakia: Profile of a Socialist Republic at the Crossroads of Europe* (Boulder, Colo.: Westview Press, 1981)
Pelikán, Jiří, *Socialist Opposition in Eastern Europe: The Czechoslovak Example* (London: Allison and Busby, 1976)
Skilling, H. Gordon, *Czechoslovakia's Interrupted Revolution* (Princeton, NJ: Princeton University Press, 1976)
—— *Charter 77 and Human Rights in Czechoslovakia* (London and Boston: Allen and Unwin, 1981)
Suda, Zdeněk, *Zealots and Rebels: A History of the Communist Party of Czechoslovakia* (Stanford, Cal.: Hoover Institution Press, 1980)
—— *The Czechoslovak Socialist Republic* (Baltimore, Md.: Johns Hopkins Press, 1969)
Wolfe-Jancar, Barbara, *Czechoslovakia and the Absolute Monopoly of Power: A Study of Political Power in a Communist System* (New York: Praeger, 1971)

8   German Democratic Republic

BASIC FEATURES

According to article 1 of the constitution adopted by a referendum on 6 April 1968 and amended on 7 October 1974,[1] the German Democratic Republic (GDR) is a 'socialist state of workers and peasants'. The reference to the German character of the socialist state and the mandate for reunification (of the two German states) in the original version of the constitution have been eliminated. As a 'political organisation of the urban and rural working population' the GDR is under the 'leadership of the working class and its Marxist-Leninist Party' (article 1); that is, the Socialist Unity Party of Germany (SUPG), whose leading position in state and society is unconditionally recognised by the other four parties still existing.

The 'inviolable foundations' of the socialist order of state and society are, according to article 2, (1) the 'firm alliance of the working class with the class of co-operative farmers, the intelligentsia, and other sectors of the population', (2) the 'socialist ownership of the means of production' and (3) the 'management and planning of social development in accordance with the most advanced scientific knowledge'. Relations within the SUPG and within the state as well as between party and state are based on the principle of democratic centralism. The resolutions and directives of the SUPG are binding on all state organs and thus have priority over the norms of the state.

THE COMMUNIST TAKEOVER

The takeover by the SUPG which emerged from the forced fusion of the Social Democratic Party with the Communist Party in the Soviet zone of occupation in April 1946, took place within the phase of 'antifascist-democratic' radical changes between 1945 and 1949. This stage, which preceded the foundation of the GDR, was marked by the nationalisation of distinct sectors of the industry, the expropriation of large-scale land-holdings as well as the reorganisation of the educational and judicial system. The SUPG, in which at the beginning of its existence members of the former Social Democratic Party had the majority, termed itself in its 1946 Statute as 'a political organisation of the German working class and of all working people', and did not claim the leadership in state and society. It contemplated at that time the possibility of a peaceful development of the revolution and thus a 'special German road towards socialism'.[2] During the following two years, however, the SUPG was transformed step by step into a Leninist cadre party, based on production enterprises and attached to the principle of democratic centralism. During this period the party was purged of unreliable former Social Democrats; leaders of bourgeois parties which opposed the socio-economic course were eliminated. As a result the SUPG established its absolute rule, not by revolutionary means but not through free and competitive elections either.

At the beginning of December 1947, on the occasion of the London Conference of the allied foreign ministers, dedicated to German unity, the First German People's Congress convened on the initiative of the SUPG. In March 1948 the Second German People's Congress elected the German People's Council as its permanent body, which appointed a committee to draft a constitution. In March 1949 this draft was accepted by the German People's Council. The subsequent elections of delegates to the Third German People's Congress were held on the basis of a unity list of the Democratic Bloc, consisting of the SUPG, four other parties and mass organisations. Only 66.1 per cent of the votes cast, however, were for the single list, because the citizens largely made use of their right to delete candidates. On 7 October

1949 the People's Council became the Provisional People's Chamber, which passed the first constitution. With its coming into force the GDR is considered to have been founded.

The constitution was that of a 'people's democracy' which has been considered to be a preliminary stage on the way to a socialist state. The SUPG and its leading role in state and society were not mentioned in it, thus concealing the actual structure of power. This aspect was finally acknowledged in the constitution of 6 April 1968, which brought constitutional norm into line with constitutional reality.

On 17 June 1953 communist rule was confronted with a serious threat when construction and industrial workers went on strike against the increase in work norms imposed on them in order to fulfil the economic programme laid down in the first five-year plan of 1950. The strikes, at first only economically motivated, soon took on the character of a popular rebellion against the regime, which was ultimately suppressed by Soviet military force.

THE MARXIST-LENINIST PARTY

According to the preamble of its Programme of May 1976, the SUPG bases its leading role on the claim that it is 'the conscious and organised vanguard of the working class and the labouring people' of the GDR. Its task is to form a 'developed socialist society' in pursuit of the final aim, the establishment of a communist social order. In 1984 the SUPG claimed a membership of 2.24 million (roughly 13 per cent of the population), of which 58.1 per cent are supposed to be workers, 4.8 per cent co-operative farmers, and 22.3 per cent members of the intelligentsia.[3]

Recruitment to the party is effected by primary organisations; a probationary year precedes full membership; anyone may become a candidate at the age of eighteen. According to the production principle, primary organisations are formed when there are at least three members in factories, co-operatives, offices, institutions of social welfare or, furthermore, in urban or rural residential places and in the armed forces. In line with the political-administrative division of the country, the primary organisations are united into district, city and city district party organisations, all within regional party organisations. District organisations have also been set up in large enterprises, central administrative bodies, the army and in universities.

According to the Party Statute, the Party Congress is the supreme organ of the SUPG. Its delegates are elected by secret ballot at the regional delegate conferences. As a rule the Congress takes place every five years. It has the power to pass the Party Programme and the Statute, to establish the general line of the party, to elect the members of the Central Committee (CC) and the members of the Central Auditing Commission, and to decide on the report of the CC. Between the Congresses the CC may call a Party Conference to decide formally on party policy and questions of personnel; it may dismiss and replace members of the CC. The CC, which, formally, is the highest party organ between Congresses and convenes at least twice — as a rule four times — a year, elects the Political Bureau, the Secretariat, the secretary general and appoints the members of the Central Party Control Commission.

The Political Bureau — with twenty-one full members and four candidates in May 1984 — is the permanent organ of the CC. Entitled to direct the work of the CC, it is practically the highest decisive organ of the SUPG, and in view of its power to issue directives to state organs, it is *de facto* an authority above the state. The Secretariat, with the first secretary or secretary general — since May 1971 Erich Honecker, successor to Walter Ulbricht — deals with the implementation and control of party decisions and with the selection of cadres. Through its departments, which partly correspond with the ministerial departments, it has a decisive influence on governmental activity. Some secretaries of the CC, including the secretary general, are also members of the Political Bureau. High party and state offices are linked through personal union. The secretary general is chairman of the Council of State and the National Defence Council; Willi Stoph, the chairman of the Council of Ministers, as well as the ministers of national defence and of state security, are also members of the Political Bureau; other members of the Political

Bureau, who are concurrently secretaries of the CC, are also vice-chairmen of the Council of State.

The SUPG feels itself to be fraternally linked to the CPSU; it considers the attitude towards the CPSU and the USSR to be 'a criterion for loyalty towards Marxism-Leninism' (preamble and section IV of the Programme of 1976). The 'uncompromising struggle' against all appearances of 'anti-Sovietism' is made compulsory for all party members (article 2 of the 1976 Party Statute).

BLOC PARTIES, SOCIAL ORGANISATIONS, AND THE NATIONAL FRONT

Apart from the SUPG there are four other political parties: the Christian Democratic Union of Germany, the Liberal Democratic Party of Germany, the Democratic Peasants' Party of Germany and the National Democratic Party of Germany, all of which were founded between June 1945 and May 1948. In 1982 they filed 125,000, 82,000, 103,000 and 91,000 members, respectively.[4] They are represented in the People's Chamber but do not compete with the SUPG for seats. They consider themselves as allies of the SUPG in the construction of socialism. Their pre-eminent offical function is to integrate those citizens into the socialist system who have a critical attitude towards the SUPG or who because of their social and/or political background cannot obtain membership in the Communist Party, and to secure these citizens' support for the aims of the party and the state. Whereas the Democratic Peasants' Party endeavours to stimulate the political commitment of the peasants, the members and addressees of the Liberal Democratic Party and the National Democratic Party come from the urban middle class — the latter party was founded in order to mobilise, above all, craftsmen, retailers and small employees, as well as former professional soldiers and members of the Nazi party who broke with their past. In addition, the bloc parties have to propagate decisions of the SUPG and the state organs among the respective sections of the population, to consult the SUPG and the state organs and to inform them about the mood prevailing in the population.

They also, however, articulate the interests of their members and make possible (limited) prospects of promotion for them. In the 1950s, in a phase when the future of both German states was still the subject of negotiations, these parties were a useful link with the parties in the Federal Republic of Germany (FRG).

The SUPG's claim to leadership is also recognised by the mass and other social organisations: the Free Confederation of German Trade Unions with 9.1 million members; the Free German Youth, with 2.3 million members and filing about three-quarters of the young people between the ages of fourteen and twenty-five; the Pioneer Organisation 'Ernst Thälmann', with 1.4 million youngsters between six and thirteen; the Democratic Women's League of Germany with 1.4 million members; the Society for German-Soviet Friendship with 6 million members;[5] the Culture League, the German Society for Sport and Technology, which provides paramilitary training and scientific education, and so on.

The organisations serve (1) to mobilise the citizens belonging to various social sections and professions for the aims of the SUPG; (2) to socialise the citizens into the system of values set up by the SUPG; (3) to recruit people for leading positions in the party, the state and the economy, and (4) to control all social activities. It would be wrong, however, to reduce the functions of these organisations to those of 'transmission belts' for the SUPG. They also represent the specific interests of their members, though not autonomously and only to the extent to which the interests of society as a whole, and as defined by the SUPG, are not affected. For party and state leadership this articulation of particular interests forms a source of information about attitudes, wishes and the potential of support among the citizens, making corrections to the political line possible. In addition, party and state can make use of the specialised knowledge accumulated in the organisations. Consultation is effected, *inter alia,* by the fact that the chairmen or secretaries of the most important organisations are members of high party organs. Thus the organisations are included in the decision-making process of the SUPG and the state, making appropriate decisions more likely, and are considered a feature of socialist democracy. The Free Confederation of German Trade Unions, the unity organisation of sixteen industrial and other trade unions, for example, does not only have the duty to see to the realisation of the economic plan and of 'socialist emulation' but through its organs also has limited rights concerning the organisation of the production process and the adoption of measures for the improvement of the working and living conditions of the workers; furthermore, it is entitled to initiate legislation.

The five parties, as well as the mass organisations and other social organisations, are united in the National Front of the GDR, which emerged from the People's Congress Movement in October 1949. It is not considered a mass organisation but an 'alliance of all sections of the population' (article 3 of the constitution) without a formal membership of the parties, organisations or individual citizens. The supreme organ of the National Front is the Congress, which is directly elected by the populace and which in turn elects a National Council and its president. It is the task of the National Front to mobilise the citizens for the support of state activities, to appoint candidates for the people's representative bodies at all levels of state organisation, to explain the election programme, to prepare and carry out the elections, to support the representative bodies in their activity and to implant into the citizens of household communities — the smallest organisational units of the National Front — the pattern of thought and behaviour determined by the SUPG.

OPPOSITION AND DISSENT

Outside the National Front, the parties and the social organisations, political activity is not possible. Since the state claims to put into effect the will of the whole nation, there is 'no objective political or social basis' for any opposition or dissent whatsoever.[6] Yet, apart from the workers' opposition and the revolt of June 1953, there has been, and still is, severe criticism of 'real socialism' and of the defence policy of the GDR and the Soviet Union among officials of the party and state apparatus, intellectuals from the rank and file of the SUPG, prominent philosophers, sociologists, writers, pacifist clergymen and ordinary citizens. This behaviour, however, is suppressed by a restricted interpretation and rigorous application of the criminal code's provisions on propaganda hostile to the state and on 'slandering of the state', which amounts to a *de facto* annulment of the freedom of opinion guaranteed by article 27 of the constitution. Offenders are sentenced to imprisonment, expatriated or officially allowed to emigrate to the West. From the construction of the Berlin Wall in August 1961 until 1977, roughly 177,000 citizens fled from the GDR to West Germany.[7]

CENTRAL GOVERNMENT

The representative body at the national level is the People's Chamber. Its 500 deputies are elected for a five-year term in multi-member constituencies. (Up to 1981 only 434 were elected directly, the other 66 — considering the Four Powers' status of Berlin — were elected by the East Berlin City Councillors' Assembly.) Every citizen who is eighteen years of age is entitled to vote and to be elected. The election turn out is usually about 99 per cent (1981: 99.2 per cent). The percentage of votes cast for the single list of the National Front is nearly 100. The candidates are proposed by the working collectives in enterprises and co-operatives and nominated by the parties and the mass organisations. They are obliged to introduce themselves to the electors, which may apply for the removal of a candidate from the list of candidates. Their opinion, however, is not binding on the National Front. Ultimately, the SUPG decides on the inclusion in the list of the National Front and the order of the candidates — the People's Chamber mandates belong to the *nomenklatura* of the CC. The list contains more candidates than mandates allotted to a constituency. A ballot without any deletions is counted as a vote for the candidates at the top of the list, whose number corresponds to the number of mandates entitled to a constituency. Because of heavy propaganda and social pressure for an open vote, deletions which require the use of screened-off booths, are very rare (1981 only 16,645 out of 12,251,967 valid votes), and the election results are practically identical with the single list. This has made it possible to keep the ratio of the distribution of the 500 seats between the SUPG, the other four parties and four major social organisations unchanged since 1963.

The SUPG gets 127 seats, the bloc parties 52 seats each, the Free Confederation of German Trade Unions 68, the Free German Youth 40, the Democratic Women's League 35 and the Culture League 22 seats. Thus the SUPG does not have the absolute majority of seats, but, together with the deputies of the mass organisations, who are mainly members of the SUPG — only a few belong to a bloc party or to no party at all — it definitely achieves a majority. All deputiies who are members of the SUPG are united in the SUPG party group, which is subordinate to the CC of the SUPG. In fact, the number of SUPG mandates is irrelevant because of the party's undisputed claim for absolute power. The deputies of the parties and of the social organisations form parliamentary groups which, among other things, have the right to initiate laws and to send their representatives into the Presidium; they do not, however, constitute groups which could pursue policies independent of the SUPG leadership.

On the one hand, the deputies are supposed to let themselves be guided by the interests of the people as a whole; on the other hand, they have to take into account the proposals and criticisms of their electors. Co-ordination is effected by the 'explanation' of national policies (article 56 of the constitution). The deputies keep in contact with their electors through public office hours and discussions; they are obliged to render account to their electors and — on gross violation of their duties — can be recalled, but they enjoy parliamentary immunity. They are entitled to take part, in an advisory capacity, in the meetings of the local representative bodies and to put questions to the Council of Ministers and to each of its members.

According to article 48, the People's Chamber is the 'supreme organ' of the state. As such it exercises the sole constitutional and legislative power, decides on 'basic questions of state policy' and 'implements in its activities the principle of the unity of decision and enforcement'. According to this principle of the unity of powers, the People's Chamber finally and bindingly for all 'sets the development goals' of the GDR and determines the main rules for co-operation between citizens, organisations and state organs, as well as their tasks in implementing the state plans for social development. It guarantees the implementation of its laws and resolutions by laying down 'the principles governing the activities' of the Council of State, the Council of Ministers, the National Defence Council, the Supreme Court and the procurator general (article 49). Moreover, the People's Chamber approves international treaties whenever these make amendments of existing laws necessary and decides on the state of defence. Exercising its creative function, the People's Chamber elects and recalls the chairmen and the members of the Council of State and the Council of Ministers, the chairman of the National Defence Council, the president and the judges of the Supreme Court and the procurator general. Despite all these competences, however, the People's Chamber is not an original organ of decision-making. Its decisions are always, in view of its composition and in view of the leading role of the SUPG, *de facto* the decisions of the Communist Party and serve to convey its will into the sphere of the state.

This is emphasised by the fact that on an average the People's Chamber convenes only four times annually for plenary meetings, each of which lasts one day. As far as the People's Chamber is actually involved in the political decision-making process, this is effected by its committees. They are responsible for the discussion of drafts and control over the enforcement of laws and they may consult experts from outside the People's Chamber as well as demand the presence of ministers and heads of other state organs in their deliberations in order to obtain information. The committees, as well as fifteen deputies, the Council of State, the Council of Ministers or the Presidium of the Free German Confederation of Trade Unions have the right to initiate legislation. Drafts of 'basic' laws have to be submitted to the population for discussion. Bills are passed by the plenum without controversial debate and are agreed on unanimously. There has been only one single exception to this rule so far: in May 1972 fourteen members of the Christian Democratic Union voted against the abortion bill and eight deputies abstained from voting.

In a formal sense the People's Chamber has gained some importance ever since the Council of State — because of the constitutional amendments of October 1974 — has no longer had the functions of a 'substitute parliament'. In particular, the Council of State no longer has the right to pass law-decrees but may merely pass 'resolutions' in order to carry out its tasks. The powers of a constitutional court, such as the control of norms, are no longer exercised by the Council of State but by the People's Chamber. Yet in emergency cases it, instead of the People's Chamber, decides on the state of defence. On behalf of the People's Chamber it assists the local representative bodies and ensures that they observe socialist legality in their activities, and it supervises the constitutionality and legality of the activities of the Supreme Court and the procurator general. Furthermore, it passes fundamental resolutions on matters of defence and appoints the members of the National Defence Council.

In its function as collective head of state, the Council of State promulgates laws and represents the GDR in foreign relations. The Council of State consists of the chairman, the vice-chairmen (among them are the chairmen of the four bloc parties), the members and the secretary, who are elected by the People's Chamber for a term of five years. The right of nomination for the post of the chairman is held by the SUPG. The chairman — at present the secretary general of the CC of the SUPG, Erich Honecker — directs the activities of the Council of State and exercises the active and passive right of legation.

The Council of Ministers, whose importance has also increased somewhat at the cost of the Council of State, is 'as organ of the People's Chamber' (article 76 of the constitution), the government of the GDR. It is composed of the chairman — since November 1976 (as already from 1964 to 1973) Willi Stoph — the vice-chairmen and the ministers. The vice-chairmen are for the most part at the same time head of a ministry or of a governmental agency (e.g. the State Planning Commission) or have a special area of responsibility (e.g. permanent representation at the CMEA). Not all members of the Council of Ministers are heads of a department (as the chairman of the Committee of Peasants' and Workers' Inspection, the head of the Price Board, the president of the State Bank, the mayor of East Berlin).

The chairman of the Council of Ministers is nominated by the SUPG in the People's Chamber; he, as well as the vice-chairmen and the ministers, is elected by the People's Chamber for a term of five years. The satellite parties provide one vice-chairman each. In view of the size of the Council of Ministers — it has more than forty members — its efficiency is guaranteed by the Presidium of the Council of Ministers (an inner cabinet) which is composed of the chairman, vice-chairmen as well as some other members of the Council of Ministers. The Presidium prepares the decisions and concentrates the work of the Council of Ministers. The resolutions it makes between the meetings of the Council of Ministers are considered to be those of the whole body.

The Council of Ministers, as the executive organ of the People's Chamber, 'directs the uniform execution' (article 76) of domestic and foreign policy, taking into account the extensive co-operation with the USSR and other socialist states, elaborates drafts of legislation necessary for solving pending problems and provides for the realisation of political, economic, cultural, social and defence tasks assigned to it. By special branch ministries the Council of Ministers directs the national economy, ensures its development according to plan and the 'harmoniously blended formation of social sectors and territories'. It decides on industrial plants, infrastructural measures, distribution of human labour, environmental protection, and so on, as well as on matters of the GDR's economic integration within the CMEA. As the Council of Ministers basically prepares the legislation of the People's Chamber, it is predominant in the governmental process of decision-making. On the other hand, the Council of Ministers acts under the direction and control of the SUPG and is, actually, the state executor of the decisions made by the leading bodies of the SUPG. On the whole, though, there can be observed a certain displacement of powers concerning the shaping of the society in favour of the state apparatus, of which the Council of Ministers is the top organ.

LOCAL GOVERNMENT

The GDR — after the dissolution of the Länder (the federal units) in 1952 — is a centralistic unity state, and administratively divided into fifteen regions (including East Berlin), cities, rural districts, urban districts (in larger cities) as well as communes (small towns and villages). Towns and communes may, while preserving their administrative independence, merge into associations of communes in order to solve common problems.

The people's representative bodies of the administrative units are elected directly by the population from unity lists of candidates of the National Front. The seats are distributed among the parties and mass organisations according to a ratio fixed in advance. As organs of state power and following the principle of the unity of powers, the local people's representative bodies prepare, execute and control decisions of local significance in which the citizens are supposed to participate. Their tasks consist in (1) the increase and the protection of socialist property; (2) the improvement of working and living conditions of the citizens; (3) the promotion of social and cultural life of the citizens; (4) the raising of the level of consciousness with regard to the socialist state and socialist law; (5) the maintenance of public order; (6) the strengthening of socialist legality; and (7) the safeguarding of the rights of the citizens — *inter alia* by deciding upon their complaints and petitions. Observing the interests of the whole state, the local people's representative bodies decide responsibly on all matters concerning their territory and their citizens. The resolutions of a higher representative body are binding on a lower one.

Every local people's representative body elects a council and various committees as its organs. The councils prepare the decisions of the representative bodies and carry out the duties assigned to them on the basis of legal acts of the people's representative bodies and the higher state organs. A council is subordinate to the people's representative body which elected it as well as to the council at the next higher administrative level (the regional council to the Council of Ministers). The councils consist of a chairman, vice-chairmen and members responsible for the particular departments. Persons who are not members of a representative body may be appointed to permanent and non-permanent commissions. In this way well-informed citizens are enabled to participate in the preparation and implementation of the decisions of the representative bodies and to control the councils with regard to the execution of legal norms and resolutions.

The regional organs are of particular importance insofar as they direct the socio-economic development of their territory on the basis of the production targets passed by the Council of Ministers. They administer the regionally directed industry (small- and middle-scale state-owned enterprises of special branches and private enterprises) and are furthermore active in the fields of price formation and price control, trade and services, urban development and housing construction, agriculture and forestry as well as food supply, traffic, energy and water supply, environmental protection, education and health service, culture, sports, tourism, social care, law and order, as well as civil defence.

ADMINISTRATION OF JUSTICE

The adminstration of justice is intended to serve the implementation of socialist legality, the protection and development of the GDR, its state and social order, the protection of freedom, of a peaceful life and of the rights and dignity of man. The respect and protection of individual rights is binding on state organs, social forces and each individual citizen. These rights, however, are not protective rights against the state but oblige the citizen, according to the interpretation of justice and law in a socialist state, to develop his abilities 'for the good of society', and 'for his own benefit' only insofar as this fits into the interests of 'socialist society' (article 19 of the constitution). Freedom of opinion, assembly and association is limited by the constitutional principles and aims defined by the SUPG.

There is neither constitutional nor administrative jurisdiction. The control of the constitutionality of laws and other legal acts is a matter for the People's Chamber; individual rights cannot be claimed in court. In a limited number of cases the citizen may only lodge a formal complaint against intrusions on the part of the administration with the organ by whose measure he feels his rights to have been violated. This or a higher organ will decide the matter. For damage resulting from illegal acts of state organs, that organ is liable whose employee has caused the damage. Damages, however, cannot be claimed in court.

The organs of jurisdiction are the Supreme Court, the regional courts, the district courts and the social courts. In addition, there is special military jurisdiction. The professional and lay judges of the law courts are elected for five years by the corresponding representative bodies, except that the lay judges of the district courts are elected directly by the citizens. They may be dismissed if they violate the constitution or the laws, or fail in their duties.

Social courts exist in the form of conflict commissions and arbitrary commissions. The first are formed in state-owned enterprises, private enterprises, health and educational institutions, offices and social organisations. Their members are elected by the members of the enterprises, and so on, for two years. Arbitrary commissions are established in the residential areas of towns, in communes, in agricultural co-operatives and in co-operatives of manual workers, fishermen and gardeners. In towns and communes their members are elected for four years by the respective people's representative bodies on the suggestion of the National Front; in the co-operatives they are elected by the general meetings on the recommendation of their committees. The jurisdiction of the social courts applies to affairs of labour law, minor breaches of the peace, misdemeanours (misappropriation, intrusion into the home, insults and defamation), infringements of the law, truancy, work-shy conduct as well as simple conflicts in civil law. They take action at the request of the victim or, if a case is transferred to the social courts by the police, the Public Procurator's Office or a law court. The hearings take place with the active participation of the members of the workers' collective or the populace of a residential area or a commune. The decisions are supposed to achieve an educational and decriminalising effect. It is possible to raise an objection against them through the district courts.

Apart from social jurisdiction, the citizens are included in the administration of justice and in controlling adherence to 'socialist law' in the form of 'workers' and peasants' inspections' — a kind of 'social police'.

The tasks and duties of the Public Procurator's Office are to combat criminality, to direct preliminary investigations, to prefer charges, to apply for annulment of legally valid judgments at the Supreme Court and regional courts, and also especially to supervise adherence to 'socialist legality' in order 'to safeguard the socialist social and state order and the rights of the citizens' (article 97 of the constitution). When a law is violated, the Public Procurator's Office lodges an appeal with the authority which has committed the violation. If this authority does not grant the appeal, the appeal is considered rejected.

The Public Procurator's Office is directed by the procurator general, who is elected by the People's Chamber and responsible to the latter or, between its sittings, to the Council of State. The procurator general appoints the public procurators of the regions and districts, who are bound by his instructions, responsible to him and may be recalled by him.

FOREIGN POLICY

Five guiding principles underlie the foreign policy of the GDR. They are established in article 6 of the constitution in the following order: (1) The 'perpetual and irrevocable alliance' with the USSR; (2) the 'inseparable' membership in the socialist community of states, towards whose members the GDR commits itself to the maintenance and development of friendship, universal co-operation, and mutual assistance; (3) the support of all peoples 'who are struggling against imperialism and colonialism'; (4) the peaceful coexistence of states of different social orders; (5) the support for peace and co-operation in Europe, a stable peaceful order throughout the world and universal disarmament. The most important fields for external activities are the socialist states, organised in the WTO and/or in the CMEA, the FRG, and selected countries of the Third World.

The existence of the GDR as a result of the Soviet policy of occupation made the political and military presence of the Soviet Union in Central Europe possible. As one of the four victorious and occupying powers, the Soviet Union (formally) conceded freedom of action in foreign affairs to the GDR in March 1954 but reserved for itself the right of intervention on the basis of the agreements with the Western allies. In the State Treaty of September 1955 the USSR confirmed the sovereign status of the GDR. This and the admission of the GDR to the WTO in January 1956 reflected the Soviet Union's reaction to the Western integration and rearmament of the FRG, which it had endeavoured to prevent by offers of reunification — especially by means of Stalin's Note of March 1952, which contemplated a neutralisation of the whole of Germany.

The determinant factor in the GDR's foreign policy is its integration into the Soviet sphere of power resulting from the Second World War. This and the maxims of proletarian-socialist internationalism give the GDR only a limited scope of action in foreign affairs. The pursuance of its own interests is only possible to an extent that does not affect vital interests of the Soviet Union. But deviations can be recorded: the GDR advocated the transformation of West Berlin into a free and demilitarised city, as had been demanded by the Soviet government in 1958, even after the Soviet Union had given up this idea; the Four Power Agreement on West Berlin of September 1971 was concluded against the opposition of the then head of party and state, Walter Ulbricht; and the GDR adapted itself to Soviet efforts for a détente in Europe — abandoning the precondition of previous international recognition and starting negotiations with the FRG — only when it was compelled to do so by Soviet–West German negotiations.

Because of its common frontier with the FRG, the GDR is of great strategic importance for the WTO. This is underlined by the fact that the greatest part of Soviet armed forces outside the Soviet Union, about 425,000, are stationed on the territory of the GDR in accordance with the Stationing Treaty of 1957.[8] Within the CMEA, of which the GDR became a member in September 1950, it holds an important position because of its economic competitiveness — the GDR has the highest income *per capita* of all CMEA countries. As a form of 'mutual aid' it grants extensive loans to its partners and unconditionally supports all Soviet endeavours aimed at the integration of the economic policies of the CMEA member states.

Furthermore the GDR is united with the bulk of socialist countries by a network of treaties on friendship, co-operation and mutual assistance. In 1964 it concluded a treaty of this kind with the Soviet Union and other treaties in 1967 with Poland, Czechoslovakia, Hungary and Bulgaria, which confirmed the thesis of the two German states and the thesis of the independent political unit of West Berlin. A corresponding treaty was not concluded with Rumania until May 1972, because the establishment of diplomatic relations between Rumania and the FRG in 1967 caused sustained ill-feeling in the GDR. In 1977 the GDR also signed treaties on friendship, co-operation and mutual assistance with Mongolia and Vietnam, and in 1980 with Cuba and Kampuchea. These last four treaties, however, do not account for military assistance and do not refer to the internationalist duty of socialist countries to undertake the mutual defence of their achievements.

The relations between the GDR and the People's Republic of China are determined by the USSR's China policy. Right from the beginning the GDR supported the Soviet campaign against the efforts of the CP of China to gain ideological and political independence. Since 1982 relations have somewhat improved at government level but not between the two ruling parties. In October 1957 the GDR established diplomatic relations with Yugoslavia; it was disappointed, however, having hoped for a wave of recognition by non-aligned countries in whose movement Yugoslavia has a leading position.

Two phases may roughly be distinguished in the relationship between the GDR and the FRG. Until 1955 the GDR, following the course of Soviet policy towards Germany, pursued a policy of wait-and-see as against the possibility of reunification. In the following period the GDR maintained the thesis of the existence of two German states, which the FRG opposed by its claim of sole representation and corresponding implementation of the so-called 'Hallstein doctrine' based on this claim. Since the ratification of the Basic Treaty on inter-German relations signed in December 1972, the GDR has maintained relations with the FRG, accepting the reservation of the FRG that these relations do not have the character of those between separate sovereign states. The treaty made co-operation between the two German states in various fields possible. Although the GDR applies a sealing-off policy towards the FRG and in spite of the worsening of East–West relations, the GDR's interest in co-operation with the FRG has not weakened because it is of vital importance for its economic development.

The Basic Treaty paved the way for a world-wide international recognition of the GDR, also on the part of the three Western war allies of the Soviet Union. After a first futile attempt in February 1966, the GDR was admitted to the UNO in September 1973 — together with the FRG — and since 1972 has already co-operated officially in several UN special organisations.

Relations with countries of the Third World in the 1950s and 1960s were marked by efforts for diplomatic recognition by non-aligned and/or 'progressive states' such as Egypt, Syria, Algeria, Ghana, Tanzania, India, Burma and Ceylon to whom the GDR gave loans and grants for students. In several states it was able to establish consular representations or at least trade missions, sometimes with diplomatic status. The development and also military aid in the form of arms supply and the dispatch of advisers was thus in the GDR's own interest but also served and serves the cultivation of the socialist image and the Soviet Union's effort to expand its sphere of influence. Development aid in the form of goods, capital and technical aid, however, in view of the economic potential of the GDR is quite modest.

NATIONAL DEFENCE

The organisation of the country's defence depends on the Council of State, which passes the fundamental resolutions, and the National Defence Council. In case of defence, determined by the People's Chamber or — in urgent cases — by the

Council of State, the chairman of the Defence Council is commander-in-chief of all the armed forces.

In 1984 regular armed forces consisted of 172,000 soldiers of the National People's Army, which is under the Joint High Command of the WTO; 120,000 were in the army, 14,000 in the navy, and 38,000 in the air force.[9] Apart from them the GDR maintains paramilitary forces: 50,000 frontier guards, 7,000 security troops, the People's Police Alert Units of about 10,500 men, and about 15,000 combat groups of the Workers' Militia[10] in factories, agricultural production co-operatives and institutions, in part mechanised and equipped with heavy wagons. The latter's duties include the protection of buildings, the suppression of disturbances and logistic support for the regular armed forces. Compulsory military service, which was introduced in 1962 after the construction of the Berlin Wall, lasts eighteen months. The citizens of East Berlin are also subject to it. In the Society for Sport and Technology, with roughly 450,000 members,[11] citizens gain a paramilitary training. In 1978 'military studies' was introduced as a subject in schools in face of the protest of the Protestant and Catholic Churches.

The GDR is a reliable partner of the Soviet Union: in August 1968 it took part in the invasion of Czechoslovakia. The 'close and fraternal military relationship' with the armies of the Soviet Union and other socialist states is a constitutional principle (article 7).

NOTES

1. English text in William B. Simons (ed.), *The Constitutions of the Communist World* (Alphen aan den Rijn, The Netherlands, and Germantown, Md., 1980), pp. 164–89.
2. Anton Ackermann, 'Gibt es einen besonderen deutschen Weg zum Sozialismus?', *Einheit* (Berlin), I (1946), no. 1, pp. 22–32.
3. *Neues Deutschland* (Berlin), 25 May 1984, p. 6. (The criteria for the assignment have not been made explicit.)
4. *Neue Zeit* (Berlin), 14 October 1982, p. 3; *Der Morgen* (Berlin), 6 April 1982, p. 10; *Bauern-Echo* (Berlin), 6 May 1982, p. 34; *National-Zeitung* (Berlin), 23 April 1982, p. 10.

5. *Statistisches Jahrbuch 1983 der Deutschen Demokratischen Republik* (Berlin, 1983), pp. 395–6 (the figures refer to 1982); Free German Youth (1984): *Einheit* (Berlin), XXXIX (1984), nos. 9/10, p. 906.
6. *Kleines Politisches Wörterbuch* (Berlin, 1973), p. 617.
7. Bundesministerium für innerdeutsche Beziehungen (ed.), *DDR-Handbuch* (Cologne, 1979), p. 401.
8. *Ibid.*, p. 1158.
9. The International Institute for Strategie Studies, London, *The Military Balance 1984–1985* (Oxford, 1984), pp. 25–6.
10. *Ibid.*, p. 26.
11. *Ibid.*

FURTHER READING

Baylis, Thomas A., *The Technical Intelligentsia and the East German Elite: Legitimacy and Change in Mature Communism* (Berkeley, Cal.: University of California Press, 1974)

Beyme, Klaus von and Hartmut Zimmermann (eds.), *Policymaking in the German Democratic Republic* (Aldershot, Hants.: Gower, 1984)

Childs, David, *The GDR: Moscow's German Ally* (London: Allen and Unwin, 1983)

Legters, Lyman H. (ed.), *The German Democratic Republic: A Developed Socialist Society* (Boulder, Colo.: Westview Press, 1978)

Ludz, Peter Ch., *The Changing Party Elite in East Germany* (Cambridge, Mass.: MIT Press, 1972)

McCardle, Arthur W. and A. Bruce Boenau (eds.), *East Germany: A New German Nation under Socialism?* (Lanham, Md.: University Press of America, 1984)

McCauley, Martin, *Marxism-Leninism in the German Democratic Republic: The Socialist Unity Party (SED)* (London: Macmillan, 1979)

—— *The German Democratic Republic since 1945* (London: Macmillan, 1983)

Scharf, C. Bradley, *Politics and Change in East Germany: An Evaluation of Socialist Democracy* (London: Pinter, 1984)

Schulz, Eberhard *et al.* (eds.), *GDR Foreign Policy* (Armonk, NY: Sharpe, 1982)

Starrels, John M. and Anita M. Dasbach-Malinckrodt, *Politics in the German Democratic Republic* (New York: Praeger, 1975)

Volkmer, Werner, 'East Germany: Dissenting Views during the Last Decade', in Rudolf L. Tökés (ed.), *Opposition in Eastern Europe* (London: Macmillan, 1979) pp. 113–41

Whetten, Lawrence L., *Germany East and West: Conflicts, Collaboration and Confrontation* (New York: New York University Press, 1980)

9　Hungarian People's Republic

BASIC FEATURES

The Hungarian People's Republic declares itself to be a socialist state following the amendment on 19 April 1972 of its constitution of 20 August 1949; the preamble embeds the present state in the millenium of Hungarian history. According to the revised version of the constitution,[1] all power in the state belongs to the working people: the working class as the 'leading class of society', the collective farm peasants and the intelligentsia (article 2). The 'leading force of society' (article 3) is the Hungarian Socialist Workers' Party (HSWP). In its Programmatic Declaration of March 1975, the HSWP declared that the Hungarian People's Republic has entered the stage of the construction of the 'developed socialist society'. During this process it is supposed to level out the still existing class differences, thus gradually turning the state of the dictatorship of the proletariat into an all-people's state.

THE COMMUNIST TAKEOVER

In December 1944, about three months after an unsuccessful attempt of Admiral Horthy, an ally of Nazi Germany, to conclude a separate armistice with the Soviet Union and his removal from power, members of the Hungarian Communist Party, which had been founded in November 1918, together with members of the Smallholders' Party, the National Peasant Party and the Social Democratic Party set up a Provisional National Assembly and a provisional government in

Debrecen. Among the first measures taken by this government was an agrarian reform eliminating the large land-holdings which had so far characterised the Hungarian social and
property structure. After the war, by using 'salami tactics' —
that is, little by little — the communists took over power with
the support of the Red Army as well as of the local committees
of people's liberation, the armed forces and security organs
dominated or controlled by them. In the free parliamentary
elections of November 1945, however, they polled only 17 per
cent of the votes, whereas the Smallholders won the majority
of seats. But by forming a leftist bloc within the four-party
coalition the communists managed to outdo the Smallholders
and to enforce a socialist course resulting in the nationalisation of industry and banking, and in central planning of the
economy. In June 1948 the Social Democrats were forced to
merge with the communists into the Hungarian Workers'
Party; all other political parties were prohibited or dissolved
themselves. At the parliamentary elections of May 1949 the
single list of the People's Front polled 95.6 per cent of the
votes. In August 1949 Hungary was proclaimed a 'people's
republic', and its constitution closely followed the Soviet
model.

   After Stalin's death (in March 1953), a fierce dispute flared
up within the Communist Party between 'Stalinists' and 'reformists' about the further political course to take; in this dispute the hard-liners gained the upper hand. Finally the division within the party, led by the Stalinist Ernö Gerö, resulted
in the virtual loss of power during the people's upheaval in
October 1956. The revolution was bloodily suppressed by
Soviet armed forces; the workers' councils, which had arisen
particularly in Budapest, were broken and the rule of the communists, which had been seriously challenged, was re-established under the leadership of János Kádár. In December
1956 the purged Communist Party — its membership numbered then only about 38,000 as against 870,000 at the beginning of that year — was renamed the Hungarian Socialist
Workers' Party. At its Eighth Congress in 1962 it declared
that now that the collectivisation of agriculture had been
finished, the fundamentals of socialism had been established.

THE MARXIST-LENINIST PARTY

In 1983 the HSWP filed about 852,000 members[2] — roughly 8.5 per cent of the total population. In contrast to most other Communist Parties, since 1966 membership has not been preceded by a candidate status. Admission to the party is effected by one of about 24,000 primary organisations, which are formed mainly according to the production but also the territorial principle. It requires the recommendation of two party members; if the applicant is a member of the Communist Youth League, one of the sponsors may be the latter's primary organisation. Although recruitment of new members should, from the ideological point of view, concentrate on blue-collar workers, the HSWP shows a strong tendency to recruit members of the intelligentsia and graduates apparently in order to take advantage of expert knowledge for innovative policies.

The HSWP exercises its leading role by directives concerning matters of principle and usually abstains from interference into specialised factual questions. It works according to Lenin's principle of democratic centralism, but increasing importance is given to the democratic component of this principle, which becomes evident in the intention to strengthen the primary organisations or even more the local party committees by conceding them a limited autonomy for local decision-making. Following Kádár's slogan 'He who is not against us is with us',[3] established in 1961, the party aims at gaining the consent of the citizens to the cause of socialism. By means of the economic reform of 1968, labelled New Economic Mechanism, which allows for a certain autonomy for enterprises in industrial decision-making and for a limited market-orientation of industrial and agricultural production, the communists have succeeded in considerably improving the living conditions of the population. By some changes in the institutional structure and by granting the citizens a certain degree of participation in settling local affairs, they try to stimulate civic interest and initiative and to fight the widespread political apathy. According to the Programmatic Declaration adopted by the Eleventh Party Congress in March 1975, the HSWP is supposed to become the Marxist-Leninist vanguard of the whole people along with Hungary's transition to an all-people's state.

The organs of the HSWP are, on the national level, the Party Congress, convening every five years, the Central Committee, meeting four to five times a year, the Political Bureau and the Secretariat with János Kádár at the top, who has been first secretary since 1956. At the Thirteenth Congress in March 1985 the highest party office was renamed that of secretary general, and the office of deputy secretary general, unique among the ruling Communist Parties, created in order to relieve the former. The Political Bureau is the *de facto* supreme organ of party and state. Among its thirteen members are also the chairman of the Council of Ministers, one of his deputies, the chairman of the Presidential Council, and the president of the National Council of Trade Unions.

The HSWP supports proletarian internationalism, recognising the leading role of the CPSU within the communist world movement. Loyalty towards the CPSU and the Soviet Union does not, however, prevent the Hungarian communists from pursuing unconventional domestic policies, a fact which finds its expression especially in the economic reform resulting in a form of economic management which substantially deviates from the Soviet model, and in a relatively undogmatic cultural policy. The stressing of national peculiarities of a socialist system led the HSWP to take up a subtly different attitude towards Eurocommunism; it condemns inherent 'anti-Sovietism' but approves the right of every Communist Party to choose its own road to socialism.

SOCIAL ORGANISATIONS

Among the social organisations mention must be made of the trade unions, the Communist Youth League and the Pioneer Federation, the Women's Federation, the agricultural production co-operatives, the consumer co-operatives, the Peace Movement, the associations of the intelligentsia and of the national minorities (Germans, Slovaks, Rumanians) as well as the churches.

The most important social organisation may be seen in the trade unions. Through their top organ, the National Council, the trade unions have restricted possibilities to articulate the interests of their members; they do, for instance, have the right to initiate laws. Although it is their pre-eminent duty to ensure the fulfilment of the plans of production and the maintenance of working discipline as well as the development of socialist consciousness among workers, they also act, albeit still unsatisfactorily in the opinion of their members, as mediator between workers and management by enjoying the right to participate in decisions concerning wages, working conditions and social affairs. The decisive power on questions of planning and production, however, remains in the hands of management and state organs.

As the party exercises its role in society (and state) in a rather moderate way, recognising particular interests of different social and professional strata and, to a certain extent, taking them into account in the policy-making process, social organisations enjoy a relatively wide scope of action. Their organs are certainly channels for the transmission of party decisions to the mass of the population, but they also articulate the interests of their members and communicate them to the supreme decision-makers. They may participate in drafting bills by consulting ministries, the conceptions of which, however, usually turn out to be predominant. In view of the relatively far-reaching autonomy of industrial decision-making granted to the enterprises, the Industrial Chamber has gained considerable importance as representing the interests of managers, quite a number of whom form the driving force for economic reform. Yet autonomy for industrial enterprises as well as the development of private initiative by peasants and craftsmen certainly also raise the control function of the corresponding social organisations.

All social organisations as well as the HSWP belong as collective members to the Patriotic People's Front (PPF) founded in 1954. Under the guidance of the party it should, according to article 4 of the constitution, 'organise the forces of society to complete the building of socialism'. Every citizen who is prepared to contribute to the attainment of this goal may co-operate in the organs of the PPF at all levels of the territorial-administrative structure, irrespective of his profession and confession. Experts collaborate in working committees; for instance, for economic policy or protection of the environment. The main functions of the PPF are political instruction, the organisation of meetings for the nomination of candidates for representative bodies, the carrying through of the elections, submission of proposals for the composition of executive committees of the local government, the initiation of the recall of members of Parliament and the local councils and the submission of statements on draft bills.

DISSENT

The albeit limited liberalisation of social and cultural life, on the one hand, and dissatisfaction with certain features of the political order, on the other, stimulate the formation and the articulation of dissent. Political dissent manifests itself principally in typescript (underground or semi-underground) *Samizdat* publications of intellectuals, which criticise bureaucracy and violation of human rights, demand pluralism of opinion and individual self-determination, and disclose tabooed aspects of the revolution of 1956; they also inform about the deprived situation of the Hungarian minority in Rumania and criticise the authorities for doing too little in this matter. Another form of dissent is the unofficial peace movement formed by young people and clergymen, who condemn armament both in West and East and demand the possibility of conscientious objection for young persons liable for military service. A non-conformist attitude is also shown by Roman Catholics who reject the arrangement between Church and the regime and form grassroot groups which operate outside the official Church, thus evading control by the State Church Office.

Dissenters are widely tolerated as long as they do not in principle challenge the fundamentals of the socialist order of state and society and do not organise themselves as opposition. The HSWP, well realising that the dissenters do not represent a mass movement, tries instead to gain their loyalty by making use of their criticism for further reforms, insofar as it considers this criticism to be constructive. Discussion on economic reforms still in flux and not undisputed within the party is indeed fairly unrestricted. The party does not hesitate, however, to suppress dissenting opinions when they question its leading role and may thus jeopardise the toleration of the Kádár model by the Soviet Union.

CENTRAL GOVERNMENT

The unicameral Parliament is elected for a term of five years. 352 deputies are elected in constituencies, one each for approximately 30,000 inhabitants. The new electoral act of December 1983 provides for an additional number of seats corresponding to 10 per cent of the number of constituency seats and reserved for prominent personalities who are elected from a national list. All citizens over eighteen years of age are entitled to vote and are eligible as deputies. Candidates of the constituencies are put up at nomination meetings convened by the PPF. The HSWP, the PPF, the social organisations, representatives of the labour collectives and also any single citizen have the right of proposal. Nomination is effected in open voting with one third of the votes of the persons attending the nomination meetings. Candidates on the national list are proposed by the political and social organisations belonging to the PPF and are nominated by its National Council. All candidates have to subscribe to the Programme of the PPF, which corresponds with the objectives of the HSWP. Since 1966 multiple candidatures have been admitted. However, only forty-nine constituencies in 1971, thirty-four in 1975 and no more than fifteen in 1980, made use of this system. The present electoral law makes the nomination of at least two candidates for each constituency seat compulsory. Accordingly, at the elections of June 1985 762 candidates were put up (about one tenth of them proposed by single citizens). The number of candidates elected from the national list must, however, correspond with that of the mandates.

The candidates are elected by absolute majority; a candidate of a constituency who polls at least a quarter of the valid votes becomes a substitute deputy. At the elections of 1985 the poll was about 94 per cent; the candidates of the PPF gained 98.8 per cent of the votes. In forty-five constituencies no candidate gained the majority; this made a second ballot necessary. Inefficient or unworthy deputies of the constituencies may be recalled on the motion of at least 10 per cent of the electors and of the National Council of the PPF. The electors decide hereupon in secret vote. Parliament decides upon the recall of deputies elected on the national list on the motion of the National Council of the PPF.

According to article 19 of the constitution, Parliament is the 'highest representative organ of state power'. Meeting as a rule four times a year, each time for two days on average, it passes laws, discusses and approves the programme of the government, establishes the state budget and the plan. In addition, it elects the Presidential Council and the Council of Ministers. The deputies as well as the Presidential Council and the Council of Ministers and parliamentary committees have the right to initiate laws. Deputies may address questions to the Presidential Council, the Council of Ministers, single ministers, the president of the Supreme Court and the procurator general. Standing committees working between the sessions of Parliament discuss draft bills and are entitled to comment on drafts of law-decrees of the Presidential Council. They also become active when an interpellation has been dismissed by the plenum as unsatisfactorily answered, but so far this has only twice been the case.

The Presidential Council elected by Parliament from among its members is both 'substitute parliament' and collective head of state. It consists of the chairman, two vice-chairmen, the secretary and seventeen members. Between the sessions of Parliament the Presidential Council exercises its functions, but it may not amend the constitution or pass laws. Yet it may issue law-decrees, which merely have to be confirmed by Parliament at its next session. There is, however, no definite delimitation of legislative competence between Parliament and the Presidential Council. Further responsibilities of the Presidential Council consist in the right to call for referenda in questions of national significance and to supervise the organs of state administration by annulment of acts not in conformity with the constitution.

The Council of Ministers is elected by Parliament, formally on recommendation of the Presidential Council, *de facto* on that of the party leadership. It consists of the chairman, the vice-chairmen, ministers, the chairman of the National Planning Board and the chairman of the Central Commission of People's Control. Characteristic of the Hungarian Council of Ministers is its small size as compared with the Councils of Ministers of other socialist states. At present it has only about twenty members, thus making an inner cabinet superfluous. The small number of departments can be put down above all to concentration of the administration of industrial branches in a single department. The Council of Ministers, working on the collective principle, ensures the implementation of the laws and decrees according to the guidelines of the leading party organs, Parliament and the Presidential Council. It is its duty to prepare the economic plan and ensure its execution, to determine the direction of scientific and cultural development as well as the system of social and health services, to coordinate the activity of the departments, and to conclude international treaties. For certain fields (economy, science, defence) the Council of Ministers may create governmental commissions, which are usually headed by a vice-chairman of the Council of Ministers.

Several central governmental departments, such as the Office for Material and Prices, the Office for Water-Supply, the Councils' Office, the Church Office, the National Bank and the Post Office, are headed by state secretaries, who are responsible and accountable to the Council of Ministers and, like this organ, to Parliament and the Presidential Council.

LOCAL GOVERNMENT

The administration is organised according to the principle of democratic centralism, but the local organs enjoy a limited right of self-government. At middle level the country is divided into nineteen regions (*megye*) and at the lower level into cities and communes. The capital, Budapest, is administratively treated as equal with the regions, and it is subdivided into districts like some other large cities.

In regions, cities, districts of the capital and communes local affairs are administered by councils, their commissions and executive committees as well as administrative organs. Several communes may form a joint council. The members of the councils are elected for a term of five years: those of the regions and the capital indirectly — by the commune and city councils and the councils of the city districts of Budapest (predominantly from among their midst), in order to facilitate the coordination of urban and rural interests. The said councils are in turn elected directly by the citizens. At least two candidates have to be nominated for every seat in a council.

The councils are conceived as organs of local people's representation, state administration and self-government; the autonomous sphere of administrative activity may not be restricted, but it is not clearly separated from the other one. They ensure the attainment of central state and local goals, especially the implementation of economic plans, the fulfilment of material and cultural needs of the populace, and they are furthermore responsible for public order and the protection of socialist property. Questions of fundamental significance (e.g. concerning budget and development plans) must be presented by the councils to the citizens for discussion. Citizens have a further possibility for participation in local decision-making by joining in the work of *ad hoc* committees. The councils have to co-operate with the PPF and single social organisations.

The activities of the councils are supervised by the Council of Ministers and the Presidential Council. Ordinances and resolutions which violate 'the interests of society' (article 35 of the constitution) are annulled by the Council of Ministers. The Presidential Council protects the rights of the councils, but it may also dissolve a council if its activity violates the constitution or 'seriously jeopardises the interests of the people' (article 30). According to the principle of dual subordination, an executive committee is subordinate to the council at the same administrative level as well as to the executive committtee at the next higher level, and finally to the Councils' Office of the Council of Ministers.

ADMINISTRATION OF JUSTICE

There are three levels of jurisdiction. It is exercised by the Supreme Court, by the regional courts and the court of the capital and, at the lowest level, by the city courts and the district courts of the capital. As court of first instance the Supreme Court makes final judgments when a case is brought before it by the procurator general or if its president takes one on. As court of appeal it decides on verdicts of the regional courts and of the military tribunals. In its capacity as a supervisory body it takes action when the president of the Supreme Court or the procurator general protests against a final verdict of a lower court. Furthermore, the Supreme Court takes responsibility for uniform jurisdiction; its directives and decisions of principle are binding upon all other courts.

The president of the Supreme Court is elected by Parliament for a five-year term. Professional judges at all courts are appointed by the Presidential Council for an indefinite period upon proposal of the Ministry of Justice; lay judges are elected by the local councils for a set of time. Judges are subject to recall.

Following the conception of socialisation of state activities, social courts may be established in enterprises and co-operatives. Their members are elected by the employees or by the general assembly upon proposal of the trade union committee of an enterprise or of the committee of the co-operative. The social courts may take action in minor offences against the rules of 'socialist social life' and against labour discipline. Against their decisions a complaint may be lodged at the committee of the trade union or of the co-operative. In recent years, however, the social courts more or less withered away, not least because of their little popularity.

Like other socialist states Hungary lacks a constitutional jurisdiction. Supervision over the conformity of legal acts with the constitution has been exercised by Parliament and the Presidential Council. However, in 1984 Parliament established for this purpose a special organ, the Constitutional Council which is entitled to suspend the implementation of unconstitutional provisions.

The supervision of the legal order as well as the protection of the rights of the citizens are basically the responsibility of the Procuracy with the procurator general elected by Parliament at the top. If the procurators discover that an organ of the state has violated a law, they may protest against the decision and demand its annulment by the superior administrative organ. In a number of cases limited by law citizens may lodge a complaint at a court of law if they consider their rights to have been violated by an administrative decision.

FOREIGN POLICY

Hungarian foreign policy is based on the principles of socialist internationalism and peaceful coexistence. After Soviet armed forces had crushed the revolution of 1956, during which Imre Nagy's government had cancelled Hungary's membership of the WTO, foreign policy has again been fully identical with the goals and actions of the foreign policy of the Soviet Union and the states belonging to the Soviet bloc. In May 1957 the stationing of Soviet troops in Hungary was put on a contractual basis and by the Treaty of Friendship, Co-operation and Mutual Assistance of September 1967 Hungary was tightly bound to the Soviet Union. As a member of the WTO Hungary, in August 1968, took part in the invasion of Czechoslovakia. As a member of the CMEA it advocates further economic integration of the member countries, expecting to gain advantages in view of its lack of raw materials but possession of a relatively highly developed industry of capital goods and consumer goods.

Hungary links the maxims of proletarian-socialist internationalism with that of socialist patriotism, which, however, it subordinates to the former. Patriotism deliberately takes up the tradition of the bourgeois struggle for independence against Habsburg Austria and Tsarist Russia in the nineteenth century. This recollection of the national past found its expression in the ceremonial recovery of the Crown of St Stephen from the United States at the end of 1977, the symbolic significance of which the communists are well aware. The national component of Hungarian foreign policy manifests itself in increased, albeit cautious efforts to improve the position of the 1.7 to 2 million Magyars living in Rumania, whose cultural autonomy is being gradually cut back by assimilation, disputed, however, by Rumanian communists.

As a medium-sized country Hungary is endeavouring to achieve international repute by a foreign policy tending to balance out as far as possible differences between East and West. Being under Soviet constraint, Hungary has to adapt to the interest of the Soviet Union and of the WTO. But it felt uneasiness because of the breaking off of negotiations on arms control between the Soviet Union and the United States. Regardless of criticism, particularly from Czechoslovakia, its leaders have repeatedly affirmed their interest in maintaining Hungary's fairly good relations with capitalist countries, and their conviction that dialogue and trade contribute to a lessening of tension.

NATIONAL DEFENCE

For the country's defence Hungary maintains armed forces numbering about 105,000 soldiers, 84,000 of them serving in the army and 21,000 in the air force. In addition, there are 15,000 border guards and 60,000 members of the Workers' Militia.[4]

NOTES

1. English text in William B. Simons (ed.), *The Constitutions of the Communist World* (Alphen aan den Rijn, The Netherlands, and Germantown, Md., 1980), pp. 196–213.
2. Richard F. Staar (ed.), *Yearbook on International Communist Affairs 1984: Parties and Revolutionary Movements* (Stanford, Cal., 1984), p. 334.
3. *Népszabadság* (Budapest), 3 December 1961.
4. The International Institute for Strategic Studies, London, *The Military Balance 1984–1985* (Oxford, 1984), p. 26.

FURTHER READING

Kovrig, Bennett, *Communism in Hungary: From Kun to Kádár* (Stanford,

Cal.: Hoover Institution Press, 1979)

Molnár, Miklós, *A Short History of the Hungarian Communist Party* (Boulder, Colo.: Westview Press, 1978)

Robinson, William F., *The Pattern of Reform in Hungary: A Political, Economic and Cultural Analysis* (New York: Praeger, 1973)

Schöpflin, George, 'Hungary: An Uneasy Stability', in Archie Brown and Jack Gray (eds.), *Political Culture and Political Change in Communist States*, 2nd edn. (London: Macmillan, 1979), pp. 131-58

—— 'Opposition and Para-Opposition: Critical Currents in Hungary, 1968–78', in Rudolf Tökés (ed.), *Opposition in Eastern Europe* (London: Macmillan 1979), pp. 142–86

Toma, Peter A. and Iván Völgyes, *Politics in Hungary* (San Francisco, Cal.: W.H. Freeman, 1977)

Váli, Ferenc A.: *Rift and Revolt in Hungary: Nationalism versus Communism* (Cambridge, Mass.: Harvard University Press, 1961)

10 Democratic People's Republic of Korea

BASIC FEATURES

The Democratic People's Republic of Korea (DPRK) has had the constitution of a 'socialist state' since December 1972.[1] It rests on the 'politico-ideological unity of the entire people, based on the worker-peasant alliance led by the working class' (article 2), and 'exercises the dictatorship of the proletariat' (article 10). The DPRK claims to represent the interests of the *whole* Korean people (article 1). The constitution contains a number of features which distinguish it both from the Soviet-type and form the Chinese Constitutions.

The guiding principle of all state and social activity is the *chuch'e* idea of the Workers' Party of Korea (WPK). This political philosophy, which the leader of party and state, Kim Il-Sŏng formulated for the first time in December 1955 and further developed in the 1960s, is regarded as 'a creative application of Marxism-Leninism' to the conditions of the country (article 4). In the words of Kim Il-Sŏng, it implies *'chuch'e* [tantamount to self-reliance] in ideology, independence in politics, self-sustenance in the economy, and self-defence in national defence'.[2] The building of socialism is furthermore to be effected by the *ch'ŏngsalli* spirit and by *ch'ŏngsalli* methods (called after a mass campaign in an agricultural co-operative of the same name), and by the *taean* system of economic management (named after an industrial mass campaign at the Taean Electric Plant). Both these mass line concepts are related with the *chŏllima* movement, named after a flying horse in Korean mythology, and inspired by the Chinese Great Leap Forward. All these principles are

151

ideological and organisational devices which aim at the comprehensive mobilisation of Korea's own human and material resources by linking the decision-making power of the party and the organisational power of the state with the creative initiative and the efforts of the mass of the people.

The state is called upon to eliminate all vestiges of the old society and to introduce the new socialist way of life in all fields; to train the working people 'to be builders of socialism and communism' by equipping them with a profound knowledge of nature and society, and a high level of culture and technology (articles 38 and 36).

Kim Il-Sŏng, secretary general of the WPK, also constitutionally exercises absolute power as head of state. Thus there are two power centres closely interconnected by him. The identification of Kim Il-Sŏng with *chuch'e* as well as his charismatic style of leadership are the bases of deference and a personality cult manifesting itself in his being apotheosised as the 'great leader' and 'sun of the nation' (similar to Stalin and Mao Zedong). By virtue of his power and influence, Kim Il-Sŏng has apparently succeeded in designating his son Kim Chŏng-Il as his successor, thus creating the possibility of a 'socialist dynasty'.

THE COMMUNIST TAKEOVER

The Korean communists seized power in the northern part of the country with the support of the Red Army and under Soviet control. Between August and September 1945 Soviet and American troops, after agreement on a demarcation line at the thirty-eighth parallel, occupied Korea, which had been under Japanese rule since 1910. Communists who had been born or trained in the Soviet Union, returned to North Korea together with a group around Kim Il-Sŏng, who from the early 1930s until 1941 had led an anti-Japanese partisan band in Manchuria; from China came the so-called Yan'an (Yenan) faction. Favoured by the Soviet authorities, Kim Il-Sŏng gained the upper hand over the 'domestic' communists, who had been in prison or underground, and in December 1945 he assumed the leadership of the northern branch of the Korean

Communist Party, which was based mainly on a small number of industrial workers. The Yan'an group at first did not join the party, but formed the New People's Party, which, according to Mao Zedong's conception of the 'new democratic revolution', recruited followers among peasants, the petty bourgeoisie and the intelligentsia. In August 1946 both parties merged into the North Korean Workers' Party under the leader of the Yan'an group.

In February 1946 the North Korean Provisional People's Committee was established under the chairmanship of Kim Il-Sŏng and was the first central executive and administrative organ after the liberation. Supported by the North Korean Democratic Unity Front, which was made up of the North Korean Workers' Party and three non-communist parties, the Provisional People's Committee embarked on land reform and nationalised industries and banks. A year later the local people's councils convened for a congress, from which a legislative body, the People's Assembly, emerged. The Assembly elected the People's Committee, dominated by communists, which, with Kim Il-Sŏng as premier, replaced the Provisional People's Committee.

In November 1947 the UN General Assembly decided to hold free elections to an all-national representative body in both parts of Korea. Boycotted by the Soviet Union and the North Korean regime, these elections took place under UN supervision only in the southern part in May 1948, and on 15 August 1948 the Republic of Korea was founded. North of the thirty-eighth parallel, ten days later, the Supreme People's Assembly was elected from a unity list of the Democratic Unity Front. On 9 September 1948, one day after the adoption of the constitution, the Democratic People's Republic of Korea was proclaimed.

In June 1949 the North Korean Workers' Party merged with its southern counterpart, the outlawed South Korean Workers' Party into the WPK, the leadership of which was assumed by Kim Il-Sŏng. At its Fourth Congress in 1961 the WPK declared that the construction of socialism had been accomplished.

THE MARXIST-LENINIST PARTY

The WPK was conceived right from the beginning as a mass party. With a membership of about 3 million in 1983, it embraces roughly 16 per cent of the total population.[3] Thus the proportion of the WPK to the populace is greater than that of any other Communist Party. Until 1958 the WPK was the arena of violent struggle between the above-mentioned three groups, which competed for power and had different opinions on the question whether the WPK should follow the Chinese communists. In this struggle Kim Il-Sŏng succeeded in asserting himself by means of repeated purges, and strengthened his position as leader with the support of the partisans as his mainstay and of 'post-revolutionary' cadres, loyally devoted to him.

The supreme party organ is formally the Party Congress. Contrary to the Party Statute, it convened only three times between 1961 and 1980 inclusive, a fact which alone demonstrates the small importance attached to it. (The Statute of 1980 provides for a Party Congress every five years.) Between its sessions the direction of the party's activities is entrusted to the Central Committee (CC). This body is also responsible for the establishment, direction and control of 'political bureaux' in offices, enterprises, educational institutions, military units, and so on, for the purpose of indoctrination; it is in charge of the recruitment and education of party cadres and organises, through its Military Affairs Committee, the armed forces. The CC elects the Political Bureau (until 1980 the Political Committee) which directs party work on its behalf. The leading core of the Political Bureau is its five-member Presidium, which in fact decides all policy in the DPRK. The Secretariat, which is also elected by the CC, with the secretary general at the top, takes care of the execution of party decisions and controls all party activity.

The party members, who join the WPK via the party cells after a probationary year, are obliged, *inter alia,* to be loyal to the 'great leader' Kim Il-Sŏng; to grasp accurately the *chuch'e* ideology; to fight capitalism, Confucianism, revisionism and dogmatism; to participate in the management of enterprises; and to observe the 'mass line'. The principle of the 'mass line', however, is employed less by laying stress on the spontaneity of the masses but rather in the sense of educating them to obey.

In accordance with the nationalist ideology of *chuch'e,* the WPK advocates the equality and independence of all Communist Parties within the communist world movement. With regard to the CPSU and the Chinese Communists the WPK has maintained a balanced though not a neutral position.

SOCIAL ORGANISATIONS AND BLOC PARTIES

Out of about a hundred social organisations the major ones are: the Korean Federation of Trade Unions (consisting of several branch unions), the Union of Agricultural Working People (organising the co-operative farmers and state farm workers), the Socialist Working Youth League, the Pioneer Organisation and the Democratic Women's Union.

The social organisations are conceived as transmission belts of the WPK. Their primary task is to mobilise the masses for the construction of socialism and communism and to see to the people's loyalty to the party. They organise mass rallies and mass campaigns and have to inspire the citizens to implement the party directives voluntarily, enthusiastically and in a disciplined manner. The trade unions, in particular, have to educate the workers in Marxist-Leninist values, safeguard the fulfilment of the economic plans, increase productivity and intensify work discipline. Apart from this, however, they also are entrusted with the technical education of the workers and participate in the establishment of work rates and wages.

Two non-communist parties from the post-war years are still in existence: the Korean Democratic Party, which in 1981 was renamed the Korean Social Democratic Party, and the Chŏngu Party, whose members adhere to the *Ch'ondogyo* faith, which is a specific Korean religion, linking Taoist, Confucian and Buddhist elements. These parties have representatives in the Supreme People's Assembly and unconditionally support the WPK's policy within the framework of the Democratic Front for the Reunification of the Fatherland domi-

nated by the WPK, to which also most of the social organisations are affiliated.

CENTRAL GOVERNMENT

The national representative body is the Supreme People's
Assembly (SPA). Its members (615 in 1982) are elected
directly for a term of four years from a single list of the Democratic Front. The right to elect and to be elected is held by all
citizens who have reached the age of seventeen.

The SPA, which the constitution calls the 'supreme organ
of state power' (article 73), enacts legislation, establishes (formally) the basic principles of domestic and foreign policy,
approves the economic plan and the state budget, and decides
on questions of war and peace. It elects the president of the
republic, and — on his recommendation — elects and recalls
the vice-presidents, the secretary and the further members of
the Central People's Committee, as well as the premier;
moreover, it elects and recalls the members of the Standing
Committee, which is its permanent organ, and the president
of the Central Court, and appoints and dismisses the
procurator general. The SPA convenes once or twice a year in
sessions of only a few days. Its legislative activity is therefore
to a large extent reduced to the approval of bills, upon which
the Standing Committee decides, when the SPA is not in
session. The Standing Committee is furthermore authorised
to interpret laws, and it elects and recalls the judges and
people's accessors of the Central Court.

The SPA is, moreover, replaced by the Central People's
Committee (CPC), which the constitution calls the 'supreme
leadership organ of state power' (article 100). This body
determines domestic and foreign policy under WPK guidance. It directs the work of the State Administrative Council (SAC, which is the government), the work of the local
people's assemblies and people's committees, as well as the
work of the judicial organs and procuracies and the organs of
national defence and state security. It supervises the
implementation of the constitution, the laws and the edicts of
the president of the republic, and of its own decrees, decisions

and directives, and it is entitled to annul decisions and directives of state organs which contravene them. The CPC appoints and removes from office the vice-premiers, ministers and other members of the SAC on the recommendation of the premier; it also appoints and recalls ambassadors and high-ranking officers. It has furthermore the right to proclaim a state of war and to order mobilisation. Through overlapping membership of the CPC and the Political Bureau, both organs are closely intertwined.

The important role of the CPC in state decision-making is furthermore underlined by the fact that it is headed by the president of the republic. The president is vested with far-reaching powers, which are not counter-balanced by any constitutional provision. Elected by the SPA for a term of four years, and re-eligible, he 'directly guides' the CPC and issues edicts. He convenes and presides over meetings of the SAC 'when necessary' and directs its work; he is commander-in-chief of all the armed forces and the chairman of the National Defence Commission. By means of his right to recommend personnel for election into, and for recall from, high state organs, the president exerts a decisive influence on their composition. The president is responsible to the SPA for his activities, but he is not accountable to it — being the only holder of a high state office not subject to recall.

The SAC is the executive organ of the SPA and the CPC in the numerous fields of state activity (foreign affairs, defence, state security, public order, finance, industry, agriculture, domestic and foreign trade, construction, transport and communications, education and health, culture and science). It is responsible for the implementation of economic plans, which it draws up, and directs the work of the local administrative organs, whose decisions it is empowered to annul if they contravene its decisions and directives. Furthermore, this body concludes international treaties, which are ratified and may be abrogated by the president of the republic. The SAC is composed of the premier, his deputies, ministers, and chairmen of the state committees, such as the Planning Committee. The plenum may assign the discussion of, and decisions on, matters concerning its activities to its Permanent Commission. The SAC is accountable to the president of the republic, the CPC and the SPA.

LOCAL GOVERNMENT

The DPRK is administered in a centralistic manner. It is sub-divided into regions, to which correspond municipalities directly under the central government (among them the capital P'yongyang). The next administrative level is made up by cities, city districts and rural districts; the latter comprise (small) towns, villages and workers' settlements.

The local organs of state power are the people's assemblies, which are elected by the citizens for a four-year term at the regional level and for a two-year term at the district level. The people's assemblies convene merely once or twice a year. When they are not in session their functions are exercised by the people's committees. The implementation of the decisions made by the local and superior organs is a matter for the local administrative committees. They are responsible, in particular, for the development of the local economy. On the principle of dual subordination, a people's committee is accountable for its activities to the corresponding people's assembly, and to the people's committee at a higher level which directs its work; an administrative committee is accountable to the people's assembly and the people's committee at the same level, and subordinate to a higher administrative committee and to the SAC. A people's committee has the right to annul inappropriate decisions of the administrative committee at the corresponding level and of the people's committees and administrative committees at lower levels, and to suspend the implementation of inappropriate decisions of the people's committees at lower administrative levels.

ADMINISTRATION OF JUSTICE

Justice is administered by the Central Court, the courts of the regions and the municipalities directly under central government, the people's courts and special courts. The judges and people's accessors of the regular courts are elected by the people's assemblies at the corresponding level for a term of four or two years. The Central Court supervises the judicial activities of all the other courts, and is, in turn, accountable to the SPA, the president of the republic and the CPC; the local courts are accountable to their respective people's assemblies. All judicial activities are directed by the CPC.

The functions of the courts comprise the protection of the socialist order, the property of the state and the social and co-operative organisations, and the rights of the citizens. The courts also serve the class struggle insofar as they are obliged to ensure that all state organs, enterprises, organisations and citizens 'actively fight' not only law-breakers but also 'class enemies' (article 136). The courts have, moreover, the task to ensure that all state organs, enterprises, organisations and citizens abide by the laws.

This task is also a function of the Procuracy, which otherwise ensures that decisions and directives of state organs conform with the constitution, the laws, the edicts of the president of the republic and the decisions and directives of the SPA's Standing Committee, the CPC and the SAC.

FOREIGN POLICY

Foreign policy is determined, first, by the partition of the nation and the military presence of the United States in South Korea; second, by the DPRK's vicinity to the People's Republic of China (PRC) and the USSR; third, by its position as a developing country. The principles of foreign policy are peaceful co-existence and proletarian internationalism. With *chuch'e* as the ideological foundation, foreign policy serves, above all, as a device for safeguarding the independence of the country. Accordingly, the DPRK is outside the system of states dominated by the USSR. It is a member neither of the WTO nor of the CMEA; it has only the status of an observer in the latter organisation.

The DPRK has committed itself to driving out foreign forces and to reunifying the country peacefully (article 5 of the constitution). This commitment excludes annexation by military means, as were employed when the DPRK invaded the Republic of Korea (ROK) in June 1950. The DPRK, however, has given many proofs that it pursues a militant policy towards the ROK, be it by a heavy military build-up, be it by encouraging opposition in the ROK and by calling for revolutionary action. This 'peaceful strategy' is based on the concept of 'three revolutionary forces', outlined by Kim Il-Sŏng in the mid-1950s and elaborated in detail in February 1964. They were to be developed in the DPRK, in the ROK and on an international scale, and aim at Korea's unification. Subsequently, the DPRK adopted a hard-line 'anti-imperialist' policy, which manifested itself in armed clashes along the demilitarised zone, the seizure of an American intelligence ship, the attempted assassination of the South Korean president in January 1968, and the shooting down of a US reconnaissance plane.

At the beginning of the 1970s, against the background of the rapprochement between the USA and the PRC and of the Sino-Soviet conflict, North Korea embarked on a dual policy towards the ROK. On the one hand, it launched a peace offensive. In April 1971 it presented an eight-point plan for unification, which considered, among others, the creation of a confederation (an idea which it had already put forward in 1960), and in autumn 1971 North and South Korea commenced talks. In a joint communiqué of 4 July 1972 they stressed the fact that unification should be realised by the Korean themselves. By 1975–76, however, the dialogue had petered out. On the other hand, the DPRK harassed the ROK by the construction of infiltration tunnels and an accelerated military build-up. At the Sixth WPK Congress in October 1980 Kim Il-Sŏng stated more precisely his idea of a confederation, which was to be named the Democratic Confederal Republic of Koryŏ. He again demanded negotiations with the USA to replace the Armistice Agreement of 1953 by a peace treaty and repeated this demand in January 1983. One year later the DPRK pronounced itself officially in favour of tripartite peace talks — that is, with the participation of the ROK — and proposed that North and South Korea should issue a non-aggression declaration. During all this time, however, the North Koreans did not cease to call for a violent overthrow of the South Korean regime. When a South Korean governmental delegation became victim of a bomb attack in Rangoon in October 1983, the North Koreans were charged with responsibility.

Parallel to the offers of unification, the DPRK developed activities intended to strengthen its international position. From 1972 to 1976 the number of countries with which it established diplomatic relations was doubled. It extended economic relations towards Western Europe in order to acquire advanced technology and did not shrink from incurring heavy debts, contrary to *chuch'e,* to gain attractiveness for the ROK, where the standard of living was (and is) considerably higher. Towards Third World countries the DPRK propagates *chuch'e,* and grants military and training aid to liberation movements and 'progressive' governments. In August 1975 the DPRK was admitted to the Non-Aligned Movement. It has so far, however, been denied membership in the UN (like South Korea). In November 1975 it could record a partial success within the UN when the General Assembly, in one of its two resolutions on the Korean question, called for the withdrawal of all foreign troops from the ROK and the dissolution of the UN Command.

Concerning North Korea's relationship with the USSR and the PRC, phases consisting of an unilateral dependence on the former and of manoeuvring between both countries, exploiting the Sino-Soviet rift, may be discerned. 'De-stalinisation' in the USSR on the one hand, and the personality cult around Kim Il-Sŏng on the other, had brought about a temporary alienation between the DPRK and the USSR in the second half of the 1950s. In July 1961 the DPRK concluded treaties on friendship, co-operation and mutual assistance both with the USSR and with the PRC. It shifted closer to the latter, however, because of the Soviet Union's compliance with American demands in the Cuban Crisis of October 1962, recollecting the comradeship in arms during the Korean War of 1950 to 1953 and sharing a common 'anti-revisionist' attitude. When, in 1962, the Soviets cut off economic aid to the DPRK, relations were at an absolute low. However, in the mid-1960s, after Krushchev's fall (in October 1964), North Korea leaned towards the USSR, and relations with the PRC deteriorated. The DPRK urged the Chinese to end the Sino-Soviet dispute in favour of a unity of action of the socialist countries in the escalating Vietnam War, but the Chinese refused to make any concessions. Totally absorbed by their domestic affairs during the Cultural Revolution, the Chinese proved unable to grant the North Koreans economic and military aid, whereas the USSR met with Korean expectations.

The maintenance of political and ideological independence from the Soviet Union, however, made it possible for the DPRK also to improve its relationship with the PRC from 1969 onwards, though there had ben some strain on it in the late 1970s because the North Koreans became concerned about China's new course in domestic and foreign policies. The DPRK made some advances towards the Soviet Union, which, however, were met with reserve, presumably because the DPRK was not prepared to side with it in the Sino-Soviet conflict. Kim Il-Sŏng also gave some examples of a policy irritating the Soviets. He supported Norodom Sihanouk of Kampuchea, but the Soviet-backed Vietnamese invasion did not prevent him from maintaining friendly relations with Vietnam. He was not prepared to pronounce himself in favour of the Soviet intervention in Afghanistan but recognised the puppet government of Babrak Karmal.

In April 1975 and in September 1982 Kim Il-Sŏng paid state visits to the PRC, but not until May 1984, the first time in twenty-three years, did he also visit the USSR. The latter visit seems to demonstrate a renunciation of the see-saw policy between the two states in favour of the USSR, in view of the American–Japanese–South-Korean triangle which the North Korean and Soviet leaders agreed to oppose by strengthening the defence of their countries.

NATIONAL DEFENCE

In accordance with *chuch'e,* the DPRK follows 'a self-defensive military line' which is established in article 14 of the constitution. The Korean People's Army has a strength of about 784,500. From this total number 700,000 are in the army, 33,500 in the navy, and 51,000 in the air force.[4] Apart from the regular forces, there are the Bureau of Reconnaissance Special Forces of 100,000, the security forces and border guards, which number about 38,000, and the Worker-Peasant Red Guard (militia), which amounts to approximately 4 million.[5]

The regular armed forces are equipped with modern Soviet arms, but Korea also maintains an efficient armament industry of its own. The military build-up might not suffice for a successful attack against the ROK as long as the USA is militarily engaged there but acts as a lever and a continuous threat against the politically restless South. In any case, the high expenditure on defence forms a heavy burden on economic development, in view of scarce resources.

NOTES

1. English text in William B. Simons (ed.), *The Constitutions of the Communist World* (Alphen aan den Rijn, The Netherlands, and Germantown, Md., 1980), pp. 232–54.
2. Kim Il-Sung, *Selected Works*, vol. 2 (P'yongyang, 1965), p. 537.
3. Richard F. Staar (ed.), *Yearbook on International Communist Affairs 1984: Parties and Revolutionary Movements* (Stanford, Cal., 1984), p. 237.
4. The International Institute for Strategic Studies, London, *The Military Balance 1984–1985* (Oxford, 1984), pp. 102-3.
5. *Ibid.*, p. 103.

FURTHER READING

Chung, Chin O, *P'yŏngyang between Peking and Moscow: North Korea's Involvement in the Sino-Soviet Dispute, 1958–1975* (University, Ala.: University of Alabama Press, 1978)

Kim, Ilpyong J., *Communist Politics in North Korea* (New York: Praeger, 1975)

Kim, Se-Jin and Chang-Hyun Cho (eds.), *Korea: A Divided Nation* (Silver Spring, Md.: The Research Institute of Korean Affairs, 1976)

Lee, Chong-Sik, *The Korean Workers' Party: A Short History* (Stanford, Cal.: Hoover Institution Press, 1978)

Scalapino, Robert A. and Chong-Sik Lee, *Communism in Korea*, 2 vols. (Berkeley, Cal.: University of California Press, 1972)

——— and Jun-Yop Kim (eds.), *North Korea Today: Strategic and Domestic Issues* (Berkeley, Cal.: University of California, Institute of East Asian Studies, 1983)

Suh, Dae-Sook and Chae-Jin Lee (eds.), *Political Leadership in Korea* (Seattle, Wash. and London: University of Washington Press, 1976)

11 People's Democratic Republic of Laos

BASIC FEATURES

The People's Democratic Republic of Laos (PDRL), proclaimed by the National Congress of People's Representatives on 2 December 1975, differs from all other socialist states by its lack of a valid constitution. In May 1984 the Standing Committee of the Supreme People's Assembly decided to form a commission to draw up a constitution, but it is uncertain as to when this will be promulgated.

All power is exercised by the Lao People's Revolutionary Party (LPRP), which adheres to Marxism-Leninism. According to statements made by its leaders, Laos, having, with the foundation of the PDRL, completed the national democratic revolution, has embarked on the course of building socialism, bypassing the stage of capitalist development (as Mongolia had done in the 1920s) and considers itself to be a state of the dictatorship of the proletariat. Following the Vietnamese line on the 'three revolutions', the PDRL is carrying through the revolution in the relations of production, a scientific and technical revolution and an ideological and cultural revolution. This programme aims at the formation of state or collective ownership of the means of production, industrialisation and the political education of the citizens by permanent indoctrination until they internalise the Marxist-Leninist values as defined by the communists.

Socialism was introduced into a country with a subsistence economy (in 1975 only 10 per cent of the peasants produced for the market) and a society whose spiritual life was widely determined by the *Sangha* (order of the Buddhist monks).

There was practically no heavy industry and only a few hundred small light industrial enterprises when the communists took over. Industrial workers, as the social base of the Communist Party, were therefore, in effect, non-existent. The transformation of the relations of production refers mainly to the peasants, who have been in the process of being collectivised, step by step, since 1978. The alliance of workers and collective peasants is supposed to form the core of unity of all working people, including the intelligentsia. The implantation of a socialist consciousness is effected by (forced) attendance at 'seminars'. These may be held at places of work — for instance, for civil servants — or at other places, for politically unreliable persons.

A major concern of the rulers is the lack of what could be called a Lao nation and consequently a lack of national identity in view of the extreme ethnic segmentation: half the total population consists of more than sixty non-Lao ethnic groups. Some of them, like the Hmong (Meo) tribesmen, strongly oppose the repression of their traditional way of life and form the basis of resistance movements inside and outside the country.

Laos is practically a client state of Vietnam. Major policy decisions can only be taken with Vietnamese consent. Control is exercised through civilian advisers attached to Lao ministries, joint consultative organs and Vietnamese troops deployed on Lao territory.

THE COMMUNIST TAKEOVER

The Lao communists seized power by employing National Front strategy, with North Vietnamese support and advice in the course of their struggle against USA-backed political forces, and in the context of the struggle of the Democratic Republic of Vietnam (DRV) for unification. The political and military struggle, however, was overtly led not by the communists but by the Lao Patriotic Front (LPF). This organisation was formed in 1956 in succession to the Lao Independence Front, which had been created in 1950 as a nationalist resistance movement against the French, under the leadership of Prince Souphanouvong and had become known internationally as the Pathet Lao in 1954.

As a result of the Geneva Conference on Indo-China of 1954, which ended French colonial rule, Laos became a sovereign state in the guise of a constitutional monarchy. Yet the Royal Lao Government (RLG) soon came under pressure from the Americans. They were concerned about the power vacuum after the French withdrawal from Indo-China and feared that negotiations between the RLG and the Pathet Lao provided for in the Geneva Agreements would result in the formation of a government which, because of Pathet Lao participation, would embark on an anti-Western course.

Notwithstanding obstruction by the USA, the RLG under Prince Souvanna Phouma, who was a half-brother of Prince Souphanouvong, and the Pathet Lao signed an armistice in October 1956, and a year later formed a coalition government. In partial elections to the National Assembly in May 1958, the LPF gained nine of the twenty-one contested seats. This electoral outcome, however, provoked the fall of the government, which ended the painfully established balance of power. July 1959 saw the resumption of the civil war, in which the USA intervened. Following the Geneva Conference on Laos of 1962, at which the neutrality of Laos was agreed, the contending political forces formed a second coalition cabinet, which, however, proved as short-lived as the first. Hostilities again broke out between the armed forces of the RLG and the Pathet Lao, and the situation became even more complicated when the USA began to wage a 'secret' war against Lao neutralists, employing rebellious Meo tribesmen. Moreover, Laos became involved in the escalating Vietnam war when the DRV used the Ho Chi Minh trail, a part of which cut through Lao territory, for military supplies to the Viet Cong. The trail and Pathet Lao areas became a target for massive American bombing.

When, in February 1973, in the aftermath of the Paris armistice agreement between the DRV and the USA, the civil war in Laos ended, the Pathet Lao troops had established control over three- to four-fifths of the country. In April 1974 the Provisional Government of the National Union was formed with equal participation of the 'Government of Vientiane' and the Pathet Lao; decisions required unanimity. Parliamentary functions were widely assumed by the National Political Consultative Council, led by Prince Souphanouvong. This body adopted an Eighteen-Point Programme for National Reconstruction and a Draft Law on Ten Democratic Freedoms to rally 'progressive' forces. Shortly after the communist takeover in South Vietnam and Cambodia, demonstrations in Vientiane, called by 'patriotic' organisations, pressurised right-wing ministers and generals into resigning. On 23 August 1975 the Pathet Lao also seized power in Vientiane through a 'people's revolutionary committee'. At the end of November, King Savang Vatthana abdicated, the six-century old monarchy was abolished and the governmental institutions were reorganised on the model of other socialist states, in particular that of Vietnam.

THE MARXIST-LENINIST PARTY

In February 1972 the LPRP emerged from the Lao People's Party. This party had been founded secretly in March 1955 by Lao veterans of the Indo-China Communist Party, formed in October 1930 by renaming the CP of Vietnam and dissolved in 1951.

LPRP membership was about 35,000 in 1982 — less than 1 per cent of the total population. Membership may be attained after a probationary period, which is nine months for workers directly engaged in production and for state and army cadres, combatants and other people who have worked for five consecutive years; in all other cases the probationary period is one year. The organisational structure of the LPRP parallels the administrative division of the state, which enables it to control all activities of the state organs by local party committees. The basic organisations are the party branches in production units, business enterprises and the like, and in villages. The army and the security forces have party organisations of their own.

The formally supreme body is the Party Congress. In the past it convened at irregular intervals (in 1955, 1972 and 1982), but in future it is to meet every five years. The Central

Committee (CC), to which the Third Party Congress, April 1982, elected fifty-five members, acts for the Congress in the interim and meets twice a year. The CC elected the Political Bureau of seven members and its executive organ, the Secretariat, with Kaysone Phomvihane as secretary general at the top. He presides over the Political Bureau and has simultaneously held the post of premier since 1975. Four other members of the Political Bureau, from which three are also members of the CC Secretariat, are at the same time vice-premiers. Thus these five persons virtually concentrate in their hands all power in party and state. Another member of the Political Bureau is the nominal head of state, the former Prince, now 'comrade', Souphanouvong.

The LPRP's orientation is strictly pro-Soviet. It practises proletarian internationalism by 'strengthening special solidarity, all-round co-operation and a militant alliance with Vietnam and Kampuchea, as well as all-round co-operation with the Soviet Union and other fraternal socialist countries'.[1] Pro-Chinese party and state officials and army officers have been purged.

SOCIAL ORGANISATIONS

As in the other socialist countries, in the PDRL too there are organisations which ensure that the decisions and directives of the Communist Party are transmitted to the masses and obeyed by them. Mass and other social organisations consist of the Federation of Lao Trade Unions, the Lao People's Revolutionary Youth League and the Young Pioneers, the Lao Women's League, the Lao Federation of Peasants, the United Lao Buddhists' Association, the Lao–Soviet Friendship Association, and the Lao–Vietnamese Friendship Association.

The special tasks of just two organisations may be mentioned by way of illustration. First, the trade unions deal with the professional training and ideological education of the workers, organise emulation campaigns, see to the increase of labour discipline and are engaged in measures concerning the working and living conditions of the workers. They are, remarkably, expected to mobilise the peasants, too, for the attainment of the goals set by the party. Second, the Buddhists' Association has to ensure that the monks — many of whom have fled to Thailand or have been arrested or assigned to re-education camps — support the cause of socialism. They are expected to earn their living themselves by cultivating fields and not, as traditionally, by begging, and to engage in the anti-illiteracy campaign. They are allowed to practise their ceremonial life. The Buddhists' Association also serves as a useful device of the state for establishing and maintaining international contacts. By its relations with corresponding associations in Vietnam and Kampuchea, it contributes to the rapprochement of the three former Indo-Chinese states.

The social organisations are united, under the leadership and control of the LPRP, in the Lao Front for National Construction, created in February 1979 to replace the LPF, and presided over by Souphanouvong. Its main task is the mobilisation of the citizens, organised according to profession, sex or age, as well as of non-organised social and ethnic groups for the construction and defence of socialism.

CENTRAL GOVERNMENT

The national representation body is the Supreme People's Assembly (SPA). It succeeded the National Political Consultative Council, and its members, forty-six in 1975, were appointed by the National Congress of People's Representatives. Its president, since December 1975, Souphanouvong, is head of state. When the communists seized power, ex-King Savang Vatthana had been appointed adviser to the SPA. Refusing co-operation, he was allegedly involved in an anti-government plot, tried to flee to Thailand in March 1977, was arrested and sent to a re-education camp, where he presumably died.

The SPA, which meets twice a year, exercises legislation and approves, formally, the governmental policy. Further powers may be inferred from the constitutional provisions concerning the corresponding state bodies in other socialist states. Remarkably, as Laos has not yet a constitution, there is no supreme legal norm by which state organs have to abide and to which laws and other judicial acts must conform.

The executive organ of the SPA and supreme administrative body, installed by the National Congress, is the Council of Government. The premier is assisted by vice-premiers who simultaneously direct ministries (like the Ministry of Foreign Affairs and Ministry of Defence). Several ministries administer special economic branches. The government also includes the chairmen of some committees, such as the Planning Committee, the Nationalities' Committee, as well as the president of the National Bank. Until his death in January 1984, the premier of the former coalition governments, Prince Souvanna Phouma, had acted as adviser to the government. The Council of Government draws up the plans for economic and social development and the state budget, and is responsible for their implementation by all subordinate administrative organs. It is responsible for taking all the measures aimed at the transformation of the country on the basis of socialism, in which considerable help is supplied by Vietnamese experts.

LOCAL GOVERNMENT

The PDRL is administratively subdivided into thirteen provinces, districts, sub-districts (comprising several villages) and villages. Within the latter, agricultural co-operatives are established, comprising, as a rule, fifteen to thirty families. By mid-1984 about 2,400 co-operatives, which cultivated about 35 per cent of the arable land, had been formed.[2]

Local policies, which consist mainly in the implementation of laws, orders and directives adopted or issued by central authorities, are carried through by the people's councils and their administrative committees. Within the framework of the centrally made decisions, these organs see to the organisation of production, do cultural and educational work and ensure the maintenance of public security. The local organs of state power are strictly supervised by organs at the next higher administrative level, and finally by the Council of Government.

FOREIGN POLICY

The PDRL's foreign policy is determined by three factors: its strategic position between Vietnam and China, Sino–Soviet rivalry, and its common border with Thailand. When the communists took over power, they at first pursued a balanced policy between the Soviet Union and China, and between Vietnam and China. The latter has always evinced strong interest in Lao neutrality. However, the dependence on Soviet aid for post-war reconstruction and development, Vietnamese ambition to dominate former Indo–China, and the pro-Vietnamese attitude of the Lao leadership resulted in close relations with Vietnam and the USSR and a deterioration in relations with China.

A Treaty of Friendship and Co-operation, signed in July 1977 for a period of twenty-five years, established a 'special relationship' between Vietnam and Laos and legalised the factual control of the latter's party and state by the Vietnamese. The 'special relationship' implies close co-operation in the fields of foreign policy, defence and economy. This is ensured, *inter alia,* through regular meetings of the ministers of foreign affairs and the integration of the economic plans of both countries. In February 1983 the leaders of party and state in Laos, Vietnam and Kampuchea celebrated a summit conference and declared it their intention to hold further meetings.

Though Laos is not a member of the CMEA (unlike Vietnam), it has co-operated with it since 1976 by attending sessions on special invitation in the capacity of an observer. It receives economic and technical aid from CMEA countries — mainly from the Soviet Union, with which it co-operates also at the level of the Planning Committees. An important partner of Laos is also the GDR, with which it concluded a Treaty on Friendship and Co-operation in September 1982 and develops relations 'on the basis of Marxism-Leninism and proletarian internationalism'.

Lao–Chinese relations are characterised by constant tensions but are better than official propaganda and official hostility would suggest. Accusing China of building up forces for an invasion in March 1979, the Lao government demanded the withdrawal of Chinese road construction workers. But, apart from border incidents, factual or alleged support of anti-government insurgents among tribesmen and exiled Lao, the PDRL has avoided a complete disruption of relations. This reveals a limited leeway in Lao foreign policy.

Relations with Thailand have been strained because of numerous border incidents, trade embargoes, which the Thai authorities have repeatedly imposed on Laos, and the problem of Lao refugees. In January 1979 both governments agreed not to permit their territories to be used as bases for interference, aggression or subversion from one against the other. But relations again became strained when the Lao government felt threatened by Chinese–Thai collusion in supporting Lao exiles. In view of Thailand's dependence on hydro-electric energy from Laos, the latter's interest in trade with Thailand and in using its ports for exports, both countries endeavour to minimise their conflicts.

The PDRL is the only former Indo–Chinese country to maintain diplomatic relations with the USA. The Americans, however, refuse to help Laos with its reconstruction in spite of the heavy damages they inflicted on it during the civil war, reproaching the Lao government with insufficient efforts to find and return the remains of American pilots missing in action. The USA has confined its support to humanitarian aid.

NATIONAL DEFENCE

The defence policy of the PDRL is determined by its geopolitical situation and internal problems, and is closely linked with Vietnam's security interest. Laos protects Vietnam's western flank. But also its northern border is a matter of concern to Vietnam, in the latter's desire to prevent the Chinese from using Lao territory for another attack against Vietnam and for arms supplies to the guerrilla forces of Democratic Kampuchea, who fight the Vietnamese.

A problem of internal security is presented by some of the ethnic minority tribes, particularly the Meo, who fought with American support against the Pathet Leo. Family bonds across the Lao–Chinese border, which can easily be exploited by China, create a problem of external security, too.

The strength of the Lao People's Army is estimated at a total of 53,700, of which 50,000 make up the army, 1,700 the navy and 2,000 the air force.[3] Paramilitary forces comprise the Self-Defence Forces in towns, factories and offices, and the militia. In order to strengthen Lao defence capacity (and to control the country), Vietnam has deployed troops, which amounted to about 40,000 in 1983,[4] and helps the Lao government with military advisers and instructors.

NOTES

1. 'Report on Amendments to the Statute of the LPRP, presented to the Third National Congress' by Sisomphon Lovansai, Ch. I, in William B. Simons and Stephen White, *The Party Statutes of the Communist World* (The Hague, 1984), pp. 289–95, p. 289.
2. BBC (London), *Summary of World Broadcasts,* 13 October 1984, quoted in *Südostasien aktuell* (Hamburg), vol. 4 (1985), no. 1, p. 49.
3. The International Institute for Strategic Studies, London, *The Military Balance 1984–1985* (Oxford, 1984), p. 104.
4. *Ibid.,* p. 112.

FURTHER READING

Adams, Nina S. and Alfred W. McCoy (eds.), *Laos: War and Revolution* (New York: Harper and Row, 1970)

Langer, Paul F. and Joseph J. Zasloff, *North Vietnam and the Pathet Lao: Partners in the Struggle for Laos* (Cambridge, Mass.: Harvard University Press, 1970)

Stuart-Fox, Martin (ed.), *Contemporary Laos: Studies in the Politics and Society of the Lao People's Democratic Republic* (New York: St Martin's Press, 1982)

Toye, Hugh, *Laos: Buffer State or Battleground* (London and New York: Oxford University Press, 1968)

Zasloff, Joseph J., *The Pathet Lao: Leadership and Organisation* (Lexington, Mass.: Lexington Books, 1973)

—— and MacAlister Brown (eds.), *Communism in Indochina: New Perspectives* (Lexington, Mass.: Lexington Books, 1975)

12 Mongolian People's Republic

BASIC FEATURES

The legal foundation of the Mongolian People's Republic (MPR) is the constitution of 6 July 1960.[1] In articles 1 and 2 it defines itself as a 'socialist state of workers, *arats* (herdsmen and cultivators) organised in co-operatives, and the labouring intelligentsia', which 'is developing in the form of a people's democracy'. The 'working people' exercise state power through representative bodies — the *khurals* of people's deputies. The 'guiding and directing force of society and state' (preamble to the constitution) is the Marxist-Leninist Mongolian People's Revolutionary Party (MPRP). All activities of the state are subject to the principle of democratic centralism. To the extent that individual functions of the state will wither away under communism, corresponding provisions of the constitution are to be repealed, and the entire constitution is destined to be abolished when the state is replaced by 'a communist association of working people' (article 94). This provision is unique in the constitutions of the communist-ruled states, among which Mongolia is the second oldest.

THE COMMUNIST TAKEOVER

The Mongolian communists seized power, with Soviet military support, in the course of a struggle for liberation from the Chinese, who in 1915 had recognised, but in 1919 had cancelled Mongolia's autonomy under their suzerainty. At this time the Bolsheviks were carrying out operations against the White

Guards, who in 1920 and 1921 had taken up positions in Outer Mongolia.

In March 1921 the Mongolian People's Party, which had emerged in 1920 from two patriotic and anti-feudalist circles, held its First Congress. Shortly afterwards a Provisional People's Revolutionary Government was formed on Soviet soil which called for the independence of Mongolia and the establishment of a kind of constitutional monarchy under the head of the Buddhist Church in Mongolia. The Chinese and the White Guards were driven out of Mongolian territory by national armed forces and, on the government's request for military aid, Red Army detachments. A treaty with the RSFSR of November 1921 guaranteed Mongolia's existence, however, China formally exercised suzerainty till 1946. In August 1924 the Mongolian People's Party was renamed the Mongolian People's Revolutionary Party. It decided to embark on a non-capitalist path of development, from feudalism directly towards socialism — practically without any industrial proletariat. Ideologically, however, it found itself justified by Lenin, who at the Second Comintern Congress in July 1920 had argued that backward countries could skip over to a Soviet system without passing through the capitalist stage of development if they were supported by the proletariat of the advanced countries.[2]

In June 1924 Mongolia proclaimed itself a 'people's republic', and in November of that year the people's assembly, called the Great Khural, adopted a constitution which was modelled on the constitutions of the RSFSR and the USSR. Thus Mongolia became the first country after the USSR with a Soviet-style regime. In 1925 Soviet troops withdrew, but party and government continued to be supported (and controlled) by Soviet advisers because Mongolia possessed only a small political and administrative élite of its own. Throughout the following years this élite was educated in the USSR. In 1940, according to official historiography, Mongolia started to lay the foundations of socialism, after it had de-feudalised society, especially by the dissolution of the Lama monasteries which owned most of the livestock. The anti-religious policy, aiming at the elimination of Buddhism, had caused considerable unrest, and even several upheavals, in the 1930s. By 1960, when Mongolia adopted its third constitution, the phase of the establishment of socialist relations of production is considered to have been concluded—in particular by the collectivisation of the herdsmen — and Mongolia has then entered a new stage, in which it aims at completing the socialist social order.

THE MARXIST-LENINIST PARTY

In 1981 the MPRP, the sole political force in Mongolia, claimed a membership of about 76,000;[3] its share of the total population is 4.2 per cent. Regarding recruitment and its composition, the party is confronted by the fact that the working class is rather weak. Only by keeping the total membership low can the party manage to maintain a fairly substantial proportion of workers among its rank and file: 31 per cent in 1976. Nineteen per cent of the party membership at that time consisted of *arats*, and 50 per cent of members consisted of the intelligentsia (officials and bureaucrats) or employees.[4]

Central party organs, apart from the Party Congress, are the Central Committee, the Political Bureau, as the guiding body, and the Secretariat. Since August 1984 the latter has been headed by Jambyn Batmunkh as secretary general. He succeeded Yumjagiin Tsedenbal, who had held this office — with a short interruption — since 1940. The organisational base of the MPRP consists of the party cells in factories, livestock co-operatives, state farms (dealing with grain farming), schools and military units. They are formed when there are at least five party members. Party cells in enterprises, state farms and co-operatives have the right to supervise the activity of the management.

The MPRP's relationship with the CPSU is characterised by unconditional subordination to the Soviet claim to leadership in world communism, whereas the relationship with the Chinese communists, reflecting the Soviet–Chinese confrontation, is strained.

SOCIAL ORGANISATIONS

The social organisations operate under the leadership and control of the MPRP; this is also a constitutional norm (article 82). Among these organisations the following should be mentioned: the trade unions, which consider themselves as instruments for the popularisation and implementation of party directives and economic plans; the Mongolian Revolutionary Youth Union, which was founded as early as 1921, being at that time more radical than the Communist Party, and is an important instrument of indoctrination; the Mongolian Pioneer Movement; the Committee of Mongolian Women; cultural and scientific societies; Friendship Societies; and the Society for Promotion of Defence. Two of the social organisations, the trade unions – through their Central Council – and the Youth Union may exercise the right of legislative initiative.

CENTRAL GOVERNMENT

The supreme organ of state power is formally the Great People's Khural (GPK). It is elected for a five-year term by citizens who have reached the age of eighteen. Elections are held in single-member constituencies, and from a unity list of MPRP and non-party candidates which, as a rule, obtains between 99 and 100 per cent of the votes cast. Of the 370 deputies elected in June 1981, 60 per cent were elected for the first time, 344 were party affiliated, 100 were claimed to be workers, 106 members of livestock co-operatives and the rest administrative personnel and members of the intelligentsia. The deputies are declared to be responsible and accountable to their electors and may be recalled at any time. They are entitled to question members of the Council of Ministers.

The GPK, which convenes only once a year, confirms and adopts the constitution; passes laws, establishes the 'basic principles and measures' of domestic and foreign policy (article 20 of the constitution), approves the national economic plan and the state budget, and decides on questions of peace and defence. In view of the leading role of the MPRP, the jurisdiction of the GPK cannot be but a formal one. A good deal of its work, such as for the budget and economic and foreign affairs, is done by permanent commissions.

Between the sessions of the GPK the highest organ of state power is its Presidium, consisting of the chairman, vice-chairmen, the secretary and members, of all whom are elected by the GPK. It has the authority to adopt decrees which need the confirmation of the GPK, to control the implementation of the constitution and the laws (and to interpret the latter), to repeal decrees and regulations of the Council of Ministers and local *khurals* if they fail to conform to the law, to appoint and to dismiss ministers upon the recommendation of the chairman of the Council of Ministers, to establish and abolish ministries and other central agencies, and to ratify and denounce international treaties.

The Presidium is the collective presidency. For practical reasons its chairman exercises the functions of head of state. In December 1984 the GPK elected the secretary general of the MPRP, Batmunkh, as chairman, who succeeded Tsendenbal in this office too.

The Council of Ministers, formed by the GPK and responsible to it and the Presidium, is the highest executive and administrative organ. It is composed of the chairman — since December 1984 Dumagiin Sodnom (from 1952–74, Tsedenbal; from then on, Batmunkh) — vice-chairmen, ministers, and the chairmen of state committees and other central agencies. Apart from 'classic' departments, there are several ministries for the administration of various economic branches; there are, moreover, committees for labour and wages, prices and standards, information, radio and television, secondary and higher education, people's control, in addition to the State Planning Commission and the Commission for CMEA Affairs. Some committees and commissions are directed by vice-chairmen of the Council of Ministers. The Council of Ministers is in charge of economic planning and the implementation of economic plans; it directs affairs in the fields of foreign policy and defence, and it guides the work of the regional and city administrative organs.

LOCAL GOVERNMENT

For administrative purposes Mongolia is divided into eighteen regions (*aymags*) and cities; below the regional level are the rural districts (*somons*), which roughly correspond to large livestock-cooperatives, and towns of local subordination; the cities and other population centres are divided into sub-districts.

State power in the local administrative units is exercised by the *khurals* of people's deputies, which are elected for a term of three years, and their executive organs. Both direct local economic and cultural affairs; they confirm and implement local economic plans, ensure observance of the laws and the fulfilment of decisions of superior agencies. On the principle of dual subordination the executive organ of a local *khural* is responsible and accountable to the *khural* which elected it, and to the executive organ of the *khural* at the next higher administrative level. A superior *khural* is empowered to change or to repeal decisions of an inferior *khural*, and decrees and regulations of its executive organ; the executive organ of a higher *khural* has the right to change or to repeal decrees and regulations of the lower executive organs, and to suspend decrees of inferior *khurals*.

ADMINISTRATION OF JUSTICE

Jurisdiction is exercised by the Supreme Court of the Republic, *aymag* and city courts, as well as precinct people's courts. Judges and people's accessors at all courts are elected: those of the Supreme Court by the GPK for a five-year term, those at the *aymag* and city courts by the *khurals* of the corresponding administrative unit for three years, and those at the precinct people's courts by the citizens for three years too. As judge or people's accessor citizens may be elected who have attained twenty-three years of age and have not been convicted.

Supervision over the observance of laws by all state organs, institutions and organisations, officials and citizens is entrusted to the Procuracy. It is directed by the procurator of the republic, who is appointed by the GPK and is responsible and accountable to it and its Presidium.

The citizens are granted the right to complain in written or oral form against illegal actions of state organs and individual officials, or against manifestations of bureaucracy or inefficiency of any organs of state power and administration. These organs and officials are obliged to consider complaints and applications, and to take measures to eliminate violations of laws and regulations. The exercise of individual rights and freedoms, guaranteed by the constitution, is restricted by such duties as: the devotion of all individual efforts to the cause of the building of socialism; the protection of social property; the respect for the priority of the interests of state and society over personal interests; and the strengthening of the unity and solidarity of the peoples of the socialist camp.

FOREIGN POLICY

In the preamble to its constitution the MPR declares that it conducts a peace-loving foreign policy directed towards ensuring co-operation with all peoples on the basis of the principle of peaceful coexistence and strengthening fraternal relations and relations of friendship, co-operation and mutual assistance with the socialist countries on the basis of the 'unshakeable' principle of proletarian internationalism.

The vicinity to the USSR and to the People's Republic of China (PRC) has a determining influence on Mongolian foreign policy. The MPR was and is linked to the USSR by treaties of friendship and mutual assistance of 1936, 1946 and 1966. The USSR regards the MPR as a buffer zone against China and uses it as a strategic area of deployment. Just as between 1921 and 1925 as well as between 1937 and 1956, the Soviet Union has again stationed troops there since 1966. The close ties with the Soviet Union, however, coincide with Mongolian security interests.

Whereas Soviet Russia and Mongolia established relations in the early 1920s, the Guomindang government of China did not recognise Mongolia's independence until January 1946 after a referendum; not until 1949 did the communist government establish diplomatic relations. In 1960 the MPR and the PRC also signed a Treaty of Friendship and Mutual Assistance, and in 1964 they concluded a treaty on the common border which, however, the PRC terminated in 1969. The MPR fears that, in view of the Sino-Soviet conflict, without backing by the USSR it might be drawn into the maelstrom of Chinese policy and in the extreme case become a victim of Sinianisation just like Inner Mongolia. The PRC, in turn, regards the MPR as a Soviet satellite and feels threatened by the Soviet military presence in Mongolia. In 1983 the Sino-Mongolian relationship reached a new low, when several hundred Chinese were expelled from the MPR.

The MPR is not a member of the WTO but is admitted as an observer. In 1962, however, it became a member of the CMEA and maintains trade almost exclusively with its member countries, particularly with the Soviet Union. Not until October 1961 did Mongolia become a member of the UNO. In the 1960s it established relations with Western European countries, among them Great Britain, and in 1972 with Japan. It is expanding contacts with African and Middle East countries.

NATIONAL DEFENCE

Mongolia's defence policy is entirely subject to Soviet strategic considerations. Its regular forces total about 36,500, of which 33,000 are formed by the army, and 3,500 by the air force. The paramilitary forces comprise the Ministry of Public Security troops of about 15,000, internal security troops and frontier guards.[5] The strength of troops which the USSR has stationed in Mongolia is estimated at about 75,000.[6] They are said to be equipped with medium-range ballistic missiles.

NOTES

1.   English text in William B. Simons (ed.), *The Constitutions of the Communist World* (Alphen aan den Rijn, The Netherlands, and

Germantown, Md., 1980), pp. 262–81.
2. V.I. Lenin, *Polnoe Sobranie Sochineniy*, 5th edn, vol. 41 (Moscow, 1962–63), p. 246.
3. Richard F. Staar (ed.), *Yearbook on International Communist Affairs 1984: Parties and Revolutionary Movements* (Stanford, Cal., 1984), p. 255.
4. Robert Rupen, *How Mongolia is Really Ruled: A Political History of the Mongolian People's Republic, 1900–1978* (Stanford, Cal., 1979), p. 101.
5. The International Institute for Strategic Studies, London, *The Military Balance 1984–1985* (Oxford, 1984), p.105.
6. *Ibid.*, p.22.

FURTHER READING

Bawden, Charles R., *The Modern History of Mongolia* (London: Weidenfeld and Nicolson, 1968)
Friters, Gerard M., *Outer Mongolia and its International Position* (London: Allen and Unwin, 1951)
Murphy, George G.S., *Soviet Mongolia: A Study of the Oldest Satellite* (Berkeley, Cal.: University of California Press, 1966)
Rupen, Robert, *How Mongolia is Really Ruled: A Political History of the Mongolian People's Republic, 1900–1978* (Stanford, Cal.: Hoover Institution Press, 1979)

13 Polish People's Republic

BASIC FEATURES

The Polish People's Republic defines itself as a 'socialist state'
by amendment on 10 February 1976 of its constitution of 22
July 1952.[1] Power is vested in the 'working people of town and
country' (article 1), who exercise the undivided state authority indirectly through their representatives in the Sejm (parliament) at the national level and in councils at the local level.
According to article 3, the Polish United Workers' Party
(PUWP) is the 'leading political force of society in the building
of socialism'. Reflecting reality, the Party Statute (article 27)
establishes the leading role of the communists, too, with
respect to the state. The PUWP decides on the guidelines of
policy, on the basis of which the Sejm 'passes resolutions
determining the fundamental directions of activity of the
state' (article 20). Besides the PUWP there are two other
political parties which are not permitted to compete with it for
power; they accept its claim of leadership and do not question
the socialist system.

There is, however, one strong force which competes
ideologically with the communists: the Roman Catholic
Church. Though the PUWP has the monopoly of political
power, it does not therefore have that of ideological power
too. To this extent Poland is fundamentally distinct from all
other socialist systems. Further features unparalleled among
socialist systems are the albeit transitory existence of
autonomous trade unions, and a limited but legally guaranteed right of the worker to strike. Finally, Poland differs from
other socialist states, with the exception of Yugoslavia, in its

large private agricultural sector: in 1981 about 70 per cent of all productive land consisted of private plots.[2] The individual family farms are protected by constitutional amendment of 20 July 1983.

THE COMMUNIST TAKEOVER

The mode and course of the communist takeover was largely determined by the geopolitical situation of the country and its liberation from Nazi rule by the Red Army. In July 1944 the Polish Committee of National Liberation was set up near Lublin. It was based upon an alliance between the Polish Workers' Party, which had been set up clandestinely in January 1942 as the successor of the Polish Communist Party dissolved in 1938, the Union of Polish Patriots founded in Moscow in 1943 by communists and Soviet-orientated leftist intellectuals, the left wing of the Polish Socialist Party as well as by pro-Soviet politicians of the People's (or Peasants') Party and the Democratic Party. Acting on behalf of the National Council of Poland, which had been established in December 1943 and which regarded itself as the provisional people's representation, with Soviet support the Lublin Committee took over executive power in the territories occupied by the Red Army.

On 1 January 1945 the Lublin Committee, headed by the Socialist Osóbka-Morawski but dominated by communists, constituted itself as Provisional Government and was recognised by the Soviet Union a few days later. It competed with the Polish exile government under prime minister Mikołajczyk, which resided in London and was backed by the Western allies. The latter had its own armed forces on several fronts in the West and the Home Army in Poland, which on 1 August 1944 inititated the unsuccessful Warsaw upheaval in order to gain an advantageous political position for bourgeois forces with respect to the distribution of power in post-war Poland. Negotiations between the Lublin Committee and the exile government on the formation of a government of national unity first came to nothing because both sides demanded the majority in that government. It was finally set up in late June 1945 on the basis of an agreement which had been made at the Conference of Yalta and shortly afterwards was also recognised by the Western powers. It comprised but a few bourgeois politicians, among them the leader of the pro-Western Polish People's (or Peasants') Party, Mikoljczyk, as deputy prime minister. By a land reform, the formation of local national councils dominated by communists, the filling of the most important ministries and administrative posts with followers of the Lublin coalition, the control of the security police and the armed forces, the communists, not without support from workers, peasants and members of the intelligentsia, paved the way for their ultimate rule.

At the manipulated elections to the Constituent Sejm of January 1947 the unity list of the Democratic Bloc, formed by the parties of the Lublin coalition, polled 80.1 per cent, whereas Mikołajczyk's party, the sole oppositional party, was given only 10.3 per cent of the votes. After Mikołajczyk's flight to the West in October 1947, this party was likewise forced into line and the whole party system restructured: in December 1948 the Polish Socialist Party, purged of anti-communist elements, merged with the Polish Workers' Party into the PUWP; in 1949 the Polish People's Party was reorganised as the United People's Party (also known as the United Peasants' Party); in 1950 the (Christian-Social) Party of Labour was incorporated into the Democratic Party. On the pattern of a people's democracy, all three parties were combined in the National Unity Front under the unchallenged domination of the PUWP.

Under the leadership of Władisław Gomułka, the communists first pursued their 'own course towards socialism', which, in September 1948, however, was condemned as 'right-wing deviation' and given up by the expulsion of the national communists around Gomułka.

THE MARXIST-LENINIST PARTY

The PUWP in July 1980 claimed about 3.1 million members and candidates.[3] Due predominantly to withdrawals – as a reaction against revelations on abuse of power by the party leadership, in connection with the formation of the trade union Solidarity, out of protest against the proclamation of martial law – and because of expulsions, in December 1982 membership had dropped to about 2.3 million (9 per cent of the adult and approximately 6.4 per cent of the total population).[4]

The party is organised on production and territorial principles; that is, primary organisations at the place of work and the place of residence form the party's base. Full membership is preceded by two probationary years. The central organs are the Party Congress, which convenes every five years, the Central Committee (CC) elected by the Congress and convening at least every four months, as well as the Political Bureau and the Secretariat, headed by the first secretary – since October 1981 General Wojciech Jaruzelski.

The Ninth Extraordinary Party Congress of July 1981 adopted a new Statute which provides for a limited democratisation of the PUWP, *inter alia*, by secret election to all leading party organs, the number of candidates having to exceed the number of office-holders. In principle it allows for only one successive re-election into an executive party office, and lays down the fundamental separation between leading executive party offices and leading offices in the administration of state and economy at the same organisational level; for example, between the Political Bureau and the Council of Ministers. (Exceptions are possible, however, as the combination of the top party office and top government office in the person of General Jaruzelski demonstrates.) Trends towards democratisation had already become obvious before the Ninth Congress, when primary organisations began to co-operate horizontally, circumventing higher party organs as the usual channel of communication, and when numerous candidates for election to the Congress, designated by the party apparatus, were not accepted by the rank and file. Consequently, about 95 per cent of the delegates were new. Another proof of democratisation was the re-election of the then first secretary of the CC of the PUWP, Stanisław Kania: he was elected by the Party Congress and not by the CC from two candidates, with only 67.6 per cent of the valid votes.

Stressing national peculiarities with respect to the building of socialism, the PUWP is a loyal follower of the CPSU to which, according to the Chapter I of its Statute, it feels tied by bonds of solidarity and brotherhood.

BLOC PARTIES, CHRISTIAN ASSOCIATIONS AND SOCIAL ORGANISATIONS

The two non-communists parties integrate and mobilise for the goals of the PUWP sections of the population which show a rather reserved attitude towards the latter. The United People's Party, whose membership is restricted principally to the rural population, had about 464,000 members at the end of 1982; roughly 71 per cent of them were peasants.[5] The Democratic Party had about 107,000 members at the end of 1982;[6] it recruits its members from the urban population: white-collar workers, members of the intelligentsia and private craftsmen. These parties may articulate their own ideas on the form of socialism and on the methods and pace of its construction, and they are now and again consulted by the PUWP. They must, however, submit to its domination and strictly observe its decisions in their political activity. They are, therefore, neither opposition parties nor coalition parties, though represented in high state organs (Council of State, Council of Ministers), because government policy is not the result of compromises.

The socialist system and the leading role of the PUWP are not questioned in principle by the three Christian associations, which lack the status of a political party but hold a few seats each in the Sejm: (1) Pax, founded in 1949 and recruiting its members mainly from the Catholic intelligentsia; (2) the Christian Social Association, founded in 1956 by some former Pax members and also comprising non-Catholics; (3) the Polish Catholic Social Association, which developed from neo-Znak, a group of pro-regime Sejm deputies. Neo-Znak, in turn, developed in 1976 by splitting off from Znak (the 'Sign'), which since 1957 had represented the clubs of the Catholic intelligentsia in the Sejm and had maintained close relations with the Polish episcopacy. By its critical attitude towards the PUWP and the government, it formed a kind of opposition in the Sejm. After the proclamation of martial law in December 1981, however, the leader of neo-Znak, Janusz Zablocki, expressed some criticism of the regime and had to resign. The same had happened to the leader of Pax, Ryszard Reiff, and the former leader of Znak, Stanisław Stomma. The former, whose organisation, like the Christian Social Association, had always been more or less pro-regime, refused to sign the decree on martial law; the latter abstained from voting in favour of the 1976 amendment of the constitution.

Social organisations include, among others, the trade unions, professional associations, the League of Polish Socialist Youth, the League of Rural Youth, the League of Polish Socialist Students, the Women's League, the influential Veterans Union of Fighters for Freedom and Democracy (Polish abbrev.: ZBoWiD). After the proclamation of martial law on 13 December 1981 some of the social organisations were dissolved and later reorganised. This happened, for example, to the writers' association (which had been accused of pursuing an autonomous cultural policy), to the journalists' association, to the students and particularly to the trade unions. In 1980–81 there were three types of trade unions: twenty-two branch trade unions, formerly united in the Central Trade Unions' Council and dominated by the PUWP, about a hundred independent trade unions and about thirty autonomous professional unions. On the basis of a law of 8 October 1982 new trade unions may be set up. First, factory unions which may organise themselves at the national level in federations on the branch principle (e.g. in the Federation of Miners); second, professional unions for the members of a certain profession (e.g. engineers). The trade unions, which have to recognise the leading role of the PUWP, are granted the right to strike when an attempt at mediation proves unsuccessful. Excepted from this guarantee are political strikes, sympathy strikes as well as strikes in institutions important for the defence and the security of the state, in the food industry and in some other branches.

The three political parties, the three Christian associations, social organisations and individual (well-known) personalities loyal to the regime are organised within the Patriotic Movement of National Rebirth (Polish abbrev.:

PRON). It was founded in July 1982 in order to overcome the socio-political crisis by mobilising support of all 'patriotic' forces for the government. In May 1983 PRON held its First Congress and replaced the National Unity Front, which was dissolved two months later. PRON assumed such tasks of the National Unity Front as preparing and holding the elections to the representative bodies, proposing candidates and drawing up election programmes. Accordingly, article 3 of the constitution was amended in July 1983, and PRON is now the common framework for the co-operation of political parties, social organisations and associations, as well as citizens, irrespective of their *Weltanschauung*, for the solution of the problems of the socialist state and for the development of the country. PRON has cells in enterprises and at places of residence; councils in cities, urban districts, communes and at the voivodship (regional) level; and a National Council with a Presidium and an Executive Committee at the top. Though PRON has also articulated demands deviating from the PUWP and the government, it is considered to be an instrument of the communists and ultimately acts as such.

DISSENT AND OPPOSITION

In the wake of strikes which took place in July 1980 resulting from discontent about economic failures, and helped by the decline of the regime's authority, 'independent, self-managing trade unions' came into being. In the Gdańsk agreement of 31 August 1980 between representatives of the workers and government, the latter agreed upon the establishment of such trade unions on condition that they recognised the leading role of the PUWP in the state; it also guaranteed the right of the workers to strike and accepted the demands of the workers of a reduction of censorship, plurality of opinion in the mass media, the broadcasting of the Mass and the release of dissenters. In September 1980 delegates from numerous enterprises and representing founding committees of the new trade unions set up the National Coordinating Commission, under the chairmanship of Lech Wałęsa (the leader of the Gdańsk Interfactory Strike Committee). It was to act as an advisory body for independent trade unions which were formed according to industrial branches, joined together in regional unions and rallied around the name of Solidarity (*Solidarność*). In October 1980 Solidarity gained legal status by registration at the Warsaw voivodship court. (Polish farmers founded the Rural Solidarity, which was also registered.)

In the following months Solidarity, whose membership at the end of 1980 is said to have reached 8 to 10 million,[7] developed into a political force which seriously challenged the monopoly of power of the PUWP. At its First Congress in September and October 1981 it demanded free elections and advocated the foundation of independent trade unions in other socialist countries. On the basis of martial law proclaimed in view of the threat of a general strike and the imminent danger for the regime, the activities of Solidarity were prohibited, and its leaders were interned or went underground; on 8 October 1982 Solidarity was dissolved by law. Its ideas, however, which deeply changed the political consciousness of the population, are still alive.

Apart from Solidarity, mention must be made of the Committee for the Defence of the Workers (Polish abbrev.: KOR). It was formed by some intellectuals in the aftermath of strikes and demonstrations which broke out in summer 1976 because of the government's attempt to increase food prices and were partly suppressed by force. In September 1977 it changed its name to Committee for Social Self-Defence (Polish abbrev.: KSS), which later also served as a sort of a political brains trust for Solidarity. After the proclamation of martial law, it was prohibited and some of the leaders were put on trial in 1983; they were accused of having questioned the leading rule of the PUWP, the system of government and Poland's membership in the WTO. In March 1977 dissent was also organised in the Movement for the Defence of Human and Civil Rights, which required from the government adherence to the commitments established in the 1975 Helsinki Final Act and in the UN Covenant on Civil and Political Rights. Radically opposed to the regime was the Confederation Independent Poland; it stood for the abolition of the communist one-party rule and of Poland's subordination to the Soviet Union.

A very strong, organised intellectual and moral force which seriously challenges the materialistic Marxist-Leninist doctrine of the PUWP is the Roman Catholic Church. Because of its great capacity to mobilise the population and to shape public opinion — it is estimated that about 90 per cent of the population is Catholic and about 60 per cent are practising believers — it also constitutes a significant element of political power. This becomes evident from the fact that the Church succeeded in opposing attempts of the state to limit its sphere of action to the performance of mere religious functions. Party and state have even shown the readiness to make concessions to the Church, well realising the common interest to safeguard national integrity and internal peace, and the ability of the Church to contribute to the preservation of both, particularly in critical situations as in 1956, 1970–71 and 1980–81. The Ninth Extraordinary PUWP Congress emphasised the patriotic attitude of the Catholic Church and advocated the dialogue between it and the state on sociopolitical questions. The Church, however, refused to collaborate with the regime within the framework of PRON.

CENTRAL GOVERNMENT

The national representative body and, according to article 20 of the constitution, 'the supreme organ of state power' is the Sejm. Its members are elected every four years by universal, equal, direct and — facultatively — secret suffrage in plurimember constituencies. (Because of political instability the Sejm elected in March 1980 has prolonged its term until August 1985.) The citizens have the right to vote after reaching the age of eighteen and may be elected deputies after attaining the age of twenty-one. Up to 1980, elections took place on the basis of single lists of the National Unity Front. The lists had to contain up to half as many candidates more than seats assigned to a constituency; in the 1980 elections 646 candidates were put up for 460 seats. The elector thus had a limited opportunity to choose between different candidates and may have favoured a candidate who was placed at the bottom of the list by deleting the name of the candidate who was at its top. As a rule, however, voting has been open and deletions have been rare. Consequently, the officially favoured candidates usually polled about 99 per cent of the votes, and the ratio of seats distributed among the parties and associations has remained unchanged during more than two decades, the PUWP retaining a slight but secure majority. In the Sejm of 1980 the communists were allocated 261, the United People's Party 113, the Democratic Party 37 seats. The remaining 49 seats went to the Christian associations or to deputies who do not belong to any party or association.[8]

By a new electoral act adopted in May 1985, two major changes have been introduced to the election of the Sejm. First, in addition to the constituency lists there shall be a national list (of prominent personalities), from which shall be elected a number of deputies, which corresponds to at the most 15 per cent of the constituency deputies; second, the nomination of two candidates for one constituency mandate shall be mandatory. The single list candidates shall be nominated at national and at voivodship conventions composed of representatives of the leading organs of PRON, of the political parties and of the Christian associations (three fifths), and of representatives of the leading organs of social organisations (two fifths). Concerning the constituency mandates, the elector shall have as many votes as seats shall be allotted to a constituency, and shall have the choice between two candidates placed alternatively for the same mandate. Leaving on the ballot the names of both candidates undeleted, the elector's vote shall be considered as cast for the first candidate; in case of deletion of this candidate the vote shall be considered to be cast for the alternate candidate. A vote shall be considered as valid but cast against the list if the elector shall strike off all candidates. On the national list the number of candidates shall correspond to that of the seats, and the vote shall be considered as cast for those candidates whose names shall not be deleted.

The electors have the right to recall a deputy but have never made use of it. The deputies who belong to one of the parties are organised in deputy clubs whose main task is to ensure uniform voting behaviour. The PUWP club acts under the guidance of the CC of the PWUP. The non-party deputies may join together in circles, the formation of which requires the approval of the Presidium of the Sejm, or they may join the PUWP club, where, however, they have non-voting status.

Ratifying the decisions of the supreme organs of the PUWP the Sejm passes laws, adopts the state budget and the national socio-economic plans, appoints and dismisses the Council of Ministers or its individual members, and supervises the organs of the state administration through the Supreme Board of Control. The Sejm convenes for sessions at least twice a year, and these usually last for two to three months; during a session the Sejm holds on average four plenary sittings lasting one or two days each. Many of the parliamentary tasks, such as the discussion of law bills, are performed by permanent committees, which correspond to the branches of state administration and also meet between the sessions. The committees may demand to be informed about the activities of the Council of State and the Council of Ministers, and make recommendations for the work of these bodies. The recommendations are not binding, but both organs are obliged to comment on them. Single deputies of the Sejm may interpellate the chairman of the Council of Ministers or individual ministers as well as the procurator general, who are obliged to answer the interpellation.

In critical situations such as in 1980–81 the PUWP usually concedes the Sejm greater authority in order to counteract the challenge to its rule by legitimising its policy with the help of the constitutionally 'highest exponent of the will of the working people' (article 20). The increased activity of the Sejm and the self-confidence of its members became evident in the high number of interpellations and questions. Since additional questions to members of the government were allowed by changing the rules of procedure, the employment of these instruments of control produced lively debates. The proceedings of the plenary sittings were directly broadcast, whereby the behaviour of deputies became known to the public. The lessening of the PUWP's control and of its reputation in state and society resulted in a relatively high proportion of no-votes and and abstentions from voting. In October 1981 the Sejm even refused to grant the government special power for managing the crisis. Non-conformist voting behaviour continued after the proclamation of martial law, albeit not on questions of principle.

The Sejm gained further influence when, in autumn 1980, the Supreme Board of Control, which had been temporarily put under the control of the president of the Council of Ministers, was again subordinated to the parliament. This body supervises the economic, financial and administrative activities of the central and local organs of the state administrations, and the social and co-operative organisations, from the point of view of the implementation of the socio-economic plan, legality, efficiency and honesty. The Supreme Board of Control becomes active on its own initiative, on complaints or petitions from the citizens, on behalf of the Sejm or the Council of State and on the initiative of the president of the Council of Ministers. It has to inform these organs of the result of its investigations.

In March 1982 the Sejm created the Socio-Economic Council as an organ of social consultation. Its members are elected by the Sejm from among candidates nominated by industrial enterprises, state and co-operative agricultural enterprises, social organisations and individual persons. Concurrent membership of the Sejm and of the Council is incompatible, except for the latter's chairman. The Council is obviously intended to detect social and economic shortcomings, to articulate interests of certain social groupings and to inform the decision-makers on the chances of enforcing necessary measures without running the danger of undue unrest.

In periods between the sessions of the Sejm its legislative function and its competence to appoint and recall the members of the Council of Ministers are performed by the Council of State. It is elected by the Sejm from among its members and is composed of the chairman, four vice-chairmen, the secretary and eleven further members, including representatives of the non-communist parties and one independent. The Council of State is also the collective presidency of the republic, and its chairman — at present Henryk Jabłoński, who is also a member of the Political Bureau of the PUWP — virtually acts as head of state. In this capacity the Council of State is empowered to proclaim martial law, if this is necessitated by 'considerations of the defence or security of the state' (article 33, paragraph 2, of the constitution). Such a measure, being in conformity with the constitution was adopted by the Council of State on 13 December 1981. It violated the constitution, however, when it issued decrees concerning the martial law having the force of law although the Sejm was still in session.

The Council of Ministers is the supreme executive and administrative organ of the state, acting in close contact with the Political Bureau and the Secretariat of the PUWP. It is composed of the president as its chairman, vice-presidents, ministers, and the chairmen of committees and commissions (e.g. the Planning Commission and the State Price Commission). The president and his deputies make up the Presidium of the Council of Ministers. Membership of the Council of Ministers is not incompatible with membership of the Sejm; on the other hand, a parliamentary mandate is not a precondition for the tenure of a government post. The Council of Ministers takes care, *inter alia,* of the implementation of laws and with this aim issues ordinances, draws up the state budget and the national socio-economic plan over a series of years, exercises 'general guidance' in the fields of foreign relations and national defence (article 4), ensures the protection of public order, of the interests of the state and of the rights of the citizens, and directs the work of the local administrative organs. It is responsible and accountable to the Sejm and, when the Sejm is not in session, to the Council of State.

On 13 December 1981, in connection with the proclamation of martial law, an extra-constitutional but omnipotent political body, the Military Council of National Redemption, consisting of twenty-one high officers, assumed power. Its chairman, General Jaruzelski, already held four other posts: he was first secretary of the CC of the PUWP, president of the Council of Ministers, chairman of the National Committee of Defence, minister of defence and, in this capacity, commander-in-chief of the armed forces. When martial law was abolished in July 1983 the Military Council dissolved itself.

LOCAL GOVERNMENT

Poland has a two-tier territorial administrative structure: on the one hand, forty-nine voivodships (among them three so-called urban voivodships), and on the other hand, towns, city districts and (rural) communes. The local representative bodies are the national councils, whose members are elected by the citizens for a four-year term. According to the new rules for the election of the national councils of February 1984, two candidates have to be nominated for one seat. The lists of the candidates who may be proposed by the basic organisations of PRON, are drawn up by electoral colleges consisting of PRON-representatives and of representatives of the political parties, Christian associations and social organisations. A candidate is considered to have been elected upon obtaining the majority of the valid votes, whereby a poll of 50 per cent is sufficient. At the elections of June 1984 the official turnout was only 75 per cent,[9] *i.e.* about 6.5 million citizens abstained from voting.

The national councils are conceived as 'organs of state power', 'fundamental organs of social self-government' and 'organs of territorial self-government'. In the latter capacity they are supposed to take independently responsibility for local economic, social and cultural tasks, as far as these are not assigned to the jurisdiction of other organs, linking the local needs with the targets of the whole state. Yet local self-government is rather limited. The national council at a higher administrative level is entitled to repeal a decision of a national council at a lower level, if the decision is illegal or if it is not in conformity with the political line of the party and the state. The activities of the national councils are supervised by the Council of State.

On the other hand, a law of July 1983 provides for wider decision-making powers of the national councils. A decade before, their presidia, as far as they had acted as collective administrative and executive organs, had been replaced by one-man organs: the *voivods* and the presidents of the cities at voivodship level, who were appointed by the chairman of the Council of Ministers; and the heads of towns, city districts and communes, who were appointed by the *voivods*. Now the national councils have been granted a say in the appointment of *voivods*; the heads of towns, city districts and communes are elected by the national councils. The national councils have also been strengthened by conceding them their own revenues, by broadening their jurisdiction in local planning and by granting them the right to participate in decisions concerning the establishment of state enterprises.

The *voivods,* heads of towns, and so on, exercise a dual function. They are organs of state administration, and in this capacity they are subordinate and responsible to the higher administrative organ, which in the case of the *voivods* is the Council of Ministers. When, however, they act as executive organs of the national councils within the latter's scope of jurisdiction, they are also responsible to the representative bodies, according to the principle of dual subordination.

Social self-government in the towns and villages serves, among others, to ensure co-operation between the citizens and the national councils in fulfilling the socio-economic plans and the election programmes, in controlling the communal services and in restoring dwellings, roads and the like.

ADMINISTRATION OF JUSTICE

The administration of justice is carried out by the Supreme Court, the voivodship courts, district courts (for the most part at the places of the former district administration) and special courts like military, industrial, social security courts, the Supreme Administrative Court and the State Court. The members of the Supreme Court are appointed by the Council of State for a term of five years; the judges of the other courts are appointed by the Council of State for an indefinite period. The people's accessors at the voivodship and district courts are elected by the national councils. Judges and people's accessors may be recalled.

The Supreme Administrative Court in Warsaw, with eight branch offices, was established in autumn 1980. Its jurisdiction, however, is, limited to an examination of administrative decisions in certain fields enumerated by law; decisions concerning fundamental rights of the citizens (such as the freedom of press, of association, and of assembly) are exempted.

The State Court was established in March 1982 by an amendment to the constitution. Its president is the president of the Supreme Court by virtue of his office; the other members are elected by the Sejm. The State Court is empowered, but only on the initiative of the Sejm, to call to account members of the Council of State, of the Council of Ministers and the heads of other central state bodies, if they have contravened the constitution or the laws in the execution of their office. Its jurisdiction does not, however, apply to the holders of high party posts.

The same constitutional amendment provided for the establishment of a Constitutional Court. The legal implementing regulations, however, have not yet been enacted. It will have the right to check the constitutionality of laws; the definite decision on the conformity or non-conformity of laws with the constitution, however, will be left to the Sejm as the body representing the unity of state power. Once constituted, the Constitutional Court will be a unique institution within the Soviet sphere of influence.

Overall control over the legality of the activity of state organs, over the protection of social property and over respect for the rights of the citizens falls within the competence of the Procuracy. It is headed by the procurator general, who is appointed and recalled by the Council of State.

FOREIGN POLICY

Polish foreign policy is determined by the country's contiguity with the Soviet Union and its membership of the CMEA and the WTO. Friendship and co-operation with the USSR and other socialist states is a constitutional principle.

Until 1970 the pre-eminent aim of foreign policy was the German recognition of the annexation of East German territories, which, by the Potsdam Agreement of August 1945, had been handed over to the Poles for administration in exchange for territorial concessions which Poland had to make to the Soviet Union. The annexation was striven for not only by the Committee of National Liberation but also by the exile government in London and was supported both by the Soviet Union and by the Western allies. The Manifesto of the Committee of 22 July 1944 not only showed readiness to cede Polish territory to the Soviet Union but also contained a commitment to co-operate closely with the Eastern neighbour. This was established in the Treaty on Friendship, Co-operation and Mutual Assistance of April 1945, which was in the interest of Polish security in view of the fact that the Soviet Union guaranteed the shift of the Polish frontier towards the West. By signing this treaty and similar treaties with a number of East and South-East European states and by refusing to participate in the Marshall Plan — after an originally positive reaction — Poland became fully absorbed into the Soviet sphere of hegemony. Within the Eastern system of alliances Poland is a very loyal partner; in August 1968 it took part in the invasion of Czechoslovakia and it supports Soviet efforts for integration within the CMEA.

In accordance with its partners in the Eastern bloc, Poland has developed some initiatives which reveal its endeavour to place its security on a broader basis. In October 1957 the then foreign minister, Adam Rapacki, presented a plan before the UNO to establish a nuclear free zone in central Europe. A year later this plan was extended by a proposal for a reduction of armed forces and conventional weapons, and in December 1963 Poland suggested the 'freezing' of nuclear weapons in central Europe. These plans were replaced by the conception of a system of collective security in Europe on the basis of non-aggression and the preservation of the territorial *status quo* which Poland brought before the UN General Assembly in December 1964. An important step in this direction was taken on 7 December 1970 by the conclusion of a treaty between Poland and the FRG in which the latter — as the GDR had already done in July 1950 — recognised the inviolability of the Polish western frontier pending a peace treaty with Germany, which decreased the Polish fear of West German revisionism. The territorial and political *status quo* in Europe was confirmed in summer 1975 by the Final Act of the CSCE, in which Poland played a constructive role hoping that détente would result in increased economic co-operation between East and West, which would be of special advantage to

Poland.

Since the mid-sixties, when General de Gaulle showed understanding for the Polish boundary problem, the Poles have maintained close relations with France, with which in October 1972 they signed an agreement on mutual consultations. Since the beginning of the 1970s they have also intensified their relations towards the USA on the basis of the principle of peaceful coexistence. In May and June 1972 President Nixon visited Poland, in September 1974 the then first secretary of the CC of the PUWP, Edward Gierek, paid a return visit to Washington. The improvement in political relations with the West resulted in increased economic and technolog ical aid. Poland's reputation in the West, however, suffered a setback when the regime proclaimed martial law and suppressed Solidarity. The USA and other Western countries, accusing the Poles of violating human rights, froze their political relations and cut economic ties with Poland. This aggravated the economic crisis which the Poles have experienced since the end of the 1970s and the beginning of the 1980s.

NATIONAL DEFENCE

Poland maintains regular armed forces of about 323,000 soldiers: 210,000 in the army, 22,000 in the navy and 91,000 in the air force.[10] In addition, there are paramilitary forces (frontier guards and internal defence troops), which total about 218,000, a citizens' militia of about 350,000 members and the League for National Defence, of some 200,000 active members,[11] which takes responsibility for the paramilitary education of the citizens.

NOTES

1. English text in William B. Simons (ed.), *The Constitutions of the Communist World* (Alphen aan den Rijn, The Netherlands, and Germantown, Md., 1980), pp. 288–310.
2. *Rocznik statystyczny 1982* (Warsaw, 1982), p. 231.
3. *Trybuna Ludu* (Warsaw), 16/17 July 1983.

202   The Political Systems of the Socialist States

4. *Ibid.*
 5. *Rocznik polityczny i gospodarczy 1981–1983* (Warsaw, 1984), p. 165.
 6. *Ibid.*, p. 175.
 7. *Polityka* (Warsaw), 31 January 1981.
 8. *Rocznik polityczny,* op. cit., p. 67.
 9. *Rzeczpospolita* (Warsaw), 20 June 1984.
10. The International Institute for Strategic Studies, London, *The Military Balance 1984–1985* (Oxford, 1984), pp. 26-7.
11. *Ibid.*, p.27.

FURTHER READING

Ascherson, Neal, *The Polish August: The Self-Limiting Revolution* (New York: Viking Press, 1982)

Bromke, Adam, *Poland's Politics: Idealism vs. Realism* (Cambridge, Mass.: Harvard University Press, 1967)

—— and John W. Strong (eds.), *Gierek's Poland* (New York: Praeger, 1973)

Dziewanowski, Marian K., *The Communist Party of Poland: An Outline of History,* 2nd edn. (Cambridge, Mass.: Harvard University Press, 1976)

Kolankiewicz, George and Ray Taras, 'Poland: Socialism for Everyman?', in Archie Brown and Jack Gray (eds.), *Political Culture and Political Change in Communist States,* 2nd edn. (London: Macmillan, 1979), pp. 101–30

Morrison, James F., *The Polish People's Republic* (Baltimore; Md.: Johns Hopkins Press, 1968)

Pirages, Dennis C., *Modernization and Political Tension Management: A Socialist Society in Perspective. Case Study of Poland* (New York: Praeger, 1972)

Raina, Peter K., *Political Opposition in Poland, 1954–1977* (London: Poets' and Painters' Press, 1978)

Rakowski, Mieczysław F., *The Foreign Policy of the Polish People's Republic* (Warsaw: Interpress Publishers, 1975)

Sanford, George, *Polish Communism in Crisis* (London: Croom Helm, 1983)

Simon, Maurice D. and Christine M. Sadowski, 'Attitudes toward Participation in the Polish Political Culture', in Donald E. Schulz and Jan S. Adams (eds.), *Political Participation in Communist Systems* (New York and Oxford: Pergamon Press, 1981), pp. 197–233

Touraine, Alain, *et al., Solidarity: The Analysis of a Social Movement: Poland 1980–1981* (Cambridge and New York: Cambridge University Press 1983)

Wiatr, Jerzy J. and Jacek Tarkowski (eds.), *Studies in Polish Political System* (Warsaw: Ossolineum, 1967)

14 Socialist Republic of Rumania

BASIC FEATURES

Rumania declares itself to be a 'socialist republic' in its constitution of 21 August 1965, still in force in the revised version
of 27 December 1974.[1] The power of the people is supposed to
be based on an alliance of workers and peasants with the
working class as the determining force. The people are 'building the socialist system and creating the conditions for the
transition to communism' (article 2) under the leadership of
the Rumanian Communist Party (RCP). As laid down in the
constitution, the RCP directs the activities of social organisations and state organs, thus also *de jure* being superordinate to
all other organs and institutions of society and state. Party and
state are to a large extent merged into one by joint organs, by
multiple holding of party and state offices, as well as by the
simultaneous subordination of institutions to high party and
state organs. The pre-eminent position of the head of state,
who is exempted from the principle of collective leadership,
gives Rumania some features of a presidential system.
Numerous institutional and procedural peculiarities of the
Rumanian political system are specially created for the present president in office, Nicolae Ceauşescu.

THE COMMUNIST TAKEOVER

As in other East European countries, the assumption of
power by the RCP, which originated from the splitting of the
Socialist Democratic Party in May 1921, took place step by

step. Having entered the war against the Soviet Union on the side of the Axis Powers in 1941, on 23 August 1944 Rumania surrendered to the Red Army and changed allies. In November 1944 the Communist Party, Social Democrats and other parties united in the National Democratic Front formed a government in which the communists exerted no decisive influence. In a new government, however, formed under Soviet pressure in March 1945, they received several key positions (Ministries of Domestic Affairs and of Justice). At the parliamentary elections in November 1946 the Bloc of Democratic Parties emerging from the National Democratic Front and supporting the government, polled nearly 80 per cent of the votes. In the second half of 1947 the National Peasants' Party, the Liberals and the right wing of the Social Democratic Party were dissolved and thus — in the presence of Soviet troops, who remained stationed in Rumania till 1958 — the way had further been paved to the monopoly of power of the RCP. On 30 December 1947 King Mihai I was forced to abdicate and Rumania was proclaimed a people's republic.

In the new government the communists took over further important departments such as the Ministries of Foreign Affairs and of Defence. On 13 April 1948 a new constitution, similar to that of the Soviet Union was adopted; likewise in 1948, industry, banking, insurance, and so on, were nationalised, and in the following year collectivisation of agriculture was initiated. In February 1948 the RCP, in which 'home communists' and the 'Muscovites' (emigrants from the USSR) competed for power, united with the left wing of the Social Democratic Party and formed the Rumanian Workers' Party. The next constitution of 24 September 1952, which orientated itself even more closely on the Soviet model, established *de jure* what had already become a fact: the leading role of the Communist Party in state and society. In 1965 it resumed the name Rumanian Communist Party.

THE MARXIST-LENINIST PARTY

According to article 26 of the constitution, 'the most advanced and conscientious citizens from among workers, peasants, intellectuals and other categories of working people' are united in the RCP. Citizens, who apply for admission to the party, need the recommendation from two party members; a probationary period is not provided for. A member has to consecrate his life, among others, 'to the defence of the SRR's independence and sovereignty' (article 5 of the Party Statute of 1974). In 1984 the RCP filed about 3.4 million members[2] — about 15 per cent of the total population. At the end of 1982 it comprised nearly 21 per cent of the adult population and 31 per cent of the 'active' population; more than 75 per cent of the members were employed in the 'productive sector'; women made up 30.6 per cent of the members. Workers accounted for 55.6 per cent, peasants for 15.8 per cent and white-collar workers for 20.8 per cent of the membership.[3] The share of the national minorities is supposed to correspond approximately to their share in the populace.

The supreme organs of the RCP are, formally, the Party Congress, which meets every five years, and within that period the Central Committee (CC), to which the Thirteenth Congress of November 1984, under the decisive influence of Nicolae Ceauşescu and his wife Elena (who is chairman of the Cadres' Commission of the CC), elected 446 full and alternate members — nearly half of them for the first time. Between the meetings of the CC, the Political Executive Committee, to which the Congress elected twenty-three full and twenty-four alternate members, guides all party activity. The core of this organ is its Permanent Bureau (consisting, since December 1984, of eight members) which co-ordinates and directs the activities of party and state. It was established in March 1974 and was originally conceived for the holders of high positions in the party and state apparatus. In December 1974 *ex officio* membership was dropped, and members have since then been appointed — formally — by the Political Executive Committee from among its members. Headed by Nicolae Ceauşescu, who since 1965 has been first secretary of the CC or secretary general of the RCP, and composed of close and reliable collaborators (among them, at present, his wife and brother-in-law), the Permanent Bureau virtually forms an instrument of his very personal rule. Further organs on the national level are the CC Secretariat, which ensures the execution of party decisions, the Central Party Collegium as supreme organ to watch over party discipline, the Central Auditing Commission to administer party finances, and the National Party Conference (the 'small Party Congress').

In regard to the CPSU the RCP pursues an independent line, theoretically laid down for the first time at the Ninth Party Congress of July 1965. First signs had, however, already been visible before then. The striving for emancipation from the CPSU's claim for leadership in the communist world movement is based on a conception of the nation quite different from the Soviet view. From the point of view of the Rumanian communist party and state are supposed, also in the socialist stage of development, to work primarily for the benefit of the nation. Because of this conviction they reject a unilateral interpretation of the principle of internationalism; that is, in the sense of a subordination of the national interest to that of the USSR. The stressing of the nation and the national interest serves to manifest theoretically an independent road towards socialism, which takes into account the special historically developed character of a people. This claim has not, to be sure, resulted in a deviation from the Soviet model of rigid communist one-party rule, but has yielded an independent foreign policy and a position within world communism which is based on equality of status for each Communist Party. In line with this attitude the RCP rejects a leading centre of world communism and advocates the 'new unity' of all progressive forces in the world instead of proletarian internationalism. The independent course of the Rumanian communists became clearly evident in their close contacts with the Eurocommunists.

SOCIAL ORGANISATIONS

The social organisations comprise the General Confederation of Trade Unions, the Union of Communist Youth, to which the Union of Rumanian Student Associations is attached, the National Women's Council, the National Union of Agricultural Production Co-operatives, and the associations of the national minorities (Hungarians and Germans). The social organisations are merely belts for transmitting party decisions and institutions for mobilising support for the party. The task of the trade unions is to ensure the implementation of economic plans and the observance of labour discipline and to take care of the social affairs of the workers. Their participation in industrial management is reduced more or less to debating questions of production and wages within the Working People's Councils set up in all enterprises, in which, however, the decisive authority rests with the party secretary and the managing director, who in their turn are bound by party directives. Although the enterprises have been granted certain responsibilities concerning the drafting of production plans and budgeting, the Working People's Councils are by no means organs for workers' self-management but rather for supervision of the workers.

Most social organisations as well as the various religious communities (the Orthodox Church and others) are collective members of the all-embracing Front of Socialist Unity and Democracy (FSUD), which includes the RCP as its leading force. It was founded in 1968 after the Soviet intervention in Czechoslovakia and until 1980 was called Socialist Unity Front. The supreme organ of the FSUD is the National Council, with Nicolae Ceauşescu as chairman. Its main task is to mobilise citizens to help build socialism according to the guidelines of the Communist Party. The FSUD possesses the exclusive right to nominate candidates, thoroughly screened by the party, for the elections to the Grand National Assembly and to the local people's councils. Further activities consist of consultations with members of the people's councils, the discussion of draft bills, the initiation of laws, the supervision of the people's representatives and the initiation of their recall.

CENTRAL GOVERNMENT

The 'supreme body of state power' is, according to article 42 of the constitution, the Grand National Assembly (GNA). The deputies are elected directly for a five-year term. Citizens have the right to vote on reaching the age of eighteen and become eligible for election at the age of twenty-three. Candidates are proposed at election meetings in enterprises, socio-cultural institutions, city districts, villages and units of the armed forces. Election takes place in single-member constituencies from a single list of the FSUD. In some of the at present 369 constituencies two candidates each have been nominated. The single list usually obtained between 99 and 100 per cent of the votes; in March 1985, however, nearly 2.3 per cent no-votes were polled. The deputies are responsible to the electors and are subject to recall. The GNA decides upon the recall on the recommendation of the FSUD, and this decision must be discussed at a meeting of the electors. The deputies have the right to address questions and interpellations to the Council of Ministers and any of its members, to the president of the Supreme Court and the procurator general; these have to be answered within three days, orally or in writing.

The GNA, meeting for sessions twice a year, is only formally the sole legislative body. Its constitutional position is greatly reduced by the right of the Council of State to issue law-decrees and by the participation of the RCP in the legislative process. The rules of procedure of the GNA provide that the CC of the RCP has the priority to initiate a law before the National Council of the FSUD, the Council of State, the Council of Ministers, the standing committees of the GNA and thirty-five deputies. (In view of this fact, the Communist Party becomes also *de jure* the real source of legislation.) Apart from the National Council of the FSUD, the party has the right to propose the members of the Bureau of the GNA; that is, of its presidency. Also the members of the Council of State, the permanent organ of the GNA, are elected on the proposal of the CC of the RCP. As Ceauşescu is secretary general of the RCP, it is in practice he who largely determines the composition of these organs and much of the work of the GNA. The GNA does, however, exert a certain influence on legislation through its standing committees, which examine and debate bills as well as other matters at the request of, and acting for, the plenary assembly or at the request of the Council of State. Debates on bills in the plenary assembly — just as their discussion in the mass media — basically serve their explanation and popularisation in order to mobilise support.

Only very seldom are citizens' proposals taken into consideration.

The Council of State, formally elected by the GNA from among its members, is, in contrast to many other socialist countries, merely a 'substitute parliament' and not also the collective head of state. It is responsible and accountable to the GNA, and its members may be recalled by the latter at any time. Yet the 'norms having the force of law', which the Council of State establishes during the period between the sessions of the GNA, must merely be submitted to (formal) debate in the next session (article 64 of the constitution). Between the sessions of the GNA the Council of State is also empowered to appoint and dismiss the prime minister, to interpret the laws in a general mandatory way, to control their enforcement and the activity of the Council of Ministers, and to order partial or total mobilisation and declare a state of war in cases of emergency. If, owing to exceptional circumstances the GNA cannot meet, the Council of State appoints and recalls the Council of Ministers and the Supreme Court, and may adopt the economic plan and the state budget. Permanent functions of the Council of State are, *inter alia,* the ratification and termination of international treaties — as far as this is not incumbent on the GNA — and the organisation of the ministries and other central state bodies. The powers of the Council of State were substantially reduced by the creation of the position of the president of the republic by constitutional amendment of 28 March 1974.

The president of the republic is elected by the GNA with at least a two-thirds majority, on recommendation of the CC of the RCP or the National Council of the FSUD, for the duration of a legislative term, and is formally responsible to it. He presides over the Council of State and the Defence Council, and is commander-in-chief of the armed forces. He may chair the meetings of the Council of Ministers and on the proposal of the prime minister appoints and dismisses members of the Council of Ministers, and appoints and dismisses members of the Supreme Court. Between the sessions of the GNA the president of the republic appoints and dismisses the president of the Supreme Court and the procurator general. In cases of urgency he proclaims a state of emergency in some localities or throughout the entire country. Apart from representative functions in relations with foreign countries, he also has the right to conclude international treaties. In performing his duties, he issues presidential decrees or decisions. All these functions and the holding of this position by the secretary general of the RCP, Ceauşescu, make the incumbent president of the republic the most powerful organ of the Rumanian state and the object of a leadership cult.

The Council of Ministers, as the supreme organ of state administration, takes the necessary measures for the execution of domestic and foreign policy. It consists of the prime minister, vice prime-ministers, ministers, heads of other central administrative bodies (e.g. the State Planning Committee) and ministers' state-secretaries (of some important ministries and other central bodies). In addition, the chairmen of four social organisations are members of the Council of Ministers by virtue of their office. Altogether this body comprises more than fifty members. The Council of Ministers as a whole, and each of its members individually, are responsible to the GNA and, during the period between its sessions, to the Council of State. The responsibility of each member refers both to his own activity and to that of the whole body.

LOCAL GOVERNMENT

Rumania's state structure is centralistic. The country is administratively divided into forty counties (judeţe), cities and communes. The Municipality of Bucharest is subdivided into districts and is administratively on a level with the counties; other large cities may be organised as municipalities. (This administrative organisation, dating from 1968, brought about the dissolution of the Hungarian Autonomous Region, which had been established in 1952.)

The local organs of state power are the people's councils, which are elected for a term of five years in the counties and in the Municipality of Bucharest, and for a term of two and a half years in all other territorial administrative units. For each constituency one deputy is elected; multiple candidacies are possible. Among the functions of the people's councils men-

tion should be made of the administration of local economic
and cultural affairs, the maintenance of public order and the
election of judges and lay judges of the local courts. According to the principle of 'self-guidance' the people's councils are
furthermore supposed to see to the self-budgeting of their
affairs and to providing the necessities of the citizens,
whereby the central bodies shift the responsibility for bottle-
necks to the local organs without granting them any real
powers of self-government.

The implementation of the decisions of the people's councils as well as of the laws, decrees and ordinances of central
organs of state administration devolves upon the executive
committees (in the counties, the capital, its districts and other
municipalities) or executive bureaux (in the cities and communes). They are responsible and accountable to the people's
councils which have elected them, but also to the higher-rank-
ing organ of state administration and to the Council of Ministers.

Limited participation in the formation of local affairs is conceded to the citizens, for instance by involvement in the work
of the standing committees of the people's councils and by
participation in meetings at which the chairmen of the
people's councils have twice a year to report on the activities
of the councils.

ADMINISTRATION OF JUSTICE

Jurisdiction is exercised by the Supreme Court, county courts,
the court of the Municipality of Bucharest, local courts in the
cities and military courts. With the exception of the Supreme
Court, the courts are composed of professional judges and lay
judges. Being subject to recall and bound by the party line,
the independence of the judges is greatly restricted. The Supreme Court supervises the activity of all the courts and sees to
uniform application of the laws by issuing directives. These
directives, however, are controlled by the GNA, whereby the
unity of state power is maintained.

Apart from the courts of law, in Rumania there are also
organs of social jurisdiction: the arbitration commissions.

These commissions are established in enterprises, agricultural production-cooperatives and at the local executive bureaux, and their members are elected by the labour collectives or the people's councils. Being understood as a product of socialist democracy, they decide upon offences against work ethics, minor criminal cases and civil disputes involving small amounts. They are entitled to issue reprimands and warnings and to impose fines. It is possible to appeal against their decisions to a court of law.

The surveillance of the conformity of laws, law-decrees and other acts of normative character with the constitution is exercised by the Constitutional and Judicial Commission of the GNA, up to one-third of whose members may be experts without being deputies. At the request of the GNA Bureau this commission also checks the constitutionality of bills and, at the request of the Council of State, the constitutionality of law-decree bills.

In contrast to many other socialist states, the courts of law may examine decisions of the administrative organs and decide upon infringements of law by verifying the legality of administrative acts. This jurisdiction does not, however, include administrative acts from the sphere of national defence, state security, planning and decisions of the Council of Ministers.

The Procuracy, with the procurator general at the top, supervises the observance of the law by administrative organs, officials and citizens. Unlike the practice in other socialist countries, the Procuracy is obliged to take action *ex officio* only when it learns about infringements of law through its participation in a criminal or civil case or through the activity which it exercises as the authority responsible for criminal prosecution. In the event of infringements of law by administrative organs, the Procuracy may intervene only on the grounds of a complaint or a charge, and if the case does not come within the jurisdiction of a court of law.

THE FUSION OF PARTY AND STATE

The manifold institutional blending of party and state is based on the conception of the 'socialisation' of the state. This implies an increasing influence on state activity by the social organisations, above all, indeed, by the Communist Party, which is considered to be the leading social organisation.

The fusion is realised, first, by organs of dual (party and state) nature. They are established, according to the Statute of the RCP, by its CC, and are subordinate to the CC on the one hand and the Council of State or the Council of Ministers on the other. Among these bodies are the Supreme Council for Economic and Social Development, which supervises the economic branch ministries and whose members are appointed by the CC of the RCP, the Council of State, the Council of Ministers, the Central Council of the General Confederation of Trade Unions (and further social organisations); the Central Council of Workers' Control of Economic and Social Activity, which is subordinate to the CC and the Council of State and supervises the observance of party resolutions and laws concerning economic and socio-political affairs; the Committee for the Problems of the People's Councils, which directs and controls their activities; the Council of Socialist Culture and Education; the National Council for Science and Technology and the Defence Council. Second, the fusion is realised by the representation of social organisations in supreme state organs, which is effected by the *ex officio* membership of the chairmen of the Central Council of the Trade Unions, the National Union of Agricultural Production Cooperatives and the National Women's Council, as well as of the first secretary of the Union of Communist Youth in the Council of Ministers. Third, it is realised by the multiple holding of high party and state offices. This applies especially to Nicolae Ceauşescu and his wife, who is a member of the Permanent Bureau and First vice prime-minister and chairman of the National Council for Science and Technology, but also to further members of the Permanent Bureau and the Political Executive Committee of the CC of the RCP, who are concurrently members of the Council of Ministers. Finally, fusion of party and state is effected by the rotation of cadres; that is, the alternating maintenance of a party or state post at various levels of party and state organisation.

The blending of party and state organs and the accumulation of party and state posts in one person are supposed to avoid parallelism, to economise in personnel but above all to strengthen and secure party control of all state and social activities; it has also, however, resulted in a confusion of competences.

FOREIGN POLICY

The principles and objectives of Rumanian foreign policy are established in three documents. First there is the 'Declaration of Independence' of the CC of the Rumanian Workers' Party of 22 April 1964, in which the CC refused further subordination to the CPSU and demanded respect for the independence and sovereignty of Rumania. Second, there is the Declaration of the GNA of 22 August 1968, in which it condemned the abuse of the WTO for the military intervention in Czechoslovakia and emphasized the exclusive responsibility of each single Communist Party for the construction of socialism. Third, there is the Resolution of the CC of the RCP of 16 December 1975, which stressed the principles of national independence, sovereignty, equality of rights, non-interference in internal affairs and mutual advantage, and set down the following aims: development of friendly relations and fraternal co-operation with *all* socialist states; strengthening of relations with developing and non-aligned countries; intensification of relations with developed capitalist states in the spirit of peaceful coexistence. According to these maxims, rooted in its national consciousness and resulting from its contiguity with the Soviet Union, Rumania pursues an unconventional course in foreign policy. Unlike the constitutions of other socialist states and the constitution of 1952, the present constitution neither mentions everlasting friendship with the Soviet Union nor refers to the part the Soviet Union played in establishing the conditions for the construction of socialism in Rumania.

Rumania's relationship with the Soviet Union is burdened with the annexation of Bessarabia and Northern Bukovina in 1940 and again in 1944; furthermore, by the Soviet effort, beginning at the end of the 1950s, to assign to Rumania, in contrast to its ambitious plans of industrialisation, but in accordance with the principle of socialist division of labour, the position of a supplier of raw materials and agricultural products to the industrially developed members of the CMEA; and finally by the so-called 'Brezhnev doctrine', restricting the sovereignty of socialist states and exposing Rumania to the threat of military intervention by the Soviet Union.

In order to demonstrate and safeguard a foreign policy serving the national interest, Rumania has extended its relations in all directions. It cultivates political and economic relations with industrialised capitalist states especially with the United States (which granted Rumania the status of a most-favoured nation), France, Great Britain and the Federal Republic of Germany, which in 1967 it was the first WTO country to recognise. It maintains close ties with Yugoslavia and the People's Republic of China on the common basis of the rejection of Soviet hegemonial policy. It has repeatedly tried to reconcile the CPSU and the CPC in order to safeguard its scope of manoeuvre by defusing the Soviet-Chinese conflict. Rumania co-operates closely with Yugoslavia not only at party level but also in the economic-technical and military-strategic fields. Its relations with Hungary, however, are not free from tensions because of the Hungarian minority in northern Transylvania, whose cultural rights the Rumanians are gradually curtailing. In the Trianon Peace Treaty of June 1920 Hungary had to cede this territory to Rumania; in 1940 Rumania lost it to Hungary but regained it in 1947 (*de facto* in 1945). Because of the RCP's conception of a nation, attributing to it a pre-eminent significance in the building of socialism (and of Rumanian socialism in particular) and the establishment of a continuity between the Rumanian socialist state and the Dacians and Romans, Rumania considers the situation of the Hungarians in Transylvania to be an internal affair.

Rumania maintains friendly relations with the majority of developing countries in Africa and Asia, with the Arab countries but also with Israel. It was the only member of the WTO which refused to break off diplomatic relations in 1967, and this enabled it to mediate between Egypt and Israel and to support their peace negotiations. Rumania is a member of the

Group of 77 (developing countries) and has a guest status in the Non-Aligned Movement. It strongly condemned the Vietnamese invasion of Kampuchea.

Rumania's largely independent foreign policy also found expression during the CSCE and the follow-up meetings in Belgrade and Madrid, as well as before the UNO, where it often shared the positions of the neutral and non-aligned countries and deviated from those of the other WTO states. Also at the Conference on Disarmament in Europe, which is taking place in Stockholm, Rumania develops ideas deviating from those of the Soviet Union and widely congruent with those of the NATO and neutral states. In summer 1984 Rumania was the only country of the Soviet bloc not to join the boycott of the Olympic Games in Los Angeles.

Concerning the deployment of medium-range arms in Europe, however, the Rumanian communists adopted the Soviet point of view, that only the withdrawal of the US missiles would make resumption of the INF negotiations possible. This attitude shows that Rumania is at present anxious not to overstrain its relationship with the Soviet Union, on whose supplies of energy and raw materials it is increasingly dependent because of its lack of hard currency for the purchase of these goods on the world market. Its heavy debts to the West and the low quality of its industrial products force Rumania to intensify its trade with the Soviet Union and other CMEA countries, after having reduced it considerably in the 1960s and 1970s. Nevertheless, Rumania is anxious that co-ordination of economic planning within the CMEA should not harm its interests, and it stresses its status as a less developed country to which the rich Soviet Union should render support by granting it favourable terms of trade.

NATIONAL DEFENCE

Rumanian defence policy is determined, on the one hand, by its membership in the WTO and the Treaty on Friendship, Co-operation and Mutual Assistance, concluded with the Soviet Union in July 1970 and, on the other hand, by the wish to pursue an independent foreign policy, rejecting the Soviet claim for hegemony and advocating the dissolution of the military alliances in East and West. Rumania refuses to allow WTO troop manoeuvres on its territory and co-operates only symbolically by sending staff personnel to the WTO manoeuvres. It has furthermore (so far) refused to comply with the Soviet demand to put its armed forces under a joint command.

In 1984 the regular armed forces totalled 190,000 soldiers: 150,000 in the army, 32,000 in the air force and 7,500 in the navy.[4] In addition, there are 17,000 border troops, 20,000 security troops and also the Patriotic Guards, a militia of at present 900,000, which was established in 1968 immediately after the occupation of Czechoslovakia.[5] It is responsible for safeguarding military objects in the hinterland and for combating air-borne troops. The mobilisation of all citizens who are fit for military service and the prohibition of capitulation are supposed to demonstrate to a possible attacker Rumania's determination to protect its territorial integrity by all available means.

NOTES

1. English text in William B. Simons (ed.), *The Constitutions of the Communist World* (Alphen aan den Rijn, The Netherlands, and Germantown, Md., 1980), pp. 318–42.
2. *Scînteia* (Bucharest), 20 November 1984.
3. *Buletinul Oficial al Republicii Socialiste România* XIX, no. 22, part I (31 March 1983), pp.4–7.
4. The International Institute for Strategic Studies, London, *The Military Balance 1984–1985* (Oxford, 1984), pp. 27–8.
5. *Ibid.*, p. 28.

FURTHER READING

Fischer-Galati, Stephen A., *The Socialist Republic of Rumania* (Baltimore, Md.: Johns Hopkins Press, 1969)
Gilberg, Trond, *Modernization in Romania Since World War II* (New York: Praeger, 1975)
Ionescu, Ghiţa, *Communism in Rumania, 1944–1962* (London and New

York: Oxford University Press, 1964)

Jowitt, Kenneth, *Revolutionary Breakthroughs and National Development: The Case of Romania, 1944–1965* (Berkeley, Cal.: University of California Press, 1971)

King, Robert R., *A History of the Romanian Communist Party* (Stanford, Cal.: Hoover Institution Press, 1980)

Nelson, Daniel N. (ed.), *Romania in the 1980s* (Boulder, Colo.: Westview Press, 1981)

—— 'Development and Participation in Communist Systems: The Case of Romania', in Donald E. Schulz and Jan S. Adams (eds.), *Political Participation in Communist Systems* (New York and Oxford: Pergamon Press, 1981), pp. 234–53.

15 Union of Soviet Socialist Republics

BASIC FEATURES

In its constitution of 7 October 1977,[1] which followed the 'Stalin Constitution' of December 1936, the Union of Soviet Socialist Republics (USSR) claims to be a 'socialist all-people's state' (article 1). With this a conception of state has found its way into the constitution which — deviating from the Marxist-Leninist view of the state as an instrument of rule by one class — can already be found in the Programme of the Communist Party of the Soviet Union (CPSU) of October 1961. It is based on the perception that Soviet society — its social groups (workers, collective farm peasants and intelligentsia) as well as the nationalities — forms 'a socio-political and ideological unity' (preamble of the constitution). State power is no longer vested only in 'the *working people* of town and country *as represented* by the Soviets of Working People's Deputies', as article 3 of the constitution of 1936 determined;[2] according to article 2 of the present constitution, it belongs to the *'people'* which exercises it *'through* the Soviets of People's Deputies' (my italics in both quoted articles). Accordingly, the CPSU as 'the leading and guiding force of Soviet society and the nucleus of its political system' (article 6) is no longer just 'the vanguard of the working people' (article 126 of the constitution of 1936) but 'the vanguard of the whole people' (preamble of the constitution of 1977).

Abandoning the utopian idea of the CPSU Programme that the Soviet Union is supposed to have already entered the stage of 'comprehensive construction of communism', the preamble of the constitution determines that state and society are in the stage of 'mature socialist social relationships' in which 'a new historical community of people — the Soviet people' has taken shape. The political system of this society is supposed to be marked by the 'effective administration of all public affairs', and the state is supposed to create 'the material and technical basis of communism'.

The USSR, which was founded on 30 December 1922, is formally a federal state. It consists of fifteen union republics, a number unchanged since 1956. In contrast to former provisions, the constitution takes into account the political reality that never allowed the republics real scope to pursue their own policies. The decline of the federal character of the Soviet Union is evident in its characterisation as 'a *unitary,* federal, multinational state' (article 70; my italics). Although each republic continues to retain the constitutional right to secede from the USSR freely, the exercise of this right is virtually excluded by the provision that the territory of the USSR 'is one and includes the territories of the union republics' (article 75). Like the Communist Party, the Soviet state is organised according to the principle of democratic centralism, which declares the decisions of the union organs to be binding on all lower organs; that is, also on the organs of the republics.

THE COMMUNIST TAKEOVER

The Marxist-Leninist party seized power in the so-called 'October-Revolution' of 1917. The party was the Bolshevik wing of the Russian Social Democratic Labour Party, founded in March 1898. Because of a basic disagreement over the nature of the party, it had split into two factions on its Second Congress in 1903, when Lenin's followers gained a majority and hence called themselves Bolsheviks ('the majoritarians') to distinguish themselves from the defeated Mensheviks (the 'minoritarians'). From the Bolshevik faction Lenin formed a party of professional revolutionaries, who, with the support of the Petrograd Soviet and the Red Guard, overthrew the Provisional Government on 7 November 1917 (25 October according to the Julian calendar used at that time in Russia). The Provisional Government was formed in March 1917 after Tsar Nicholas II had been forced to abdicate. Yet it, too, failed to change the course of the war in favour of Russia, to overcome the economic crisis and to prevent the increasing internal decline of Russia caused by the lack of a strong central power. Soviets of workers and soldiers were formed at first in Petrograd (later Leningrad) and Moscow, then also in other places, resulting in a kind of 'dual rule'. Lenin, having returned from Swiss exile to Petrograd in April 1917, made use of the Soviets' gain in strength and called for 'all power to the Soviets'. In fact, it was the Second All-Russian Congress of Soviets which convened in Petrograd on 7 November 1917 and by proclaiming the seizure of power in the name of the Soviets set the seal of legality on the Bolshevik *coup d'état*. It dismissed the Provisional Government of Alexander Kerenski, and the Council of People's Commissars under the chairmanship of Lenin took over the government. At the elections to the Constituent Assembly held three weeks later, however, the Bolsheviks polled only 25 per cent of the votes, whereas the other socialist parties polled about 63 per cent and the bourgeois parties 13 per cent. Ignoring the vote of the citizens for socialist not Bolshevik rule, Lenin dissolved by force the Constituent Assembly, which met on 18 January 1918.

In the following years the Bolsheviks, having changed the name of their party into Russian Communist Party (Bolsheviks) in March 1918, had to defend their power both inwardly and outwardly. In Brest-Litowsk they signed a separate peace treaty with the Central Powers. (This prompted the left-wing Socialist Revolutionaries to withdraw from the Council of People's Commissars, which they had entered in December 1917.) On the other hand, the Bolsheviks had to defend themselves against the invasion by Polish troops (May 1920), to repel military interventions of the Allied Powers (March 1918 until summer 1920) and to uphold their power in a civil war (spring 1918 until November 1920) against the followers of tsarism, bourgeois democrats, Socialist Revolutionaries and Social Democrats (Mensheviks). During and immediately after the civil war the Bolsheviks, with the help of local communists, also took over power in Belorussia, the Ukraine, Azerbaidzhan, Armenia and Georgia, parts of

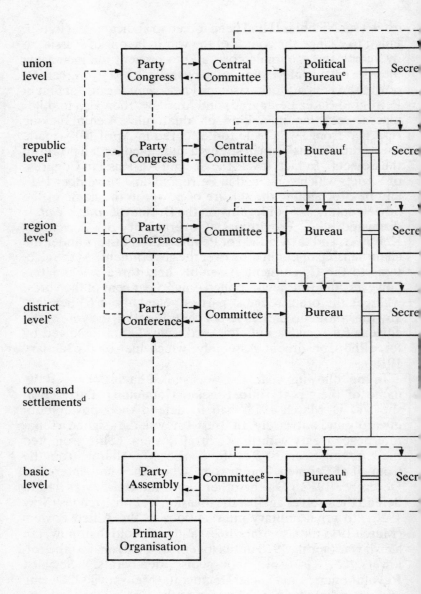

union
level

republic
level[a]

region
level[b]

district
level[c]

towns and
settlements[d]

basic
level

Figure 15:1 *The organisational structure of party and state in the USSR*

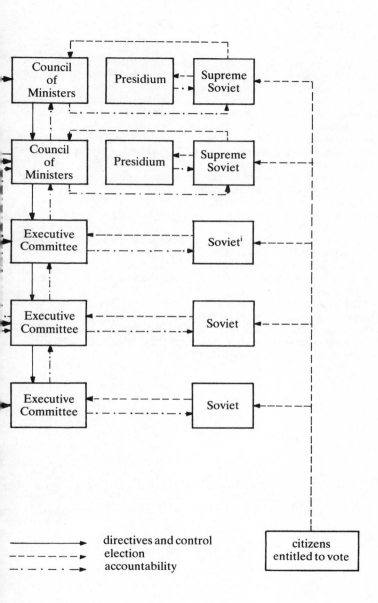

directives and control
election
accountability

citizens
entitled to vote

Notes to Figure 15.1

(a) Some union republics are directly subdivided into districts. The RSFSR has no Communist 'Party'; its party organisations are directly subordinate to the central CPSU apparatus.

(b) Regions, territories, autonomous republics; the capitals of the republics and the cities of Leningrad and Sevastopol; autonomous regions. (The autonomous regions in the RSFSR are situated within a territory and form there a further regional administrative tier; the same is true for the autonomous districts in the RSFSR which are a part of a region or a territory).

(c) Rural districts, large cities (directly under the republics or regions), city districts (of the capitals of the republics).

(d) In detail: small towns, city districts (of the cities at the district level), urban settlements (worker's settlements, housing schemes, health resorts) and rural settlements (villages). At this administrative level there are no party organisations corresponding to the Soviets, except in a part of the towns; in larger cities there are district party organisations which are subordinate to the city party organisations.

(e) As a rule the deciding party organ (Political Bureau or Bureau) is *de facto* formed by co-optation.

(f) In the Ukraine: Political Bureau.

(g) Only in large primary organisations.

(h) Very small primary organisations have no Bureau but only a Secretary.

(i) The autonomous republics have a Supreme Soviet with a Presidium; the executive organ is the Council of Ministers.

the former tsarist empire which had declared independence between November 1917 and May 1918. By suppressing the revolt of sailors and workers in Kronstadt (and Petrograd) in February and March 1921, the Bolsheviks finally consolidated power. The Mensheviks and Socialist Revolutionaries were prohibited.

At the Tenth Party Congress of March 1921 the Bolsheviks decided to prohibit factions too. This measure was directed particularly against the Democratic Centralists, who opposed the predominance of Lenin and advocated a co-operative party leadership. This step was likewise directed against the Workers' Opposition, which took up syndicalist ideas, and demanded the administration and control of factories by the producers organised in trade unions. In this respect the Workers' Opposition conflicted with Lenin, Stalin and Trotski, who wanted to use the trade unions as instruments of the party and the state. Trotski and his followers came to oppose Lenin as they called for rapid industrialisation at the expense of agriculture and, by disregarding the principles of the New Economic Policy, supported a rigorous policy against the peasantry. In 1922 Stalin became secretary general of the party and — apparently against Lenin's advice — was confirmed in this office after Lenin's death in 1924. Under his leadership all communists not supporting his political line, first the 'left' then the 'right' oppositionists, were systematically expelled from the party. In the second half of the 1930s they were for the most part liquidated physically.

At the Fourteenth Party Congress in 1925, after the foundation of the USSR, the Russian Communist Party (Bolsheviks) changed its name into All-Union Communist Party (Bolsheviks). The historical reference to the split in 1903 was not ommitted until the Nineteenth Party Congress in 1952, when the party was named the Communist Party of the Soviet Union.

THE MARXIST-LENINIST PARTY

The actual leading position of the CPSU in state and society is put in concrete terms in article 6 of the constitution to the effect that the party 'determines the general perspective for the development of the society and the course of the domestic and foreign policy of the USSR'. This provision implies the authority to issue binding directives to all state organs, and consequently the party's organisational structure at all levels but the lowest corresponds to the administrative structure of the state (Fig. 15:1).

Organs of the CPSU at the union level are the Party Congress and the Central Committee (CC), its Secretariat and the Political Bureau. Similar organs — Party Congress, CC, Secretariat and Bureau — can also be found in the Communist Parties of the union republics (with the exception of the RSFSR, which has no party organisation of its own). The republic parties, however, are not independent parties but merely territorial sub-organisations of the union party. The next level of the CPSU organisation is made up of the autonomous republics, the regions, the territories and the autonomous regions with their organs: Party Conference, Committee, Bureau and Secretariat. The same organs can be found on the lowest territorial level — in the districts, cities and city districts. The basis of the party pyramid is organised fundamentally according to the production principle. It consists of primary organisations in industrial enterprises, *sovkhozes* (state farms) and *kolkhozes* (agricultural co-operatives), offices and trading, educational, cultural and scientific institutions as well as in units of the armed forces. In addition, territorial primary organisations can be formed in villages and housing areas.

According to the Statute the supreme organ of the party is the Congress of the CPSU. It is supposed to be summoned every five years. The duties of the approximately 5,000 delegates actually amount to nothing more than (a) the formal election of the CC and the Central Auditing Commission (which controls the party's finances), (b) the approval by acclamation of decisions already made by the Political Bureau and Secretariat and presented to the Party Congress in the form of a report of the CC and (c) the passing of the Party Programme and Party Statute. Between Congresses the CC is formally the supreme party organ. The CC elected at the Twenty-Sixth Party Congress in February and March 1981 consists of 319 full members and 151 candidate members (who have no voting status). About 85 per cent of the CC full members are leading party, state and economic functionaries and high army officers. The CC, which convenes as a rule two or three times a year, elects the Political Bureau, the Secretariat and the secretary general of the CPSU as well as the Committee of Party Control (supreme disciplinary organ of the party).

The Political Bureau is the real policy-making organ of the CPSU and, due to the special relationship between party and state, is the real government of the USSR. It virtually regenerates itself by co-optation, and its composition often varies, which is also a sign of changing political preferences and reflects the distribution of power among the most influential personalities of the party, state, military and security apparatus. At present the Political Bureau consists of thirteen full members and five candidate members without voting status. Among the former are, apart from the secretary general of the CC (since March 1985 Mikhail Gorbachev), the chairman of the Council of Ministers of the USSR (Nikolay Tikhonov*), the chairman of the Presidium of the Supreme Soviet (Andrey Gromyko), the minister of foreign affairs (Eduard Shevarnadze), the chairman of the Committee for State Security (Russian abbrev.: KGB), the chairman of the Council of Ministers of the RSFSR, the first secretaries of two republic parties; the minister of defence is a candidate member.

The preparation and the control of the implementation of party decisions is the duty of the Secretariat of the CC, consisting of the secretary general and the secretaries, and is divided into departments. Apart from specifically party tasks, such as organisational work, propaganda and relations with the Communist Parties of the socialist countries, there are departments more or less corresponding to some governmental departments. The Secretariat is further responsible for the appointment of personnel to key positions in the party, state and economy, in the armed forces and social organisations according to the *nomenklatura* (see p.11). It has the supreme authority to issue directives to state organs, is responsible for the supervision of all party activity and controls the armed

---

* In September 1985 80 years old Tikhonov was replaced by Nikolay Ryshkov.

forces through the Main Political Administration of the Soviet Army and Navy.

The distribution of competences in the party organs of the union republics, autonomous republics, territories and regions and their interrelationship roughly corresponds with the regulations at the union level. The secretariats of the regional committees are particularly important among the organs which are responsible for the implementation of the central party resolutions and directives. They have the authority to issue directives to the party organs of the districts and cities and are responsible for their activities. These activities consist particularly of the establishment and supervision of the primary organisations.

A primary organisation is set up when there are at least three communists at a place of work or residence. The primary organisations are directly responsible for the implementation of party decisions in the enterprises and other places of work. They have the right and the duty to control the management in order to ensure its efficiency (which often causes friction). They are supposed to take measures in order to improve the work of the administrative apparatus and to report short-comings either of institutions or single persons to the higher party organs. It is likewise their duty to ensure the loyalty of communists to the party line and to urge them to obey the communist moral code. (This includes such virtues as devotion to the cause of communism and intolerance of its enemies; conscientious work for the benefit of society; maintenance and increase of social property; intolerance of infringements on social interests; honesty, love of truth and modesty in social and private life.) They are supposed to educate the mass of non-party citizens in the spirit of communism, to set a good example in fulfilling the production plans, to organise socialist emulation and to propagate the work and the goals of the party. With all this in mind, at least three communists form party groups at congresses, conferences and consultations of the social organisations to safeguard party influence. The 414,000 primary organisations and more than 618,000 party groups (in 1981)[3] form a tight network which guarantees that the party's will reaches every Soviet citizen.

The recruitment of members into the CPSU is effected by the primary organisations — until the age of twenty-three by the Leninist Communist Youth League (Komsomol). The minimum age is eighteen years. The applicant has to be recommended by at least three party members who have known him at work for at least one year, and they themselves must have been party members for at least five years. Full membership is preceded by a probationary year.

At the Twenty-Sixth Party Congress of February and March 1981 the CPSU had about 17.5 million members (candidates included) — approximately 10 per cent of the adult population. Of party members, 43.4 per cent were claimed to be workers, 12.8 per cent collective farm peasants and 43.8 per cent members of the intelligentsia (in the broader sense), state officials and members of the armed forces.[4] As compared with their share of the working population, the two first groups, particularly the peasants, are under-represented, the last, however, are heavily over-represented.

SOCIAL ORGANISATIONS

The claim of the CPSU to represent the interests of all Soviet citizens and its aim to create a communist society leave no room for other political parties. The constitutionally guaranteed fundamental right of the freedom of coalition merely permits the citizens to form — 'in accordance with the goals of communist construction' (article 51) — social organisations, of which the CPSU is the central core.

These organisations may be divided up into (1) professional associations, such as the trade unions and the associations of teachers, writers, journalists, composers and so on; (2) youth organisations, such as the Komsomol, to which Soviet citizens belong from the age of fourteen to twenty-eight, and the Pioneers' Union; (3) leisure organisations, among them the paramilitary Voluntary Association for the Promotion of the Army, Air Force and Navy (Russian abbrev.: DOSAAF), the Association of Societies for Friendship and Cultural Relations with Foreign Countries and the Association for the Spreading of Political and Scientific Knowledge. In addition, the

Soviets, consumer co-operatives, construction co-operatives, scientific-technical associations, and so on, are considered to be social organisations. The big professional group of collective farm peasants, however, is not organised.

It is the duty of social organisations to support CPSU policy and not to represent or force through the decision-making process policies favouring particular interests arising from profession, income or education. On the other hand, they are no longer, as in Stalin's times, merely 'transmission belts' for the execution of the party's will. They do in fact play a certain part in making decisions concerning economic, social and cultural policies, being guided of course by the common interest as bindingly defined by the CPSU. The trade unions participate in labour legislation through their leading organ, the Central Council. Although they do not have the right to free collective bargaining with the state as the sole employer, they are heard when wage categories and wages are fixed. And although they have to provide for the fulfilment if the production plans, the enterprise trade union committees can influence working conditions within the framework of collective agreements which they negotiate with the management. In addition, the social and, even if only limited, protective function of the trade unions is of some importance. They supervise the construction of houses and recreation centres, administer the social insurance fund and workers may only be dismissed with the consent of the enterprise trade union committee.

On the whole, the numerous mass and other social organisations provide abundant opportunities for participation in social affairs which, however, do not imply real political power.

DISSENT

The constitution does not permit the existence of associations which could challenge the monopoly of power of the CPSU and which operate outside party control. This also applies to associations which do not openly oppose the party and the state but whose members could merely criticise single aspects of the political and socio-economic system, articulate dissenting ideological and political views or be in conflict with the official political culture.

Among the critics of the regime, or 'dissidents', the following can be distinguished: citizens, who adhere to Marxism-Leninism but demand the democratisation of the single party; 'liberals', who advocate a multi-party system, free elections and the separation of powers; religious-nationalist protagonists, who strive for a non-communist authoritarian rule; groups of writers, who avoid censorship by circulating their works in the underground 'Chronicle of Current Events'; people who have tried to establish independent trade unions; and civil rights campaigners, who fight for respect for civil liberties such as the rights of freedom of conscience, opinion, speech, association and assembly. They refer to the Soviet constitution, to the International Covenant on Civil and Political Rights, which the Soviet Union has signed, and to the Catalogue of Principles of the 1975 Final Act of the Helsinki Conference on Security and Co-operation in Europe (CSCE), and they try to keep a record of the violations of the rights laid down in these documents. In addition, there are members of certain nationalities (Balts, Ukrainians, Georgians, Crimean Tatars, Germans) and of religious minorities (Jews, Baptists), who strive for national self-determination, freedom of religion, or emigration. All the dissident movements pursuing political aims and composed mainly of intellectuals are being systematically suppressed by prison or 'Gulag' sentences, admission to psychiatric clinics, deportation or expatriation, and are virtually crushed.

FEDERAL STRUCTURE AND NATIONALITIES

The federal structure takes into account the multinational structure of the population of the USSR — the census of 1979 itemises ninety-two nationalities.[5] The largest of them live in fifteen union republics: the Russian Soviet Federal Socialist Republic (RSFSR), the Ukrainian, the Belorussian, the Uzbek, the Kazakh, the Georgian, the Azerbaidzhan, the Lithuanian, the Moldavian, the Latvian, the Kirgiz, the Tadzhik, the Armenian, the Turkmen, and the Estonian

Soviet Socialist Republic.

In April 1917 Lenin and Stalin promised the non-Russian peoples resident on the territory of the tsarist empire self-determination, and they reasserted this right in their Declaration toward the peoples of Russia of November 1917. In the course of the takeover by communists orientated towards the Communist Party of Russia and by Soviets controlled by them, however, the right of self-determination was interpreted as a right (and a duty) to establish a socialist Soviet system according to the political and socio-economic pattern of the RSFSR. Federalism and the granting of cultural autonomy, the social revolution (from above), and the co-operation of the national élites, eliminating those who refused to co-operate, became the instruments for the integration of the numerous nationalities.

The constitutions of the union republics have basically to conform with the constitution of the USSR. Divergencies are limited to the settling of specific features of the republics; for example, the federal structure of the RSFSR. How insignificant the rights of the republics are is evident from the competences assigned to the Union. In the field of foreign and defence policy these are (1) the representation of the USSR in international relations, (2) the admission of new republics to the USSR, (3) questions of peace and war, (4) the organisation of defence and the direction of the armed forces of the USSR and (5) foreign trade (on the basis of the monopoly of the state). In the field of domestic affairs they are (1) the control over the observance of the constitution of the Union, (2) the ensuring of uniform legislation, (3) the establishment of general principles for the work of the republic and local governments, (4) the confirmation of boundary changes between the republics, (5) the ensuring of state security and (6) the establishment of general outlines of legislation in the fields of industrial law, legal proceedings and the administration of justice, and in civil, criminal and citizenship law. In the economic field they are (1) the drawing up of economic plans and of the state budget of the USSR, (2) the establishment of banks and industrial, constructive, agricultural as well as commercial enterprises directly subordinate to the central government, (3) the ensuring of a uniform monetary and credit system, (4) the determination of prices and wages policy and (5) the determination of guidelines for the utilisation and protection of national resources.

Although the constitution of the USSR declares the union republics to be sovereign states, they have no inalienable rights. The general clause that the Union may 'resolve other questions of all-union importance' (article 73) gives the federal organs the right to settle practically all affairs. A precisely outlined exclusive competence of legislation is not guaranteed to the republics. A union law has priority over a law of a republic. A uniform, compulsory production plan worked out by the State Planning Committee of the USSR does not leave the republics any scope for an economic policy of their own. Cultural autonomy is also limited, the Soviet Union having a uniform educational system. In all important spheres of state activity the organs of the republics are virtually organs executing centrally made decisions. Although the republics are represented in the Supreme Soviet of the USSR, in its Presidium as well as in the Council of Ministers of the USSR, and thus can participate in all-union decision-making, the compliance with their particular interests — if any — depends on the influence which their party leaders are willing and able to exert within the *de facto* supreme organs of the CPSU.

The right to have armed forces of their own as conceded to the union republics in the constitution of 1936, is now no longer conceded to them even formally. The right to the maintenance of foreign relations, which the former constitution had conceded to the republics with the evident intention of safeguarding more than one vote for the Soviet Union in the UN General Assembly, has been restricted. (This step has anyway been successful only with respect to the Ukrainian and Belorussian republics.) The organs of the Union not only establish the 'general procedure' for relations between the republics and foreign states and international organisations but also reserve to themselves the right of their 'co-ordination' (article 73).

Finally, the real status of the union republics must be judged by taking into account the centralist, strongly hierarchical organisation of the CPSU. Through its central organs, where Russians are predominant and to which the organs of the republic parties are subordinate, the CPSU directs the politics of the union republics. The deputy of the first secretary of the republic party organisation is usually a Russian who outweighs potential nationalist aspirations of republic party leaders.

For the smaller nationalities an autonomous status is provided. According to size they are organised in Autonomous Soviet Socialist Republics, autonomous regions and autonomous districts. In the twenty autonomous republics, sixteen of them being on the territory of the RSFSR, the autonomy of those people is supposed to be taken into account who, because of their location within a union republic or because of their small number, may not obtain the status of a union republic. (This refers, for instance, to the Bashkirs, the Kalmyks, the Kareliens, the Tartars, the Udmurts and the Yakuts.) The autonomous republics have constitutions of their own which in general have to be in conformity with the constitution of the USSR and the constitution of the respective union republic, but they do not retain a defined area for the execution of own state power. Their autonomy is limited to the preservation of national peculiarities in the cultural field. Thus their status does not differ essentially from that of the eight autonomous regions, of which five are on the territory of the RSFSR (for instance, the Jewish one) and one each in the Azerbaidzhan, Georgian and Tadzhik republics. The rights of the ten autonomous districts, situated entirely within the boundaries of the RSFSR, do not exceed the rights of the normal administrative units.

Federalism and cultural autonomy contrast conspicuously with the trends towards Russianisation through migration and linguistic assimilation. Although the migration of Russians to the Asian and Trans-Caucasian republics stopped in the 1960 and 1970s, it still continues to the Ukraine, Belorussia, Moldavia and the Baltic. Migration as well as generative behaviour resulted in an increase of the titular population in the five Asian and the three Trans-Caucasian republics and in a decline of the titular nations in the Ukraine, Belorussia, Moldavia and in two Baltic republics between 1959 and 1979 (Table 15:1). The proportion of non-Russians who consider their language as the native language dropped between 1959

Table 15:1   *The national structure of the Soviet union republics*

Union republic	1959			1979		
	Total (000s)	Titular nation (%)	Russians (%)	Total (000s)	Titular nation (%)	Russians (%)
RSFSR	117,534	83.3	83.3	137,410	82.6	82.6
Ukrainian SSR	41,869	76.8	16.9	49,609	73.6	21.1
Kazakh SSR	9,310	30.0	42.7	14,684	36.0	40.8
Uzbek SSR	8,106	62.2	13.5	15,389	68.7	10.8
Belorussian SSR	8,055	81.1	8.2	9,532	79.4	11.9
Georgian SSR	4,044	64.3	10.1	4,993	68.8	7.4
Azerbaidzhan SSR	3,698	67.5	13.6	6,027	78.1	7.9
Moldavian SSR	2,884	65.4	10.2	3,950	63.9	12.8
Lithuanian SSR	2,711	79.3	8.5	3,392	80.0	8.9
Latvian SSR	2,093	62.0	26.6	2,503	53.7	32.8
Kirgiz SSR	2,066	40.5	30.2	3,523	47.9	25.9
Tadzhik SSR	1,980	53.1	13.3	3,806	58.8	10.4
Armenian SSR	1,763	88.0	3.2	3,037	89.7	2.3
Turkmen SSR	1,516	60.9	17.3	2,765	68.4	12.6
Estonian SSR	1,197	74.6	20.1	1,465	64.7	27.9

Sources: *Itogi Vsesoyuznoy perepisi naseleniya 1959 goda,* svodnyy tom (Moscow, 1962), pp. 202–8; *Naselenie SSSR: Po dannym Vsesoyuznoy perepisi naseleniya 1979 goda* (Moscow, 1980), p. 27–30.

and 1979 from 87.6 per cent to 85.6 per cent; in 1979 16.3 million out of 124.7 million non-Russians regarded Russian as their native language.[6]

Since 1979 Russian lessons have been introduced in kindergartens, and at universities, colleges and technical colleges teaching must only be held in the Russian language. Furthermore, the language policy aims at turning Russian more and more into the official language and the language of the courts and at confining the language of the nationalities to the private sphere. This policy, however, meets with opposition. (Demonstrations brought it about that in their constitutions of 1978 the three Trans-Caucasian republics were able to declare the national language to be the official language.) Nationalist tendencies are counteracted by filling more and more leading positions in party, administration, industry, commerce and the educational system with the new, Russianised national élites. It is uncertain to what extent this produces unconditional loyalty to party and state and counteracts identification with the respective nationality. Developments at present seem to weaken this assumption, especially in Estonia and Lithuania. (In the latter republic opposition against Russianisation is combined with the defence of Catholicism.)

A special problem of the Soviet multinational state and the Soviet policy towards the nationalities (and religions) is presented by the estimated 30 million Muslims in Central Asia and in Azerbaidzhan. The over-average birth rates of the Asian (Islam) peoples reduced the proportion of Russians, who in 1979 amounted to only 52.4 per cent (1959: 54.6 per cent) of the whole population of 262.1 million, whereas the proportion of the Uzbeks, Tadzhiks, Kazakhs, Turkmenis and Kirgiz increased from 6.2 per cent in 1959 to 9.9 per cent in 1979. Although the Soviet Muslims came to terms with the socialist order by tracing socialism back to Mohammed's teachings, they continue to practice their traditional customs and are developing a strong consciousness of belonging to the community of all Muslims.

The 'comprehensive development and rapprochement' of the nationalities of the USSR (article 36 of the constitution) and their education in the spirit of Soviet patriotism obviously aim at their amalgamation as the ultimate goal of the CPSU. For the time being, however, the official propaganda seems to stress harmonious relations between the nationalities more than their amalgamation in order to avoid an increase of national tensions. Opposition against Russianisation is condemned as 'chauvinism, nationalism and nationalistic deviation',[7] and is suppressed by legal and administrative measures.

THE SYSTEM OF THE SOVIETS

At all levels of state organisation the Soviets of People's Deputies constitute a uniform system of state power and thus form its basic organisational and structural element. All other state organs are subordinate and accountable to them.

The right to nominate candidates for the election to the Soviets is reserved to the organisations of the CPSU, of the trade unions and of the Komsomol, to co-operatives and other social organisations, to the labour collectives in enterprises, institutions, *sovkhozes* and *kolkhozes* as well as to the units of the armed forces. Membership of the CPSU is not a prerequisite for nomination. Non-party candidates might owe their nomination to the reputation which they enjoy among the citizens because of their social function or their work. In any case, a candidate's devotion to the party goals and his reliability have to be beyond doubt. The citizens and the social organisations are entitled to question the candidates. Although the electoral law allows several candidates for one mandate, in practice only one candidate is put up. The elector only has the alternative of voting for the candidate or crossing out his name on the ballot paper. The deputies are elected by absolute majority of votes in one-man constituencies.

Elections are universal, direct and equal; voting is formally secret. The citizens who have reached the age of eighteen years have the right to vote and to be elected deputy, with the exception of the deputies for the Supreme Soviet of the USSR, who have to be twenty-one years of age. The election turnout is usually nearly 100 per cent. The very small number of those who abstain from voting as well as the overwhelming majority of votes cast for the single list of the 'bloc of communists and non-party people' — at the elections to the Supreme Soviet of the USSR, likewise almost 100 per cent — is considered to be a proof of full support for the party and the government by the population. Now and then the candidate in the elections to a local Soviet fails to receive the required majority of votes. Then a second ballot is necessary. Abstention from voting or a vote against a candidate does not necessarily signify disapproval of the political system but may merely express criticism of a certain candidate or of local misgovernment; a vote for a candidate might be motivated by a sense of patriotic duty and does not necessarily imply acceptance of the nominated candidate.

The Soviets of the People's Deputies 'directly and through organs created by them, control all branches of state, economic and socio-cultural construction, ensure their execution, adopt decisions and supervise their implementation' (article 93 of the constitution). The electors have the right to instruct their deputies, but these, in turn, are considered to be plenipotentiary representatives of the people and thus have to let themselves be guided by the 'general interests of the state' (article 103). The Soviets are required to consider the voters' mandates and to take them into account while formulating the economic plans and drawing up the budget, and to see to the implementation of the electors' mandates as far as these are not in conflict with broader interests. On the basis of the fundamental right to 'participate in the administration of state and public affairs' (article 48), the citizens are included in the activities of the Soviets, their standing commissions and other organs.

The deputies are obliged to inform the electors, the social organisations and the labour collectives which nominated them about their activity and may be recalled by a decision of the majority of the constituents, when they no longer enjoy their trust. The right of recall, however, has to be seen in the light of the leading role of the party, which decides not only on the nomination but also — which seldom happens — on the recall. The deputies have the right to address enquiries to state organs and officials; these are obliged to answer the enquiries at a session of the Soviet. Furthermore, the deputies themselves are entitled to address to all state and social organs, organisations, enterprises and institutions questions relevant to their scope of activity. The heads of the organs, and so on, are obliged to receive the deputies and to consider their proposals.

Compared with earlier regulations, the Soviets have gained at least a formal increase of functions and rights. Nevertheless, the Soviet system has little in common with the conception of councils which Karl Marx developed on the basis of the Paris Commune of 1871. Because the Soviets at all levels are directly elected — in contrast to the practice until 1936 — an essential feature of a council's democracy has been replaced by that of a parliamentary democracy. The imperative mandate, another characteristic of a council's democracy, is combined with the elements of a free mandate. The possibility of a collision of interests is obviously not contemplated either legally or practically, because particular interests are assumed to merge into the interests of the society as a whole, and because the deputies belong to the party which claims to represent these interests, or to the social organisations dependent on it. Thus the deputies are directly or indirectly subject to party discipline and the principle of democratic centralism. Moreover, the Soviets are not autonomous decision-making organs but, in view of the leading role of the CPSU in state and society, implement the decisions of the party organs at the same or a higher level of party organisation. This becomes clear, for example, from the fact that the sessions of the Supreme Soviet are usually preceded by sessions of the CC of the CPSU, which passes resolutions binding on the Supreme Soviet and are transformed into law by the Supreme Soviet.

CENTRAL GOVERNMENT

The highest organ of all-union state power is the Supreme Soviet of the USSR. It consists of two chambers with equal rights; the Soviet of the Union and the Soviet of Nationalities. The chambers, which have 750 members each, are simultaneously elected for five years. Whereas the deputies to the Soviet of the Union are elected in electoral districts with an equal number of inhabitants, the deputies to the Soviet of Nationalities are elected according to the following ratio: thirty-two from each union republic, eleven from each autonomous republic, five from each autonomous region and one from each autonomous district. Both chambers convene on the same date twice a year, together or separately.

The Supreme Soviet is empowered to decide all questions assigned to the jurisdiction of the Union by the constitution. It exercises the exclusive power of legislation; it may decide, however, that a law should be adopted by a referendum. Its chambers have the right to initiate legislation. (Other organs with the right to initiate legislation are the Presidium of the Supreme Soviet and the Council of Ministers of the USSR, the commissions of the Supreme Soviet and the standing commissions of its chambers, single deputies, the Supreme Soviets of the union republics, the Supreme Court of the USSR, the procurator general of the USSR, and the all-union organs of the social organisations.) Draft bills and 'other highly important questions of the life of the state' (article 114) may be submitted to the citizens for discussion by a decision of the Supreme Soviet or its Presidium. A good deal of legislative work is done by the standing commissions of the chambers of the Supreme Soviet, where, with the participation of outside experts, draft bills are discussed thoroughly, though for the most part not controversially. These commissions have gained substantial authority in the recent past.

A law is considered adopted if in each chamber a majority of the total number of deputies voted in favour of it. In case of disagreement between the chambers, the constitution provides for the formation of a conciliation commission on a parity basis. If both chambers at a joint meeting fail to reach an agreement on the proposal made by the conciliation commission, the Supreme Soviet may submit the question to a referendum. The provisions are quite academic, however, because since 1937 the chambers of the Supreme Soviet have adopted all decisions unanimously and concurrently, and because conduct deviating from this practice is unimaginable in view of the fact that the CPSU is the real source of legislative power. As the party claims to represent the will of all Soviet people, the bicameral structure of the Supreme Soviet can by no means serve to even out controversial views and to bring about a mutual correction of decisions.

Since the Supreme Soviet meets only twice a year for sessions lasting only two or three days, it is obvious that it needs a permanent organ to work on its behalf. The Supreme Soviet therefore elects in joint session a Presidium, consisting of thirty-nine members: the chairman; the first vice-chairman; fifteen vice-chairmen, who are in virtue of their office the chairmen of the Presidiums of the Supreme Soviets of the union republics; twenty-one (ordinary) members, and the secretary.

The Presidium of the Supreme Soviet of the USSR has original functions and functions which it exercises on behalf of the plenum of the Supreme Soviet. It is the collective head of state. Some duties of a president of the republic, however, such as the reception of heads of foreign states or the accrediting of ambassadors, are exercised by its chairman — since July 1985 the former minister of foreign affairs, Gromyko. (From 1977 until 1985 this office had concurrently been held by the secretaries general of the CPSU, Leonid Brezhnev, Yuriy Andropov and Konstantin Chernenko.)

Other original functions of the Presidium apart from the ceremonial ones are the formation of the Council of Defence, chaired by the secretary general of the CPSU and the appointment and replacement of the Supreme Command of the armed forces; furthermore the surveillance of the conformity of the constitutions and the laws of the union republics with the constitution and the laws of the USSR, as well as the interpretation of the laws of the union, which is a jurisdictional function; and in its legislative capacity the Presidium issues decrees. Among the functions which the Presidium exercises between the sessions of the Supreme Soviet are the amendment of legislative acts of the USSR 'when necessary' (article 122), the formation and abolition of ministries and state committees (at the proposal of the Council of Ministers of the USSR), and the appointment and dismissal of members of the Council of Ministers (on the recommendation of its chairman). These measures and decrees which the Presidium adopts, acting for the plenum of the Supreme Soviet, require the confirmation of the latter, although this may be only a formal act.

The Council of Ministers of the USSR is the supreme executive and administrative organ of the union. It is, formally, set up by the Supreme Soviet of the USSR; in practice the Supreme Soviet merely confirms by acclamation the decisions adopted in this respect by the Political Bureau and Secretariat of the CPSU. The Council of Ministers is, likewise formally, responsible and accountable to the Supreme Soviet and, between the sessions of this organ, to its Presidium. *De facto* the Council of Ministers exercises its functions in accordance with the party decisions, which are binding on it. Occasionally, it issues joint ordinances together with the CC of the CPSU.

The Council of Ministers is composed of the chairman (prime minister), one first vice-chairman and several vice-chairmen, the ministers, and chairmen of state committees and other central agencies; furthermore, the chairmen of the Councils of Ministers of the fifteen union republics are *ex officio* members of the Council of Ministers of the USSR. Altogether the executive branch of the government of the USSR has far more than a hundred members. In view of this, it is necessary that the chairman and the vice-chairmen of the Council of Ministers form the Presidium, a kind of 'inner cabinet', which acts as its permanent organ and, as such, coordinates the work of the departments and adopts decisions on the basis of the guidelines set by the supreme party organs. Apart from the classic departments, there are ministries for agriculture, health, culture, education and foreign trade, and ministries for the administration of the numerous industrial branches whose main task is to ensure the implementation of the production plans. Important state committees are: the State Planning Committee (Russian acronym: *Gosplan*), the Committee for Science and Technology, for Construction, for State Security, for People's Control, and so on.

There are two kinds of ministries; all-union and union-republic. The first exist only on the level of the USSR and direct an administrative branch throughout the whole union. The latter have counterparts in the union republics; they direct a branch of administration together with corresponding ministries in the republics, taking into account local conditions.

GOVERNMENT OF THE REPUBLICS

The union republics and autonomous republics also have Supreme Soviets with Presidia as permanent organs. These Supreme Soviets are again elected for a five-year term but consist of only one chamber. They exercise legislation in those fields which are not reserved to the Union or, in the case of the autonomous republics, to a union republic, and they set up Councils of Ministers, which implement the laws and other legislative acts of the USSR as well as of the union republics and of the autonomous republics. According to the principle of dual subordination, the union-republic ministries of the republics are subordinate to the corresponding union-republic ministries of the USSR, as well as to the Council of Ministers of the union republic. The directive authority of the central organ is decisive. On the other hand, the republic ministries, which can only be found in the republics, are subordinate only to the Council of Ministers of the union republic. The Council of Ministers of the USSR is empowered to suspend the implementation of decrees and ordinances of the Councils of Ministers of the union republics when the jurisdiction of the USSR is concerned. The Councils of Ministers of the union republics have the same right with respect to the execution of decrees and ordinances of the Councils of Ministers of the autonomous republics, and they can annul resolutions of the executive committees of the local Soviets.

REGIONAL AND LOCAL GOVERNMENT

Insofar as ethnic points of view do not determine the territorial-administrative structure, the large union republics are sub-divided into regions and territories. (The latter exist only in the RSFSR and differ from the first by the location of autonomous regions within their boundaries.) The next lower level is constituted by the (rural) districts into which the smaller republics, such as the Baltic ones, are directly subdivided, and by the larger cities and city districts. (The capitals of the union republics as well as the cities of Leningrad and Sevastopol, however, are directly subordinate to the central organs of the republic.) Below the district level are the small towns as well as the urban settlements and the villages (see Fig.15:1).

In these administrative units as well as in the autonomous regions and autonomous districts, state power is vested in the Soviets of People's Deputies. They are elected for only two and a half years, thus making a broad participation of the citizens in their affairs possible. The Soviets have, *inter alia,* the following rights and duties: they (1) decide on questions of regional and local importance taking into acount all-union interests, (2) implement the decisions of higher state organs, (3) ensure economic and social development within their territory, (4) confirm plans of economic and social development and the budget, (5) direct enterprises and institutions subordinate to them, (6) ensure observance of the laws by enterprises and institutions located on their territory but subordinate to higher organs, and co-ordinate and control the activities of these enterprises and institutions with respect to the utilisation of the labour force, the production of consumer goods, socio-cultural services and the protection of nature. Furthermore, they are responsible for the maintenance of public order and the protection of the rights of citizens. The regional and local Soviets participate in the discussion of, and may submit proposals in respect of, questions of republic and all-union importance which may take place in the ministries of the union republics.

Through permanent commissions, which are established by the Soviets and which usually meet once a month, citizens who are not members of the Soviets can also participate in local affairs. A further chance for (guided) citizen participation is the right of labour collectives to take part in the discussions on decisions concerning state and social questions.

The Soviets elect from among their deputies, executive committees as their administrative organs. Through their departments the committees implement laws and other legal acts of all-union and republic organs as well as decisions of the local Soviets. They have to report at least once a year to the

Soviets and to the meetings of the labour and housing-block collectives. According to the principle of dual subordination, they are responsible to the Soviet which has elected them and to the executive committee at the next higher level in the administrative hierarchy which is entitled to annul decisions of a lower executive committee.

The local organs, like the state organs at a broader administrative level, are ultimately controlled by the Communist Party or by its organs of the same level or by its higher organs (Fig. 15:1). Although the scope of local organ activity can only be judged in the light of the party's predominance, the increasing participation of the public in local government, even if only formal, may nevertheless provide for better consideration of the interests of the citizens.

ADMINISTRATION OF JUSTICE

At the top of the judicial system is the Supreme Court of the USSR. Its members (judges and lay judges), with the exception of the presidents of the Supreme Courts of the union republics who belong to it *ex officio,* are elected for five years by the Supreme Soviet of the USSR. Apart from its appellate function, its duty is to care for uniform jurisdiction by issuing interpretations of the law.

The Supreme Courts of the union republics and of the autonomous republics, the territorial and regional courts, as well as the courts of the autonomous regions, autonomous districts and large cities, are courts of first instance and appellate courts. The judges and lay judges at these courts are elected for five years by the corresponding Soviets. The lowest level is formed by the people's courts in the districts, cities and city districts. They consist of people's judges, who are elected by the citizens for a five-year term by secret ballot, and of lay judges who are elected for two and a half years by open ballot of the citizens at their place of work or residence. In civil and criminal proceedings representatives of social organisations may participate.

Judges and lay judges enjoy the same rights. The constitution guarantees their independence; virtually, however, this is restricted because both are responsible and accountable to their constituents or to the organs which elected them, and because they may be recalled, although this hardly happens and re-election is the rule. The main obstacle to a limited independent position of judges and lay judges, however, is the Communist Party's demand that jurisdiction has to observe the party line. Thus judges and lay judges are not subject exclusively to law as the constitution establishes, but also and predominantly to the will of the party, which is considered to be the expression of the real will of the people.

Outside the jurisdiction of the state, so-called comrades' courts exist in places of work, in villages and housing blocks, and are elected at a meeting of the collectives. They punish the violation of work discipline and 'socialist morals' (e.g. alcoholism and hooliganism) as well as minor criminal offences, by a mere verdict of guilty, warning, reprimand or fine. Furthermore, they are responsible for minor civil court cases. The hearings take place in the presence of the members of the collective and can be rather unpleasant for the persons involved. Against decisions of the comrades' courts a complaint can be lodged at the trade union's committee or at the executive committee of the local Soviet, but an appeal at a court of law is not possible. (Since 1965 meetings of inhabitants of villages, etc., are no longer entitled to exile citizens, regarded as 'parasites', for up to five years.)

As custodian of 'socialist legality' the procuracy controls the 'exact and uniform execution' (article 164) of the law by all executive and administrative organs, enterprises, *kolkhozes*, social organisations, officials and every citizen. It is entitled to take measures against unlawful decrees, thereby enjoying an extensive right of information. The procurators are responsible for the preliminary investigation, the preferment of charges and the supervision of places of confinement. In a criminal trial they can lodge an appeal against an acquittal or against an inadequate sentence but can also appeal against a final judgment or protest against a non-final decision when they consider the rights of the accused to have been violated. Furthermore, the procurators also participate in civil trials, in which they have the right to lodge an appeal.

At the top of the hierarchy of the Procuracy is the procurator general of the USSR, who is appointed for a five-year term by the Supreme Soviet of the USSR and is formally responsible and accountable to it or to the Presidium of the Supreme Soviet. He appoints the procurators of the union republics, autonomous republics, regions, territories and autonomous regions, and he confirms the appointment by the procurators of the union republics of the procurators of the autonomous districts, the districts as well as of the city procurators. All organs of the Procuracy are subordinate to the procurator general of the USSR. Yet ultimately their activity is bound to the party line.

The legal supervision of state organs, enterprises, and so on, through the courts and the Procuracy is completed by organs of People's Control, which are established by the Soviets at all levels of state administration, with the Committee of People's Control of the USSR at the top. These organs are supposed to check both the violation of discipline and bureaucratic excesses (as well as the fulfilment of economic plans).

Basic rights are guaranteed by the constitution with the reservation that their exercise may not 'injure the interests of society and the state or the rights of other citizens' (article 39). Furthermore, the exercise of fundamental rights is limited: by 'the needs of society' (e.g. the right to choose a profession, article 40); by the 'goals of communist construction' (e.g. the freedom of scientific and artistic creation, article 47; the right of coalition, article 51); by 'the interests of the people' and by 'the strengthening and development of the socialist system' (freedom of speech, of the press, of assembly and of meetings, article 50). This watering down of civil rights and liberties gives the authorities the option of declaring as unconstitutional any criticism of the Soviet state and social order, such as those voiced by Soviet dissidents. A further limitation of fundamental rights is possible by law. The guarantee of fundamental political and social rights is linked to the observance of fundamental obligations. Thus the Soviet citizen has not only the right but also the duty to work.

There is no (independent) constitutional and no adminstrative jurisdiction. Its existence would not comply with the principle of the unity of powers. The control of the observance of the constitution of the USSR, of the conformity of the constitutions and laws of the union republics with the constitution of the USSR as well as the interpretation of laws of the USSR falls within the competence of the Presidium of the Supreme Soviet of the USSR. The citizens, however, do enjoy a certain amount of protection from administrative acts because they can lodge a complaint to state organs against officials and file an objection at a law court against unlawful administrative acts of officials or against officials who have exceeded their authority. They can claim compensation for damage caused by unlawful acts of state organs, officials and social organisations.

SECURITY ORGANS

There are two institutions which are responsible for internal security: the KGB and the Ministry of the Interior. The KGB's duties are: external espionage and internal counter-espionage; the preliminary investigation of political crimes, such as treason, espionage, anti-Soviet agitation and propaganda, which are severely punished, and of certain economic crimes; the political control of the citizens through a close network of informers, and the protection of the frontiers by the border troops.

The Ministry of the Interior is in charge of the maintenance of public order. For this purpose it has at its disposal the internal security troops, which serve, for example, to suppress political unrest, and the milita (i.e. police). The militia is supported in the execution of its duties by millions of people's auxiliary policemen, who are active in industrial enterprises and residential areas. They are entitled to control identity cards and to hand over a real or alleged wrongdoer to the militia, but they may not detain a person.

FOREIGN POLICY

Soviet foreign policy is both programmatically and practically directed towards creating 'favourable international condi-

tions for the building of communism in the USSR' (article 28
of the constitution). The further tasks and aims of foreign policy which are functionally related to this primary goal are the
stengthening of world socialism, the support for 'struggles for
national liberation', universal disarmament and the pursuance of a policy of peaceful coexistence with capitalist
states.

Article 29 mentions the following as principles of action and
behaviour in Soviet international relations: the observance of
the sovereignty and the territorial integrity of states by abandoning the use of force, the threat of force and any interference in internal affairs; respect for human rights; the right
of peoples to decide their own destiny; co-operation between
states and the fulfilment of obligations arising for the USSR
from principles and norms of international law and international treaties. A further principle — valid for relations with
Communist Parties and socialist states — is that of proletarian-socialist internationalism. This principle supersedes the
above-mentioned rules of conduct, as the intervention in
Czechoslovakia in August 1968 and the so-called 'Brezhnev
Doctrine' justifying the invasion, demonstrate. According to
the 'Brezhnev Doctrine', the socialist states may execute the
rights of a sovereign state only in so far as they do not violate
the interests of the 'socialist community'. The right of self-
determination of these states is virtually replaced by the duty
to submit to the interests of the USSR and to copy the Soviet
model of socialism, slight deviations being possible.

The driving force of Soviet foreign policy are the world-
revolutionary impetus founded on Marxist-Leninist doctrine
and a nationalistic-missionary impetus based on the tradition
of the Russian great power policy. Both characterise, together
with considerations of strategy and security, a cumulative pattern of Soviet foreign policy aimed at territorial annexation,
the establishment of zones of supremacy or the creation of
spheres of influence. In this respect Soviet foreign policy is
essentially cautious. It orientates itself according to its own
means of power and those of its opponents. During the Berlin
Blockade of 1948 to 1949, the Korean War of 1950 to 1953,
and the Cuban Crisis of 1962, however, the Soviet Union
underestimated the will of defence of the USA and had to

reverse its actions, which had been aimed at altering the international balance of power in its favour.

The activities of Soviet foreign policy pursued according to
the above-mentioned principles and goals occasionally seem
to be contradictory. From the point of view of operational
leadership, however, they are interconnected tactical
approaches and serve a consistent strategic aim: the internal
and external consolidation and increase of the global power of
the USSR.

The ambivalence of Soviet foreign policy is evident in the
Soviet interpretation of the policy of détente and of the underlying principles of peaceful coexistence between East and
West, which were elevated to a maxim of Soviet foreign policy
towards the capitalist states by Krushchev at the Twentieth
Congress of the CPSU in 1956. On the one hand, the Soviet
Union seeks co-operation with the West in restricted fields;
on the other hand, it fights the West by exploiting every
opportunity to gain political and strategic advantages — such
as the destabilisation of Western regimes and NATO, or the
expansion (without risks) of the Soviet zone of influence into
the Third World by supporting 'struggles of national liberation', which according to the Soviets are 'just wars' and which
take place in a field of international relations to which the
principles of peaceful coexistence do not apply. The Soviet
conception of peaceful coexistence only applies to inter-state
relations and only implies the renunciation of the use of military power in East–West relations. Understood by the Soviets
as a form of class struggle at the international level, it does not
imply the renunciation of an ideological penetration of the
West or of support to radical leftists. On the other hand, to
influence the Soviet Union with liberal-democratic thought is
hardly possible, not only because of its isolation from external
ideas but also because any such effort would be denounced by
the Soviets as interference into their domestic affairs and a
violation of the principles of peaceful coexistence, since in
their view state and society cannot be separated.

The Soviet Union attained an important goal of its foreign
policy, the stabilisation of the territorial and political *status
quo* in Europe, as a result of the CSCE. Since then its foreign
policy has been directed towards (1) further political,

economic and military integration of the countries of the 'socialist community' within the framework of the CMEA and the WTO, (2) increased co-operation with Western industrial countries to relieve its own economic resources and to obtain advanced technology, (3) the continuation of its arms policy with which to guarantee, *inter alia*, an advantageous position in the negotiations on the reduction of troops in Europe and in the talks with the USA on the limitation of strategic arms, (4) the expansion of the Soviet sphere of influence by interventions in crisis areas.

Committed to proletarian internationalism, and taking advantage of opportunities to expand its sphere of influence the Soviet Union engaged itself not only in Cuba but also in Africa by giving military support to the 'progressive' governments of Angola and Ethiopia in their struggle against internal and external enemies. At the end of December 1979 it invaded Afghanistan in order to make the 'revolutionary process irreversible'.[8] It refuses to withdraw its troops, disregarding several resolutions of the UN General Assembly.

This intervention marked the end of the détente between the Soviet Union and the USA, which since the middle of the 1970s had already been under strain. The SALT II Treaty, aimed at a limitation of strategic weapons and signed in June 1979, did not come into force because the USA did not ratify it. The Soviets broke off negotiations on medium-range nuclear missiles in Europe, as well as on a reduction of strategic arms, when the USA began to deploy Pershing-2 missiles and cruise missiles in Western Europe after the Soviets had refused to dismantle their SS-20 missiles aimed at Western Europe and Asia. The declaration of martial law in Poland in December 1981, which the Reagan Administration has also ascribed to Soviet pressure, the (cautious) involvement of the Soviet Union in Central American affairs by granting economic and technical aid to the Sandinistas in Nicaragua and the massive Soviet economic and military assistance to Vietnam, further damaged Soviet–American relations. They had virtually reached a dead-lock in 1984. At the beginning of 1985 both sides, however, came to an agreement to resume talks on arms control (including space weapons) in Geneva, since the Soviets had dropped their precondition that the USA should first dismantle their medium-range weapons in Europe.

The Soviet Union has gained footholds in South and South-East Asia at the expense of its slowly improving relationship with China, whose rapprochement with the USA and Japan the Soviet Union regards as a policy of containment. On the other hand, China feels threatened by the Soviet medium-range missiles stationed West of the Ural Mountains, by the strong Soviet military presence at its borders with the Soviet Union and Mongolia, by the Soviet-backed Vietnamese policy towards Kampuchea and by the Soviet intervention in Afghanistan. Negotiations with the aim of improving mutual relations have produced only meagre results so far because Soviets refuse to comply with any Chinese demands.

NATIONAL DEFENCE

Soviet security and armament policy is guided by the claim to superiority over the West in order to ensure the Soviet Union's ability to survive in a possible war. This striving for military superiority might be explained by threat perceptions rooted in the beginnings of Bolshevik rule and the Second World War. It, however, is also intended to serve as a means of threat and pressure, in order to dictate, for instance, the conditions of détente, and to compensate for obvious economic inferiority compared with Western industrial states, which is detrimental to Soviet prestige.

The armament policy is therefore characterised by a steady and swift increase in the quantity and quality of its conventional and nuclear weapons, of its strategic arms and its maritime striking power. In 1984 the USSR maintained regular armed forces at a total of about 3,615,000, of which 885,000 belong to the (offensive and defensive) strategic nuclear forces, equipped with 981 submarine-launched missiles, 1,398 intercontinental missiles, and 596 intermediate-range/medium-range missiles (among them 378 SS-20); 1,840,000 belong to the army, 490,000 to the navy and 400,000 to the air force.[9] In addition, there are paramilitary forces: 225,000 KGB border troops, 300,000 security troops of the Ministry of the Interior and the Civil Defence, whose permanent staff amounts to 150,000; furthermore, there is the part-time military training organisation DOSAAF with about 80 million members, of whom some 5 million are instructors and activists.[10] About 565,000 Soviet troops are deployed in WTO countries (380,000 in the GDR, 80,000 in Czechoslovakia, 65,000 in Hungary, 40,000 in Poland); 115,000 in Afghanistan and 75,000 in Mongolia.[11] Western estimates of defence expenditure range from 10 to 20 per cent of the GNP.[12]

NOTES

1. English text in William B. Simons (ed.), *The Constitutions of the Communist World* (Alphen aan den Rijn, The Netherlands, and Germantown, Md., 1980), pp. 352–92.
2. English text in Jan F. Triska (ed.), *Constitutions of the Communist Party States* (Stanford, Cal., 1968), pp. 37–76.
3. Report of the Central Committee to the Twenty-Sixth Congress of the CPSU, *Pravda* (Moscow), 24 February 1981.
4. *Ibid.* In 1983 the CPSU claimed 18.3 million members — see Richard F. Staar (ed.), *Yearbook on International Communist Affairs 1984: Parties and Revolutionary Movements* (Stanford, Cal., 1984), p. 372.
5. *Naselenie SSSR: Po dannym Vsesoyuznoy perepisi naseleniya 1979 goda* (Moscow, 1980), pp. 23-6.
6. For this and the following demographic data, see *Naselenie SSSR, op. cit.*, pp. 23, 27; *Itogi Vsesoyuznoy perepisi naseleniya 1959 goda*, svodnyy tom (Moscow, 1962), p. 184.
7. Report of the Central Committee, *op. cit.*
8. Leonid Brezhnev, *Pravda* (Moscow), 16 October 1980.
9. The International Institute for Strategic Studies, London, *The Military Balance 1984–1985* (Oxford, 1984), pp. 17–21.
10. *Ibid.* p. 22.
11. *Ibid.* pp. 19, 22.
12. *Ibid.* p. 15.

FURTHER READING

Adomeit, Hannes, *Soviet Risk-Taking and Crisis Behaviour: A Theoretical and Empirical Analysis* (London and Boston: Allen and Unwin, 1982)
Armstrong, John A., *Ideology, Politics, and the Government in the Soviet Union*, 3rd edn. (London: Nelson, 1974)

The Political Systems of the Socialist States

Barghoorn, Frederick C., *Politics in the USSR*, 2nd edn. (Boston and Toronto: Little, Brown, 1972)

Bialer, Seweryn, *Stalin's Successors: Leadership, Stability, and Change in the Soviet Union* (New York: Cambridge University Press, 1980)

—— (ed.), *The Domestic Context of Soviet Foreign Policy* (Boulder, Colo.: Westview Press, 1980)

Brown, Archie H., *Soviet Politics and Political Science* (London: Macmillan, 1974)

Byrnes, Robert F. (ed.), *After Brezhnev: Sources of Soviet Conduct in the 1980s* (Bloomington, Ind.: Indiana University Press, 1983)

Carrère d'Encausse, Hélène, *Decline of an Empire: The Soviet Socialist Republics in Revolt* (New York: Newsweek Books, 1979)

Cocks, Paul *et al.* (eds.), *The Dynamics of Soviet Politics* (Cambridge, Mass.: Harvard University Press, 1976)

Feldbrugge, Ferdinand J.M. (ed.), *The Constitutions of the USSR and the Union Republics: Analysis, Texts, Reports* (Alphen aan den Rijn, The Netherlands, and Germantown, Md.: Sijthoff and Nordhoff, 1979)

Feuchtwanger, E.J. and Peter Nailor (eds.), *The Soviet Union and the Third World* (London: Macmillan, 1981)

Friedgut, Theodore H., *Political Participation in the USSR* (Princeton, NJ: Princeton University Press, 1979)

Griffith, William E. (ed.), *The Soviet Empire: Expansion and Détente* (Lexington, Mass.: Lexington Books, 1976)

Harasymiw, Bohdan, *Political Elite Recruitment in the Soviet Union* (London: Macmillan, 1984)

Hill, Ronald J. and Peter Frank, *The Soviet Communist Party*, 2nd edn. (London: Allen and Unwin, 1983)

Hough, Jerry F., *The Soviet Prefects: The Local Party Organs in Industrial Decision-Making* (Cambridge, Mass.: Harvard University Press, 1969)

—— *Soviet Leadership in Transition* (Washington, DC: Brookings Institution, 1980)

—— and Merle Fainsod, *How the Soviet Union is Governed* (Cambridge, Mass.: Harvard University Press, 1979)

Jacobs, Everett M. (ed.), *Soviet Local Politics and Government* (London and Boston: Allen and Unwin, 1983)

Jones, Christopher D., *Soviet Influence in Eastern Europe: Political Autonomy and the Warsaw Pact* (Brooklyn, NY: Praeger, 1981)

Lane, David S., *Politics and Society in the USSR*, 2nd edn., (New York: New York University Press, 1978)

Little, D. Richard, 'Bureaucracy and Participation in the Soviet Union', in Donald E. Schulz and Jan S. Adams (eds.), *Political Participation in Communist Systems* (New York and Oxford: Pergamon Press, 1981), pp. 79–107.

Löwenhardt, John, *Decision-Making in Soviet Politics* (London: Macmillan, 1981)

Meyer, Alfred G., *The Soviet Political System: An Interpretation* (New York: Random House, 1965)

Moreton, Edwina and Gerald Segal (eds.), *Soviet Strategy toward Western Europe* (London and Boston: Allen and Unwin, 1984)
Nove, Alec, *Stalinism and After* (London: Allen and Unwin, 1975)
—— *The Soviet Economic System*, 2nd edn. (London: Allen and Unwin, 1980)
Rigby, Thomas H., *et al.* (eds.), *Authority, Power and Policy in the USSR* (London: Macmillan, 1980)
Schapiro, Leonard, *The Communist Party of the Soviet Union*, 2nd edn. (London: Eyre and Spottiswoode, 1970)
Skilling, H. Gordon and Franklyn Griffiths (eds.), *Interest Groups in Soviet Politics* (Princeton, NJ: Princeton University Press, 1971)
Tökés, Rudolf L. (ed.), *Dissent in the USSR* (Baltimore, Md.: Johns Hopkins University Press, 1975)
Topornin, Boris N., *The New Constitution of the USSR* (Moscow: Progress Publishers, 1980)
Triska, Jan F. and David D. Finley, *Soviet Foreign Policy* (London: Collier-Macmillan, 1968)
Ulam, Adam B., *Expansion and Coexistence: The History of Soviet Foreign Policy, 1917–67* (New York: Praeger, 1968)
White, Stephen, *Political Culture and Soviet Politics* (London: Macmillan, 1979)

16 Socialist Republic of Vietnam

BASIC FEATURES

The Socialist Republic of Vietnam (SRV) was founded on 2
July 1976 by the merger of the Democratic Republic of Vietnam (DRV), or North Vietnam with South Vietnam. The
continuity of the DRV and SRV are symbolised by the adoption of the national flag and the national anthem of the DRV.
After the unification of the country the constitution of the
DRV of 1 January 1960 remained temporarily in force until
the National Assembly adopted a new constitution on 18
December 1980.[1]

The SRV claims to be a socialist state within the world
socialist community. Socialism is to be built up directly from a
society in which small-scale production predominates, bypassing capitalism. The constitution, according to the preamble, is a 'constitution of the period of transition to socialism on
a national scale'; this reflects the fact that overall socialisation
of the means of production, particularly the collectivisation of
the peasants, has not yet been realised in the southern part of
Vietnam. There was, however, also a substantial non-public
industrial sector in 1980.

By exercising the dictatorship of the proletariat, whose elements are leadership by the party, mastery by the working
people and management of public affairs by the state,[2] Vietnam carries out 'three revolutions: in the relations of production, in science and technology, and in ideology and culture'
(article 2 of the constitution). The 'worker–peasant alliance'
forms 'the core' of the working people, composed of the working class, co-operative peasants and 'the socialist intellectual

stratum' (article 3). In article 4 the Communist Party of Vietnam (CPV) is referred to as the 'vanguard and general staff' of the working class and 'the only force leading the state and society'. It claims to represent the interest of the whole people. Vietnamese society is to be developed on the basis of Marxism-Leninism (article 38), and the state organs work according to the principle of democratic centralism.

THE COMMUNIST TAKEOVER

The takeover by the Vietnamese communists in the north of the country was the product of a liberation struggle against the Japanese, who in 1941 occupied Vietnam, and against French colonial rule. In the south the communists seized power, emerging victorious in the war against the armed forces of the Republic of Vietnam (ROV) and the USA.

The CPV was founded by Ho Chi Minh in Hong Kong in February 1930, but since October of that year it had been called the Indo-Chinese Communist Party (ICP) in view of the task of carrying through the liberation of, and the socialist revolution in, the whole of Indo-China (Vietnam, Laos and Cambodia). In May 1941 the ICP decided to set aside the class struggle and to fight 'imperialism', relying on the League for the Independence of Vietnam (the Viet Minh), which consisted of several patriotic groups and was led by it. In June 1945, after the French colonial administration had been dissolved by the Japanese, the Viet Minh proclaimed six provinces as a 'liberated zone'. At the end of August 1945, after Japan's capitulation, Ho Chin Minh, with the participation of non-communists, formed a provisional government in Hanoi and proclaimed the independent Democratic Republic of Vietnam on 2 September 1945.

At the Potsdam Conference of July and August 1945 Indochina was divided into a Chinese and a British zone of occupation. In order to get along with the Chinese, Ho Chin Minh admitted into his government representatives of the nationalist Revolutionary League, which was protected by the Guomindang. In November 1945 the ICP was, formally, dissolved; in fact it went underground. In September 1945

French troops replaced the English in South Vietnam and six months later they also moved into North Vietnam according to an agreement between the DRV and France, in which the DRV was recognised as a 'free state' within the French Union. After the retreat of the Chinese, the non-communist parties were purged or forced into line with the Viet Minh, and all opposition was suppressed. On 8 November 1946 the National Assembly, elected in January 1946 from a unity list, adopted a constitution, the preamble of which provided for 'the transformation of the country on a democratic basis'.

An attack on French ships in the harbour of Haiphong in November 1946, retaliatory actions by the French and subsequent attacks by Vietnamese troops against French garrisons unleashed the First Indo-China War. In its course the communists, whose party was renamed the Vietnam Worker's Party in March 1951, employing the Chinese strategy of guerrilla warfare, defeated the French in the decisive battle of Dien Bien Phu in May 1954. In July 1954, at the Geneva Conference on Indo-China an armistice and a demarcation line along the seventeenth parallel were agreed upon, behind which the French and the DRV troops were to retreat. In time, however, the demarcation line, considered provisional, became a state border between the DRV and the ROV (proclaimed in October 1955). The all-Vietnamese elections, which according to the Geneva Agreements were scheduled for July 1956, did not take place because of the refusal of the South Vietnamese government. On 31 December 1959 the DRV adopted a new constitution, in which it declared itself to be a 'people's democracy, advancing step by step to socialism'.[3]

After the North Vietnamese communists had decided to wage an armed struggle in the South in 1959, the (communist) Viet Cong intensified guerrilla activities and founded the National Liberation Front (NLF) in December 1960 to rally also the non-communist opposition against the ROV government. The DRV supported them at first by propaganda, advisers and arms, and later also by regular troops against the armed forces of the ROV and the USA, which engaged themselves increasingly from 1960. This brought about the Second Indo-China War. After the armistice agreement signed in

Paris in January 1973 and the withdrawal of the US troops, the Viet Cong and the troops of the DRV succeeded in gaining control over the South Vietnamese territory. On 30 April 1975 the ROV government surrendered. Power formally passed to the Provisional Government of the NLF, already established in June 1969. Power was actually assumed by party and administrative cadres from the DRV, a fact which, however, was also due to the lack of NLF cadres, decimated during the war. In November 1975 delegates from North and South Vietnam met in Ho Chi Minh City (the former Saigon) to decide on the unification and on the election of an all-Vietnamese National Assembly, which took place in April 1976.

THE MARXIST-LENINIST PARTY

The organisation of the Vietnamese communists, which in December 1976 adopted its initial name Communist Party of Vietnam, claimed a membership of about 1.7 million in 1982.[4] This corresponds to a share in the population of only 3 per cent.

Party membership is open to any citizen who has reached the age of eighteen, has worked and has not exploited other people. Youths, as a rule, must already be members of the Communist Youth League before being admitted to the party. Admission is effected through the party branch, which is the basic party organisation, and needs the recommendation of two party members. Full membership may be attained after a probationary period, which is one year for workers who have been directly engaged in the production for at least five years and for persons who have carried out professional activities for five years or more in the party and state apparatus, the mass organisations or the armed forces. For persons who do not comply with this precondition and for members of other social strata or professions the probationary period is eighteen months. Primary organisations are established in enterprises, co-operatives, villages, wards and basic units of the Vietnam People's Army. Above the basic level the party structure corresponds with the administrative division of the state.

The central organs of the CPV are: the National Congress of Delegates, which must convene once every five years; the Central Committee (CC), to which the Fifth Congress of March 1982 elected 152 members; the Political Bureau, and the Secretariat of the CC with the secretary general at the top, elected by the CC. Among the fifteen members of the Political Bureau, formed in 1982, are the secretary general, Le Duan, the chairman of the Council of State, Truong Chinh, the premier, Pham Van Dong, the ministers of interior, defence, foreign affairs (the latter as alternate member) and the chairman of the Planning Commission. Whereas the Political Bureau leads the party's activities and *de facto* also the state activities, the Secretariat directs the work of all party organisations and sees to the implementation of the resolutions of the CC and the Political Bureau. The top leadership demonstrates unity, but there are groupings within the party, which have different views concerning the pace and depth of the socialist revolution, especially with regard to the collectivisation of agriculture in the south.

The relationship of the Vietnamese communists with the CPSU, in view of a strong tendency to an ideological orientation towards the Chinese communists, was not without problems in the mid-1950s and the first half of the 1960s. During the following years they held a neutral position in the Soviet–Chinese dispute, thus ensuring the support of both opponents in their struggle against South Vietnam and the USA. Since 1975, however, the CPV has unequivocally adopted the political and ideological line of the CPSU. At the Fourth Party Congress of December 1976 CC members having ties with the Chinese communists were not re-elected.

BLOC PARTIES AND SOCIAL ORGANISATIONS

From the days of the liberation struggle against the Japanese and the French, when the communists sought the support of other political forces in order to establish and consolidate their rule, there have been two minor parties: the Democratic Party (Dang Dan Chu), founded in June 1944, and the

Socialist Party (Dang Xa Hoi), founded in July 1946. They serve as a melting pot for elements of the population whose attitude towards the communists has been reserved. The Democratic Party has orientated itself particularly towards traders, and the Socialist Party towards members of the intelligentsia. Both parties cannot and do not compete with the CPV or oppose it but recognise unconditionally its absolute rule. Their task is to ensure the loyalty of their followers towards the state and to mobilise them for the building of socialism.

Major social organisations (mass organisations) are the Vietnam Confederation of Trade Unions, the Vietnam Association of Collective Peasants, the Ho Chi Minh Communist Youth League, and the Vietnam Women's League. Furthermore there are several professional associations and the organisations of religious communities (Catholics, Buddhists). The social organisations' principal function is to form transmission belts for the decisions of the CPV. They are also agencies for the control of the citizens, the implementation of socialist values (particularly in the southern part) and the motivation of the citizens (who display widespread apathy) for the goals of the party. The trade unions, which are organised according to the territorial and branch principles, promote emulation campaigns and mobilise the workers for the implementation of the production plans. But they are also entrusted with the professional education of the workers, the improvement of work conditions and with tasks in the field of social welfare. The Women's League is engaged not only in the political mobilisation of women but plays an important role in securing equal rights for women in economic, social and family life by fighting still-existing barriers. The Vietnamese Buddhists' Association serves the regime by proclaiming the unity of religion, nation and socialism. (Not a few Buddhists, however, who refused to compromise with the communists, were imprisoned or confined to re-education camps.)

Political parties and social organisations are united in the Vietnam Fatherland Front, which is under the guidance of the CPV. It was founded in 1955 and succeeded the Lien Viet, which had in turn grown out of the Viet Minh as an association of anti-French non-communist political groupings. In 1976 the Fatherland Front merged with the NLF and its mass organisation, the Alliance of National, Democratic and Peace Forces. Its main task is to promote patriotism and national unity, and to motivate people to build socialism.

The political parties and the four mass organisations have the right to submit draft laws to the National Assembly. The president of the Confederation of Trade Unions has the right to attend, and leading representatives of other mass organisations and the president of the Central Committee of the Fatherland Front may be invited to attend the meetings of the Council of Government. These concessions provide the organisations with the possibility of initiating legislation which is in the interest of their affiliates, and of being at least consulted, when the state decision-making refers to matters concerning them.

ETHNIC MINORITIES

Among the approximately 57 million inhabitants there are about 7 million members of 50 or so officially recognised ethnic minorities (such as the Tay, Khmer, Muong, Nung, Meo, Tho). In the 1950s Autonomous Zones had been established for some of them and the DRV constitution of 1960 provided for the creation of further zones. In 1975, however, they were abolished. One major reason for the change in policy towards the minorities was the fact that many of them live near the Vietnamese–Chinese border, which has become a sensitive area since the outbreak of a conflict between both states. A further problem was presented by the more than 1 million strong Chinese (Hoa) minority, of which a great part has been living in South Vietnam and engaged in commercial activities. Affected by the abolition of large-scale trade and accused of being a 'fifth column', reportedly some hundred thousands emigrated in 1978-79. Some minorities have joined together in resistance movements.

The constitution grants the minorities the right to use their languages and to maintain their customs, and the state has accepted the responsibility of eliminating inequalities in the levels of economic development between the nationalities. The government has embarked on a course of developing the mountainous areas, inhabited by minorities, by exploiting the resources there. The formation of large production schemes, however, destroys the traditional way of life of the Montagnards, and the moving of lowland Vietnamese into these areas has already considerably decreased the proportion of the minorities in the local population. The Council of Nationalities, elected by the National Assembly, is supposed to support the National Assembly and the Council of State in supervising the local authorities that they implement policies concerning the minorities.

CENTRAL GOVERNMENT

The National Assembly is the highest representative body and, as in other socialist states, is declared to be the supreme state organ, vested with extensive constitutional and legislative authority. It (formally) decides on fundamental questions of domestic and foreign policy, on the objectives for economic and cultural development, and on matters of war and peace; it adopts the economic plan and the state budget; it elects and removes from office the chairman and members of the Council of State and the Council of Government. The National Assembly may decide on the delegation of certain duties of state organs to social organisations for execution. The examination of draft laws is entrusted to standing committees.

The National Assembly is elected for a five year term from a unity list of the Fatherland Front. The number of candidates, whose selection and nomination is strictly supervised by the CPV, exceeds the number of seats. At the elections of April 1981 there were 614 candidates for 496 mandates in 93 constituencies. Any citizen who has reached the age of eighteen has the right to vote, and any person of twenty-one or older may be elected deputy. The deputies are obliged to maintain close contact with their electors, report to them about their activities and those of the National Assembly, answer requests and petitions and submit themselves to the supervision of the electors.

The National Assembly convenes only twice a year. This fact alone makes the Council of State a much more important state organ. The constitution (article 98) defines it as 'the highest continuously functioning body' of the National Assembly. It decides on important matters concerning the building of socialism and national defence, albeit formally in view of the powers of the Political Bureau; supervises the implementation of legal norms, and activities of the state apparatus; interprets the constitutions, laws and (its own) decrees. It is entitled to suspend the orders of the Council of Government which contravene higher norms; to revise or rescind inappropriate decisions of people's councils at the province level, and dissolve these bodies, when it considers that their activity is seriously detrimental to the interests of the people; to ratify or abrogate international treaties, except when it is deemed necessary to refer the matter to the National Assembly. Apart from these original powers, the Council of State acts for the National Assembly when this body is not in session; for instance, by appointing and dismissing the vice-chairmen of the Council of Government and ministers. Such decisions, however, need the later approval of the National Assembly.

Furthermore, the Council of State is the collective Presidency of the SRV; through its chairman it represents the state in domestic and foreign affairs. The chairman is commander-in-chief of the armed forces and presides over the National Defence Council. By the assignment of all these functions to the Council of State, this body has practically assumed the functions of the Standing Committee of the National Assembly and the president of the republic under the 1960 constitution.

The Council of Government consists of the chairman, vice-chairmen, the minister-secretary general, ministers and chairmen of state committees (such as for planning, prices, and science and technology). In view of the numerous specialised ministries for the administration of economic branches, the Council of Government has about forty members. It has the overall jurisdiction for the unified management of the political, economic, cultural, social, security, national defence and external activities of the SRV, ensuring herewith the building of socialism in all fields. With this aim it exercises control over the activities of the local representative and executive organs; it ensures that the people's councils at all levels discharge their tasks; it is entitled to suspend the execution of inappropriate decisions of the people's councils directly under central authority and to suspend the execution of, or revise or rescind, inappropriate decisions of the people's committees at all levels. The chairman has a dominant position insofar as he not only heads the work of the Council and supervises the implementation of decisions of the National Assembly, the Council of State and the Council of Government but also directs the work of the ministries and other central administrative bodies as well as of the local administrative organs.

LOCAL GOVERNMENT

Below the national level the SRV administrative structure consists of three tiers: (1) thirty-six provinces, municipalities directly under the central authority (Hanoi, Haiphong and Ho Chi Minh City) and corresponding units (special zones); (2) the (rural) districts, capitals of the provinces, and other towns and districts or precincts and townships of the municipalities under the central government; (3) villages and urban sub-districts. Apart from the administrative units, there are at the basic level the *Xa*, which unite several villages into agricultural production co-operatives. Below the lowest level of state administration, in small villages and wards, operate 'self-organisations of the masses'.

Organs of local state authority are the people's councils, elected by the citizens for a term of four years at the province level and for a term of two years at the other levels. The number of candidates must exceed the number of mandates allocated to a constituency; if candidates poll an equal number of votes, the elder ones are considered elected. Elections take place with the active co-operation of the Fatherland Front and the mass organisations.

The people's councils are in charge of carrying through the 'three revolutions' at the local level on the grounds of directives issued by the higher authorities. Of importance is also their duty to ensure the building up of national defence units and to protect socialist property. The people's councils are responsible not only to their electors but also to higher authorities. They operate under a strictly hierarchical regime. A people's council is entitled to dissolve the people's council at a lower level when the latter 'seriously harms the interests of the people' (article 115, clause 11 of the constitution). Resolutions concerning the dissolution must be approved by the people's council at a higher level or, when the dissolution is decided upon by the people's council at the province level, by the Council of State.

The people's councils elect people's committees, which are their executive organs and local organs of state administration. The committees are responsible for the fulfilment of the plans for economic development, and matters of national defence and security, for which they establish special organs, and they are obliged to deal with complaints and petitions of the citizens. According to the principle of dual subordination, a people's committee is responsible and accountable to the people's council which has elected it, and to the people's committee at the higher administrative level. There is also a hierarchical relationship between the people's committees and between them and the people's councils. Committees at a higher level are empowered to suspend the execution of, or revise or rescind, inappropriate decisions of lower level committees, and they have the right to suspend the implementation of inappropriate decisions of people's councils at a lower level and to request people's councils at the same level to revise or rescind such decisions of a lower people's council.

ADMINISTRATION OF JUSTICE

The judicial system consists of the Supreme People's Court, the people's courts of the provinces, districts and villages, and the military tribunals. Moreover, there are organs of social jurisdiction at the grass-roots level which deal with minor cases and disputes among citizens. The Chief Justice of the Supreme Court is elected by the National Assembly, and his deputies, the judges and the people's accessors are elected by the Council of State; judges and accessors of the local courts are elected by the people's councils. The term of office of the judges corresponds to that of the representative bodies; the term of office of the accessors at the Supreme People's Court is two and a half years, and that of the accessors at the local courts is two years. Judges and people's accessors have equal rights. The courts are responsible and accountable for their activities to the organs which have elected them and which are also entitled to remove judges and accessors from office, a fact which underlines the unity of state power vested in the representative bodies.

The constitution guarantees the citizens civil rights and liberties. But it assumes that there is an identity of interests between the state, the collective and the individual, and does not provide for independent constitutional or administrative jurisdiction for the protection of the citizens' rights. People who consider their rights to have been violated by an unlawful act of a state organ, social organisation, a people's armed forces unit or an individual official may merely lodge a complaint with a state authority and claim redress. The supervision of the observance of the law by state organs, organisations and citizens and the prosecution of criminal offences is entrusted to the Supreme Organ of People's Control, led by the procurator general, and the local organs of people's control. Any action prejudicial to the cause of socialist revolution and the building of socialism is severely punished. A widely employed penalty is confinement to a 're-education camp'.

FOREIGN POLICY

The main fields and goals of Vietnam's foreign policy as prescribed in the constitution are the strengthening of 'fraternal friendship, militant solidarity, and co-operation in all fields' with the Soviet Union, Laos, Kampuchea and other socialist countries 'on the basis of Marxism-Leninism and proletarian internationalism', and the struggle 'against imperialism, colonialism, hegemonism, and apartheid, and for peace, national independence, democracy, and socialism' (article 14).

After the capitulation of South Vietnam the DRV/SRV renounced the balanced policy between the USSR and the PRC and sought the unilateral support of the Soviets. This political course served the interests of both states: the intention of Vietnam to extend its domination to Kampuchea and Laos; that of the USSR to strengthen Vietnam in order to utilise the centuries-old animosity between Vietnamese and Chinese for the Soviet containment strategy toward the PRC. The close link with the Soviet Union became manifest when Vietnam joined the CMEA in June 1978 and signed a Treaty of Friendship and Co-operation in November 1978, which, among other things, provides for 'consultations' in the case of an attack or a threat of an attack against either country. The USSR supplies extensive economic and military aid to the SRV, and already during the Vietnam war this exceeded that of the PRC by far.

Relations between Vietnam and China deteriorated and finally broke down altogether because of numerous border incidents; a territorial dispute concerning the Spratly and Paracel Islands in the South China Sea, claimed by both sides; the Chinese view that the USSR is the main threat to world peace; the oppression and exodus of the Chinese minority; and Vietnamese policy towards Kampuchea and Laos. In July 1978 the Chinese suspended all aid to the SRV. The tensions culminated when the PRC invaded SRV territory in February and March 1979, to 'teach the Vietnamese a lesson'.

While Vietnam could bind Laos by a Treaty on Friendship and Co-operation, concluded in July 1977 for twenty-five years and providing for a 'special relationship', and submit Laos to its control, this idea met with strong opposition from the Khmer Rouge. This fact, as well as a controversial border and actions by both sides to change it to their advantage, resulted in the Vietnamese invasion of Kampuchea at the end of 1978 and the imposition of a puppet government. In February 1979 both states concluded a treaty equivalent to that between the SRV and Laos, and when in March 1979 the same thing happened with Kampuchea and Laos, the 'special relationship' triangle was completed. The 'special relationship' has been institutionalised in manifold ways: at the level of the party and state leaderships and by means of consultations between the ministers of foreign affairs, foreign trade and culture, the chairmen of the Planning Commissions and through committees for economic co-operation and co-ordination established in each of the three countries. Vietnam apparently aims at integrating the economies of the former Indo-China countries on the basis of a division of labour: Vietnam will develop industry, Kampuchea provide agricultural products and Laos will supply energy from its hydro-energy stations and coalmines.

Another major field of foreign policy activity comprises the South-East Asian states united in the ASEAN. The Vietnamese strove to gain their support in its conflict with the PRC. But the appeal to revolutionary forces in these states to overthrow the governments and the intervention in Kampuchea proved counter-productive to the attempt to remove the ASEAN from USA influence. Among ASEAN members, Thailand feels immediately threatened by the Vietnamese anti-guerrilla warfare on its border.

The SRV does not maintain relations with the USA. In the Paris Agreement of 1973 the USA promised comprehensive reconstruction aid but refused to fulfil this pledge, accusing the Vietnamese of having violated this agreement by hesitating to settle the question of Americans missed in action, and to return prisoners of war whom the USA assumes to be still alive. Later it made the establishment of diplomatic relations also dependent on the Vietnamese withdrawal from Kampuchea. Among Western countries, only France and Sweden give the SRV substantial development aid. (To a lesser extent Belgium, the Netherlands, Denmark and Finland.) In 1977, and only after the USA had given up its opposition, was the SRV admitted to the UNO.

NATIONAL DEFENCE

The Vietnam People's Army has a total strength of 1,227,000, of which about 1.2 million are in the army, 15,000 in the air force and 12,000 in the navy.[5] There are, additionally, various kinds of paramilitary forces: the Border Defence Forces of some 60,000; the People's Regional Force (militia) of about half a million; the People's Self-Defence Forces of about 1 million; and the Armed Youth Assault Force which amounts to an estimated 1.5 million.[6] The militia and the Self-Defence Forces are regarded as 'armed mass organisations'. While the former is entrusted with security tasks mainly in rural areas, the latter is employed more in urban areas — for the guarding of factories and administrative institutions. The Youth Assault Force serves the training of young people in the use of infantry weapons.

By numerical strength and equipment — the Vietnamese obtained a great number of American weapons and are equipped with, in part, modern Soviet arms — the SRV is by far the strongest military power in the South-East Asian region. Moreover, the SRV serves as a military stronghold of the USSR by conceding it the right to use Cam Ranh and Da Nang naval and air bases.

Vietnam's military extravagance, which contrasts with its scarce economic resources, is intended to cope with its involvement in a four-front war: against the Chinese themselves at the common border, against the China-backed guerrilla forces of Democratic Kampuchea, against resistance movements in Laos and in the mountainous areas of Vietnam, which are also encouraged or supported by the Chinese. Approximately 160,000 soldiers are deployed in Kampuchea and 40,000 in Laos.[7] The SRV has so far rejected repeated appeals of the UN General Assembly to withdraw its troops from Kampuchea. It officially declares that its military presence in this country (and in Laos) aims at nothing else than to prevent the Chinese from using these territories as infiltration bases. It therefore considers the maintenance and the international recognition of the goverment of the People's Republic of Kampuchea, which guarantees the 'special relationship' with the SRV, as a precondition for moving out.

NOTES

1. English text in *Review of Socialist Law* (Leyden, The Netherlands) VII (1981), no. 3, pp. 347–78.
2. According to Truong Chinh, Excerpt from the speech delivered at the Fourth CPV Congress (1976), *Viet Nam Courier* (Hanoi), 1977, no. 58, p. 6.
3. English text in William B. Simons (ed.), *The Constitutions of the Communist World* (Alphen aan den Rijn, The Netherlands, and Germantown, Md., 1980), pp. 400–21.
4. Richard F. Staar (ed.), *Yearbook on International Communist Affairs 1984: Parties and Revolutionary Movements* (Stanford, Cal., 1984), p. 280.
5. The International Institute for Strategic Studies, London, *The Military Balance 1984–1985* (Oxford, 1984), pp. 111–12.
6. *Ibid.*, p. 112.
7. *Ibid.* (the numbers fluctuate).

FURTHER READING

Buttinger, Joseph, *Vietnam: A Dragon Embattled*, 2 vols. (London: Pall Mall Press, 1967)
—— *Vietnam: The Unforgettable Tragedy* (New York: Horizon Press, 1977)
Duncanson, Dennis J., *Government and Revolution in Vietnam* (London: Oxford University Press, 1968)
Fall, Bernard B., *The Viet-Minh Regime: Government and Administration in the Democratic Republic of Vietnam*, rev. and enl. ed. (Westport, Conn.: Greenwood Press, 1975)
Nguyen Long and Harry H. Kendall, *After Saigon Fell: Daily Life under the Vietnamese Communists* (Berkeley, Cal.: Institute of East Asian Studies, University of California, 1981)
Nguyen Van Canh, *Vietnam under Communism, 1975–1982* (Stanford, Cal.: Hoover Institution Press, 1983)
Papp, Daniel, *Vietnam: The View from Moscow, Peking and Washington* (Jefferson, NC.: McFarland, 1981)
Pike, Douglas, *History of Vietnamese Communism, 1925–1976* (Stanford, Cal.: Hoover Institution Press, 1978)
Turley, William S. (ed.), *Vietnamese Communism in Comparative Perspective* (Boulder, Colo.: Westview Press, 1980)
Zasloff, Joseph J. and MacAlister Brown (eds.), *Communism in Indochina: New Perspectives* (Lexington, Mass.: Lexington Books, 1975)

17 Socialist Federal Republic of Yugoslavia

BASIC FEATURES

Yugoslavia is a federal state consisting of six socialist republics: Bosnia-Herzegovina, Croatia, Macedonia, Montenegro, Serbia — including the Socialist Autonomous Provinces Vojvodina and Kosovo — and, finally, Slovenia. According to article 1 of the constitution of 21 February 1974,[1] it defines itself at the same time as 'a socialist, self-managment democratic community of working people and citizens, and of nations and nationalities'. The basic elements of the political and socio-economic order are correspondingly: a real federal structure of the state, the workers' self-management, and the direct or indirect self-government of the citizens in local communities, communes, provinces, republics and the federation. (In what follows, the term 'self-management' —corresponding to the Serbo-Croat term *samoupravljanje* — will cover both workers' self-management and territorial self-government.) The self-managing democracy of the workers and citizens in Chapter 4 of the introduction to the constitution is qualified as 'a special form of the dictatorship of the proletariat'.

The inviolable and inalienable right to self-management is realised under the guidance of the League of Communists of Yugoslavia (LCY), which, in Chapter 8 of the introduction to the constitution, is declared to be 'the leading organised ideological and political force of the working class and of all working people'. Its main activity is supposed to be aimed at the 'strengthening of socialist consciousness. Despite the monopoly of political power of the LCY, Yugoslavia is a relatively open society as compared with all those which are ruled by a Communist Party.

In industry the means of production are socially owned property, yet in agriculture and trade there is a large private sector. The self-managed enterprises compete with each other. Economic activities are regulated by indicative economic planning, self-management agreements, social compacts and by market forces. This constitutes an economic system called 'market socialism'.

The relations between the republics and provinces and their Communist Parties on the one hand, and the federation and the LCY on the other, are determined by three principles. The republics and provinces are represented in the central organs of party and state on the principle of parity, whereby both are either represented equally or the two provinces have a less numerous representation than the six republics. Concerning offices held by a single person, the equality of the republics and provinces is taken into account by applying the principle of rotation. Decisions of the central organs should be adopted by consensus. A further principle to be observed is that of separation between party and state executive offices.

THE COMMUNIST TAKEOVER

The Communist Party of Yugoslavia (CPY), which was founded in 1919 and in 1952 changed its name to the LCY, took over power as a result of the victorious struggle of the Tito-led partisans against the German and Italian invaders. The takeover was essentially effected without Soviet support. Josip Broz Tito, secretary general of the CPY, pursued, at the same time as the liberation struggle, a political-revolutionary goal too: the creation of a socialist Yugoslavia. In November 1942 representatives of the People's Liberation Front established the Anti-Fascist Council for the National Liberation of Yugoslavia, which one year later formed a Presidium; for the duration of the war this declared itself to be the supreme legislative and executive body. In this capacity the Presidium set up a permanent organ consisting of thirteen members and presided over by Tito, which called itself the National Liberation Committee and considered itself to be the Provisional Government of Yugoslavia.

In May 1944 King Peter, who was living in exile in London, agreed to form a government which would co-operate with the National Liberation Committee and finally join it. In March 1945, on the basis of an agreement between Tito and the former Governor of Croatia, Ivan Šubašić, a new provisional government was formed, consisting of twenty members of the Anti-Fascist Council, five representatives of non-compromised pre-war parties and three representatives of the royal government with Tito as prime minister. This arrangement was conceived as a gesture towards the Western allies, who had supported the partisan People's Liberation Army. It was by no means dictated by the domestic constellation of forces, because at the end of the war all military and civil power resided in the partisans and the local people's liberation committees, both dominated by the communists. The anti-fascist coalition did not last long. On 11 November 1945 elections to the Constituent Assembly were held on the basis of a single list of candidates of the People's Front, which had been founded three months before, succeeding the People's Liberation Front. Out of 510 members of the Assembly 470 were communists.

When the Assembly met for the first time on 29 November 1945, it abolished the monarchy and proclaimed the Federative People's Republic of Yugoslavia. The constitution adopted two months later closely followed the Soviet model. The type of government was that of a 'people's democracy', which was considered to be a variant of the dictatorship of the proletariat; the federation was practically a deconcentrated unity state.

THE MARXIST-LENINIST PARTY

The LCY is composed of the Leagues of Communists (LCs) of the republics and autonomous provinces as well as of the organisation of the LCY within the Yugoslav People's Army (YPA). In 1983 it claimed 2.2 million members, almost 10 per cent of the total population.[2] In 1981 out of the then 2.1 million members 30.7 per cent were 'workers' and 3.9 per cent were peasants. The national structure of the LCY is supposed to have approximated to the national structure of the populace.[3] Membership of the LC of a republic involves LCY membership. Contrary to the rule in most Communist Parties, an applicant need not complete a probationary year as 'candidate'.

The basis of the LCs is formed by the primary organisations at places of work and of residence. On the territory of a commune the primary organisations are joined together in communal party organisations. These form the LCs of the republics and, in the Vojvodina and the Kosovo, they form the LCs of the provinces, which for their part are components of the LC of Serbia. The organs of the republic and the province LCs are the Congresses or Conferences and, between their sessions, the Central Committees or Committees with the Presidium as the political executive organ and a president at the top.

The organs of the LCY are: the Party Congress, which convenes every five years; the Central Committee (CC), which is elected by the Party Congress; its Presidium, the Statutory Commission and the Auditing Commission. The composition of these organs accounts for the federative feature of the LCY structure. The CC, which was formed by the Twelfth Party Congress of June 1982, consists of 163 members chosen according to the formula: twenty members of each republic party and fifteen members of each province party, who are elected by the LC Congresses or Conferences. Further members of the CC are sent by the LCY organisation within the YPA. Consequently, 'election' by the LCY Congress is a mere formality.

The same is true of the formation of the *de facto* supreme organ of the LCY, the Presidium, which determines the political course of the party and co-ordinates its activity. It consists of twenty-three members: three each are sent by the LCs of the republics, two each by the LCs of the provinces, among which are the respective party presidents by virtue of their office; the twenty-third member is the president of the Committee of the LCY organisation within the YPA, also *ex officio*. The Presidium elects from its midst the president of the CC Presidium for a one-year term of office and the secretary (for two years), and from among the CC members the executive secretaries (for four years). The president and the secretary must be elected annually from another republic or province LC according to an established schedule, and they may not come from the same LC. (The office of 'president of the LCY' was reserved for Tito for life.)

The LCs of the republics and provinces enjoy limited autonomy. They are linked together by the former struggle against Germans and Italians, a joint statute and a joint programme, aiming at the development and the safeguarding of self-management socialism, and by common central organs. Until his death Tito's authority in particular saw to the unity of the LCY. Yet the republic and province party leaderships do not always pursue a uniform policy within the framework of the LCY but hold divergent opinions on questions of political and socio-economic order, such as on the relationship between market and planning, the relationship with mass media, intellectuals and religious communities, and on the scope of inner-party democracy, and they sponsor national or regional interests. At the end of the 1960s the LCY was actually as federalised as the state. In 1971 the LCY even underwent a crucial test, when leading Croatian communists became the spokesmen of national and even separatist aspirations of a part of the Croats, who were still discontented with the constitutional amendments of 1971 providing for an extensive political and economic autonomy of the republics.

The crisis was settled by the Presidium of the LCY and especially by the direct intervention of Tito, which resulted in a purge of national elements in the Croatian party and in other republic parties as well. Since these events the principle of democratic centralism has regained strength. The eight parties are obliged to execute the decisions of the central party organs and are also responsible to them for decisions which they adopt within their own area of competence on the basis of the 'general line'. This 'general line', however, develops from a compromise of particular regional and/or national, often conflicting interests which the LCs of the republics and provinces introduce into the decision-making process of party and state on the level of the federation. Consent is often reached only at the expense of a clear-cut effective policy.

Concerning democratic centralism, it can be observed that this principle works within the regional party organisations rather than with respect to the relationship between the central organs and the republic and province LCs. And second, the principle is applied — to this extent differing from other Communist Parties — with greater emphasis on its democratic component: a party member whose opinion remains in the minority, is obliged to carry out the majority decision, but is allowed to retain his deviant opinion. The right to resign from a party post, in order to prevent a conflict between a party member's opinion and the implementation of a decision, corresponds with this regulation. Groupism or factionalism, however, is strictly prohibited; this is really a necessity in order to prevent the disintegration of the LCY and to safeguard the cohesion of the federation.

Although the LCY has declared that it does not want to rule by exercising political monopoly, it does not yet confine itself to educating the people in the values of self-management, to the definition of common interests and the co-ordination of particular interests. The LCY advocates the delegation of power but only insofar as it may be sure that the organs of self-management act in accordance with the ideological and political guidelines determined by it. However, as long as it behaves as a privileged political force and not as an equal, integral part of the system of self-management and does not adopt its theoretically anti-hierarchic pattern of decision-making, both are in irreconcilable conflict.

The relationship of the LCY with the CPSU is characterised by the former's persistent refusal to admit the Soviet claim for leadership in the communist world movement. This attitude is rooted in the independent seizure of power by the partisan army. Although there were differences about the role of the peasants in the socialist revolution, the break between both parties in 1948 was not a result of deviation from the Soviet model of socialism — the CPY did not realise its concept of workers' self-management until 1950. Instead, the conflict resulted from Stalin's unwillingness to accept the Yugoslav claim to have already entered the stage of socialism in 1946 and therefore to be recognised as equal. Since the expulsion of the Yugoslav communists from the Cominform in 1948, attempts of the CPSU to bind them to the principle of proletarian internationalism — in the sense of subordination to Soviet interests — have been repeatedly rejected by the CPY/ LCY. This also happened in June 1976 at the Conference of European Communist Parties in East Berlin, which, not least because of the insistence of the LCY, but not without resistance on the part of the CPSU, agreed to apply this principle in the sense of voluntary co-operation while maintaining the equality and independence of each Communist Party. By advocating the right to determine autonomously the national road to socialism, the LCY has much in common with the so-called Eurocommunists.

ORGANISATIONS AND ASSOCIATIONS

Besides the LCY there are four further 'socio-political organisations': the Socialist Alliance of the Working People of Yugoslavia (SAWPY), the Federation of Trade Unions, the Socialist Youth League and the Veterans' League. A distinction must be drawn between these, on the one hand, and, on the other, the 'social organisations' and the 'citizens' associations': the Red Cross, cultural, professional, scientific and leisure-time associations, the religious communities and the associations of the national minorities for fostering their culture.

Membership in the all-embracing SAWPY, which emanated from the People's Front and numbered more than 14 million people in 1981,[4] is achieved through membership in one of the organisations or associations which are united in the SAWPY, or individually. Membership of, and participation in, the activities of the SAWPY are not dependent on belief in the Marxist-Leninist doctrine but they require identification with the basic elements of Yugoslavia's political and socio-economic system. The SAWPY's pre-eminent functions are the mobilisation of the citizens for political activities, the nomination of the candidates for, and the organisation of, elections to the delegations and the representative bodies and participation in the shaping of the latter's decision-making process.

The Federation of Trade Unions — the umbrella organisation of the Federations of Trade Unions of the republics and structured on the branch principle — has the constitutional right and duty to fight for the realisation and the observance of the workers' self-management rights, to initiate self-management agreements, to co-operate with the SAWPY in the nomination of candidates for the delegations and organs of the workers' and territorial self-management, to co-ordinate individual and group interests with those of the whole society, and to be concerned with raising the educational level of the workers. The trade unions, moreover, exercise an arbitrational function in the case of strikes, which are tolerated though not legally allowed.

Although the social organisations and citizens' associations articulate special interests, they do not exert pressure on the decision-making process, so that it would not be justifiable to call them pressure groups. Nevertheless, they are in a position to introduce the interests of their members into this process through the SAWPY, which is supposed to co-ordinate and concentrate the sometimes conflicting interests under the decisive influence of the communists, who for their part, however, are exposed to the influences of their national environment.

Largely autonomous structures for the articulation of particular interests are the self-managing organisations and communities. By the system of self-management as well as by the decentralisation of decision-making through federalism, the pursuit of particular socio-economic and national group interests has been openly institutionalised.

DISSENT

Dissent can be observed in the form of demands for a multi-party system, for (further) democratisation of the LCY decision-making and for freedom of opinion, or of criticism of bureaucratic excesses, on the one hand, and of demands for the adoption of the Soviet model of socialism, for a proletarian-internationalist subordination to the interests of the

Soviet Union (denounced as Cominformism), on the other.
Though criticism and dissent are more tolerated than in other
socialist systems, any questioning of the political monopoly of
the LCY, self-management socialism and the actual federal
structure as well as nationalist sentiments, particularly when
connected with religious sentiments, are regarded as 'counter-
revolutionary' and are penalised if considered to constitute a
political criminal offence (e.g. 'hostile propaganda').

   A prominent example of dissent is the 'heresy' of Milovan
Djilas. Until his disgrace in 1954 the 'number two' in the
Yugoslav party leadership, he severely criticised the LCY for
holding the monopoly of political and ideological power, and
demanded its abolition. He was (another time) sentenced to
imprisonment in October 1957 because of his book *The New
Class* (published in the West), in which he attacked the party
élite's privileged position in society. Another example is the
case of philosophers and sociologists grouped around the
journal *Praxis*, who, emphasising humanist elements in the
teachings of Marx, condemned social differentiation,
privileges and unemployment resulting from shortcomings of
workers' self-management and the market mechanism, and
deplored the failure of self-management to overcome the alienation of man. *Praxis* had to cease publication, and in 1975
eight of its contributors were dismissed from their Chairs at
the University of Belgrade.

WORKERS' SELF-MANAGEMENT

Workers' self-management is mainly achieved (1) through an
organisation of associated labour (OAL), which may take the
form of a basic organisation of associated labour (BOAL), or
a labour organisation, or a complex organisation of associated
labour (the latter two integrate the activities of several
BOALs), and (2) through a work community. These organisations and communities are formed by people working in
industrial, handicraft, commercial, service and agricultural
enterprises insofar as they use means of production regarded
as social property; they are also established by people working
in schools, hospitals, research institutes, publishing houses,

and in the field of banking and insurance, by persons belonging to the administrative staff of state organs and of socio-political organisations, by members of liberal professions, such as artists, journalists, lawyers, and so on. What follows refers to self-management in economy.

The association of work principally takes place through a BOAL (a production unit within an enterprise), where the working process and its implications can be observed by the worker, so that he does not only have to execute orders but is supposed to be in a position to participate in the decision-making. The criterion for setting up such an organisation is the capacity to measure the economic value of work.

The rights of self-management of the workers include, among others, the administration of the OAL, the utilisation of the means of production on behalf of the organisation and the whole society, the regulation of the type and scope of production, the distribution of income, the fixing of work conditions, decisions on the possible exclusion of parts of an OAL or their fusion with others and the guarantee of the rights of self-management by control over their observation. Details are regulated autonomously in accordance with the constitution, laws (in particular the Law on Associated Labour, promulgated in November 1976), self-management agreements and social compacts.

The workers' collective makes use of its rights directly either at meetings or by referendum, or indirectly by elected or appointed executive and administrative organs. Meetings may consider reports from the administrative organs, the distribution of income, the economic plan, working conditions or the foundation of BOALs. The workers' collective decides by referendum matters such as the separation from, or the fusion with, other organisations into industrial combines.

The OALs generally have two organs of self-management: one administrative (the workers' council); one executive. The numerical composition of a workers' council, the procedure for the election and the recall of its members, and the detailed determination of its function, are the concern of the organisation. The constitution fixes the term of office, which is limited to two years. By the principle of rotation, nobody can be elected more than twice successively to the same workers' council. Implementation of the resolutions passed by the workers' collective or by the workers' council is generally the duty of the director appointed by the workers' council after public competition and on the recommendation of a commission consisting of representatives of the OAL, the trade unions and a socio-political community (e.g. a commune). His term of office is four years but it can be renewed as often as convenient.

Workers' self-management in the context of market elements, and the right of the workers' collectives to decide on the distribution of the enterprise's income, produce two problems. The one consists in the earning of different incomes for equal work, because the amount of personal income depends not only on the individual and collective work performance but also on market opportunities. The other consists in the freedom to choose between consumption and investment. The market mechanism is counteracted by self-management agreements between enterprises and by social compacts between territorial self-management organs, trade unions and other institutions, through which marketing, prices, incomes and the planning of the middle and long-term development of an economic branch and/or a region are regulated (yet competition is distorted or suppressed). The workers' inclination to favour consumption and to neglect investment is countered by also taking into consideration the value of work invested in an enterprise when calculating the amount of personal income.

The system of workers' self-management offers vast formal possibilities for participation in economic decision-making: in 1981 about 487,000 people were delegates in roughly 33,000 OAL workers' councils.[5] However, the real exercise of participation is rather poor. The discussions and decisions in the workers' councils are dominated by the management and technical experts. Their superior access to information, on the one hand, and the absence of any motivation on the part of the workers to participate in decisions, resulting from their lack of knowledge and competence, on the other hand, favour a hierarchic and technocratic pattern of decision-making. The referendum and the workers' meeting, significant because their results are binding on the workers' council and the management, are rarely used.

THE NATIONAL STRUCTURE AND FEDERALISM

Yugoslavia is a multi-national state (Table 17:1). It contains numerous regional, ethnical, linguistic, religious, cultural and economic cleavages. Through its federal system of government it is subdivided into six republics and two autonomous provinces. The 'nations' alone — the Croats, Macedonians, Montenegrins, Muslims (in Bosnia-Herzegovina), Serbs and Slovenes — speak three languages (Serbo-Croat, or Croato-Serbian, and Macedonian and Slovenian), profess three religions (Catholicism, Orthodoxy and Islam, the latter, since 1961, also being considered as an ethnic criterion) and use two scripts (Roman and Cyrillic). Furthermore, there are many national minorities, called 'nationalities', among which the Albanians, who number 7.7 per cent of the total population, are by far the strongest.[6] Economically, Yugoslavia is split into a wealthy north-eastern part (Croatia and Slovenia) and a relatively poor part (Bosnia-Herzegovina, Kosovo, Macedonia and Montenegro); Serbia 'proper' (i.e. without the provinces) and the Vojvodina occupy an intermediate position.

Because Yugoslav federalism is mainly determined by the territorial criterion, the ethnic segments, with the exception of almost homogeneous Slovenia, are distributed among several federal units, which are consequently multi-segmentary. This is particularly true of Serbia. The share of the Serbs in this republic is only 66.4 per cent; besides them there are 15 per cent Albanians, 4.2 per cent Hungarians and, furthermore, Bulgarians, Ruthenians and Slovaks, to mention but a few. In Bosnia-Herzegovina 39.5 per cent of the population are Muslims, 32 per cent Serbs and 18.4 per cent Croats; the population of Macedonia has almost 20 per cent Albanians and 4.5 per cent Turks. Regional interests are not, therefore, always identical with the interests of all subcultures within the boundaries of a republic or province.

The republics are considered to be 'self-managing democra-

Table 17:1 The national structure of the SFRY, the republics and the autonomous provinces (1981)

| | SFRY | | Republics | | | | | | Provinces | | |
	Totals	%	Bosnia-Herzegovina (%)	Croatia (%)	Macedonia (%)	Montenegro (%)	Serbia (%)	Slovenia (%)	Kosovo (%)	Vojvodina (%)	Serbia 'proper' (%)
Croats	4,428,043	19.74	18.38	75.08	0.18	1.18	1.60	2.94	0.55	5.37	0.55
Macedonians	1,341,598	5.98	0.05	0.12	67.00		0.53	0.17	0.07	0.93	0.51
Montenegrins	579,043	2.58	0.34	0.21	0.21	68.54	1.58	0.17	1.71	2.13	1.35
Muslims	1,999,890	8.92	39.52	0.52	2.07	13.36	2.31	0.71	3.70	0.24	2.66
Serbs	8,140,507	36.30	32.02	11.55	2.33	3.32	66.38	2.23	13.22	54.42	85.44
Slovenes	1,753,571	7.82	0.07	0.55			0.13	90.52		0.17	0.14
Albanians	1,730,878	7.72	0.11	0.13	19.75	6.46	14.99	0.10	77.42	0.19	1.27
Bulgarians	36,189	0.16			0.10		0.36			0.12	0.54
Czechs	19,624	0.09		0.33						0.10	
Hungarians	426,867	1.90		0.55			4.19			18.94	0.09
Italians	15,132	0.07		0.25				0.11			
Rumanians	54,955	0.25					0.58			2.32	0.11
Ruthenians	23,286	0.10		0.07			0.21			0.95	
Slovaks	80,334	0.36		0.14			0.79			3.42	0.06
Turks	101,291	0.45			4.53	5.35	0.15		0.79		
'Yugoslavs'	1,219,024	5.44	7.91	8.24	0.74	5.35	4.75	1.39	0.17	8.22	4.78

Source: Totals from Statistički godišnjak Jugoslavije 1982 (Belgrade, 1982), p. 437. Percentages by author.

tic communities of working people and citizens, and of nations and nationalities' (article 3 of the constitution) on the one hand, and as (sovereign) states, on the other. Their relationship with the federation contains federative and confederative features. They have exclusive jurisdiction in the fields of education, research, health, social welfare, mass communications and sports; furthermore, they have organisational power in respect of the communes and the right to plan the socio-economic development in their territory. They take measures in the fields of the monetary, foreign exchange and credit system, in price control, and take similar political-economic measures on the basis or in implementation of federal regulations. Within the framework of foreign policy, determined by the federal organs, the republics maintain relations with organs and organisations of foreign countries, and with international organisations; the conclusion of international treaties, however, is reserved for the federation. The rights and duties of the republics in the field of national defence derive less from their statehood than from the fact that they too are self-managing communities, and the national defence is also conceived to be a matter of self-management. Correspondingly, the republics have no regular armed forces but maintain units of territorial defence. The republics have the right of secession, which is established in their constititutions as a right corresponding to their voluntary accession to the federation, but the latter is constitutionally obliged to maintain Yugoslavia's integrity.

The autonomous provinces, which are constituent parts of Serbia, are not states, but they are approximately on an equal footing with the republics in their relationship with the federation; their rights go beyond autonomy in preserving the ethnical and cultural characteristics of the people living on their territory. Drafts of federal laws which necessitate the agreement of the republics and provinces before becoming law may be blocked by the veto of a province just as by the veto of a. republic.

The federation is considered not to be superior to the republics but to be an instrument to secure the independence of the SFRY, the constitutional order, the system of self-management, the equality of the rights of the nations and

nationalities, assistance to the economically backward regions, the unity of the market and the socio-economic development of the federation by establishing the federal social plan
and the federal budget. Enactment of the latter two requires
the agreement of the republics and provinces. The same is the
case regarding the amendment of the constitution and the
ratification of international treaties, when treaties entail the
passage of new republican or provincial laws or amendments
to existing ones or contain particular obligations for the
republics and provinces.

Because of historical animosities between Yugoslavia's
nations and nationalities, but particularly because of the
different level of regional economic development, relations
between the republics, between republics and provinces, and
between republics or provinces and the central power are
strained. Two major causes of conflict which seriously jeopardise the country's political stability can be distinguished. The
first is the demand of the more developed republics (Slovenia
and Croatia) for an unrestricted right to dispose of the returns
on their economic activity. The second is related to the provincial status of the Kosovo-Albanians, who for this reason in
1968 and again in 1981 called for their recognition as a nation
and a republic of their own, thus affecting historically rooted
interests of the Serbs. Whereas the 'Croatian crisis' of 1971,
after the articulation of economic demands and a language
dispute between Croats and Serbs, escalated in separatist
tendencies, and was then solved by means of democratic centralism, the Albanian outburst of nationalist sentiment was
suppressed by (military) force.

In order to reconcile the conflicting forces in Yugoslavia's
society by taking into consideration regional and/or national
interests in central decision-making, the Yugoslav leadership
has developed a pattern of decision-making based on inter-
regional bargaining, compromise and consensus, and labelled
'harmonisation of positions'. However, the variously
institutionalised negotiation of compromises proves to be via-
ble only if the subcultural interests permit consensus and if the
regional political élites do not block federal initiatives but are
prepared to co-operate.

THE DELEGATION AND ASSEMBLY SYSTEM

The network of political institutions is characterised by a three-tier system of assemblies based on the delegate principle. In generalised form — there are slight differences in the single republics and provinces — this complex system of functional and territorial representation contains the following elements (Fig.17:1): first, members of the self-managing organisations and work communities, individual peasants and craftsmen, soldiers and civilian employees of the armed forces, students and pupils (of at least eighteen years of age), and citizens in the local communities elect delegations. Second, these delegations, from among their midst, send delegates to the Council of Associated Labour and the Council of Local Communities of the Commune Assembly and the citizens elect directly the Socio-Political Council of the Commune Assembly from a list of candidates, who are put up from among the members of the elected leading organs (committee or conference) of the socio-political organisations. (These organs perform the function of delegations.) Third, the councils of the Commune Assembly (separately or jointly) elect from among the members of the delegations delegates to the Council of Associated Labour, the Council of Communes and the Socio-Political Council of the Republic Assembly and the Province Assembly. Fourth, the commune assemblies elect the Federal Council of the Assembly of the SFRY from among the members of the delegations, while the Council of Republics and Provinces of the Assembly of the SFRY is formed by delegates of the assemblies of the republics and provinces.

The candidates for members of the delegations of the local communities and the organisations and communities of worker's self-management are proposed by the citizens and put up by the SAWPY and the trade unions respectively. The number of finally admitted candidates usually only slightly exceeds the number of available delegation mandates. The candidates, as a rule, receive about 90 per cent of the votes.

The self-managing character of the delegation system is meant to be preserved by the delegates acting as a link between the social base and the assemblies. The delegates are

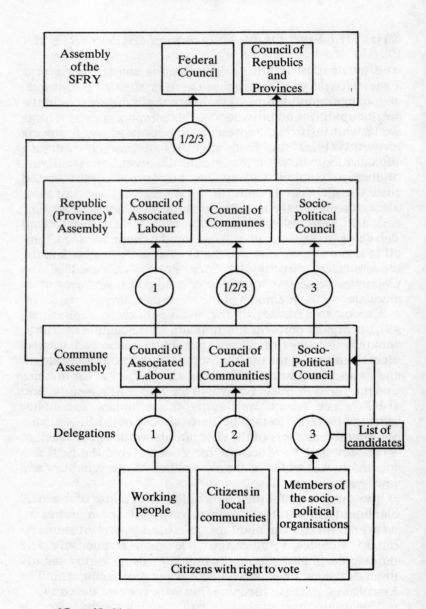

*Case of Serbia

Figure 17:1   *The Yugoslav delegation and assembly system*

expected, on the one hand, to express the interests of the BOALs and local communities, and, on the other hand, to co-ordinate these interests in the assemblies in such a way that a majority decision can be reached. The right of the self-managing organisations, local communities and socio-political organisations and their delegations to give directives, and the duty of the delegates to provide information and assume responsibility, are meant to secure the influence of the workers and citizens on decision-making in the assemblies. Recall and rotation are intended to prevent professionalisation of the elected and their separation from the electors. The duration of elected office is four years; election to the same delegation and to the same assembly is restricted to two successive terms. The delegate does not give up his job but is merely given time off for his work in the assembly. (In Slovenia the delegates to the Council of Associated Labour and the Council of Local Communities of the commune assemblies have no permanent mandate.)

If a delegate has an explicit instruction, he can bring forward in the assembly a motion for the adjournment of the debate in order to consult his organisation, community and/or the delegation. He is not, however, bound by an imperative mandate. (But an exception exists for the members of the Council of Republics and Provinces of the Assembly of the SFRY.) The constitution provides in addition that the instructions given to the delegates should take into account not only the interests of their self-managing organisation or community but also the interests of other organisations and communities, and the 'general interest'. For this purpose the delegations are supposed to co-operate and to seek solutions to questions of common interest. The Social-Political Councils should counteract local aspirations.

In 1982 there were about 66,000 delegations with roughly 730,000 members (omitting a part of the delegations elected in Slovenia). From among the members of these delegations about 50,000 delegates were sent to 527 Commune Assemblies, 2,028 to the Republic and Province Assemblies, and 308 to the Assembly of the SFRY.[7]

CENTRAL GOVERNMENT

The Yugoslav legislative body is the Assembly of the SFRY. It is divided into two chambers: the Federal Council, comprising 220 members, and the Council of Republics and Provinces, consisting of 88 members. The Federal Council constitutes the representation of the self-managing organisations and communities and of the socio-political organisations in the republics and provinces. The candidates are proposed by the delegations, nominated at candidate conferences of the SAWPY in the republics and provinces, and are elected by the Commune Assemblies for a four-year term from among the members of the delegation – thirty from each republic and twenty from each province. The Council of Republics and Provinces, which is the representative organ of the regions, consists of eight delegations. These delegations are composed of twelve delegates from each Republic Assembly and of eight delegates from each Province Assembly, elected from among their members (Fig.17:1). The delegates retain their tenure in the respective assemblies because the delegations are considered to constitute a link between the regional assemblies and the SFRY Assembly. They are not only to represent regional interests on the level of the federation but also to introduce federal interest into the regional decision-making process.

The jurisdiction of the SFRY Assembly includes, particularly, the adoption of amendments to the constitution, the adoption of federal laws, the determination of the guidelines of domestic and foreign policy, and the establishment of the federal social plan and the federal state budget. The Federal Council decides by a majority vote; the Council of Republics and Provinces decides by the vote of the individual delegations. Decisions on issues which require the participation of the regions are considered adopted only when they have received the vote from all delegations on the agreement of the regional assemblies. For this purpose the delegations have to keep their assemblies informed of the work of the Council of Republics and Provinces, and the delegates take part in the formulation of the positions adopted by the assemblies. However, if no agreement can be reached with the regional assemblies on the draft of a law which the Federal Executive Council (FEC — the federal government) considers indispensable — for example, in order to fulfil commitments of the SFRY or to prevent serious harm to the social community — the SFRY Assembly may adopt a law on 'temporary measures'. The adoption of such a law only requires a two-thirds majority of all delegates of the Council of Republics and Provinces.

Since the death of Tito (4 May 1980), who had been president of the republic for life, the functions of head of state have been performed by a collective organ, the SFRY Presidency. It consists of nine members, formed on the principle of parity: one member from each republic and province, elected by their assemblies, and the president of the CC of the LCY by virtue of his office. The term of office of the elected Presidium members is five years, and they may be re-elected for only one consecutive term. Employing also the principle of rotation, the Presidency elects from among its members the president for a term of one year according to a schedule laid down by the rules of procedure. These provide that the president of the Presidency, who represents the SFRY in domestic and foreign affairs, shall each year come from a different republic or province.

The Presidency is entitled, *inter alia*, to submit to the SFRY Assembly proposals on domestic and foreign policy, to work towards the adoption of a draft law, if it deems it to be indispensable, and to propose to the Assembly the candidate for president of the FEC. It may request the FEC to take certain measures for the implementation of laws and may introduce in the SFRY Assembly a motion of no confidence in the FEC. During a state of war the Presidency may pass decrees with the force of law and suspend individual provisions of the constitution, including also freedoms and rights of the citizens. It is not responsible to the SFRY Assembly.

In case of extraordinary or unforeseen situations the SFRY Presidency holds joint meetings with the president of the SFRY Assembly, the president of the FEC and the federal secretaries of foreign affairs, national defence, and domestic affairs. These office holders take part in the deliberations without the right to vote. A share in the work of the Presidency may also be taken by the presidents of the Presidencies of the republics and provinces as well as by representatives of the socio-political organisations.

The FEC is composed of (1) the president, vice-presidents, and Council members, who are elected by the SFRY Assembly on the principle of 'equal representation of the republics and corresponding representation of the autonomous provinces' (article 348 of the constitution) and (2) the federal secretaries (e.g. of foreign affairs, defence, foreign trade, finance, justice) and the chairmen of federal committees (for energy and industry, agriculture, transport, labour, etc.) who are appointed in consideration of the national structure of Yugoslavia. The term of office of the president of the FEC is four years; he may not be re-elected for a second consecutive term and must each time come from a different republic or province.

The FEC is responsible to the SFRY Assembly for its activities; it may ask for a vote of confidence and resign collectively; the Assembly may introduce a motion of no confidence. In view of the frequent inability of the Councils of the SFRY Assembly to harmonise their stands, the Executive Council holds a strong position in the federal decision-making process. As it considers issues from the point of view of the federation rather than from that of the regions, it proves to be that federal body which is best suited to co-ordinate diverging interests and to formulate compromises. But through its right to submit to the Assembly a draft of law on temporary measures with the approval of the SFRY Presidency, it also has at its disposal an effective means to produce willingness to compromise.

LOCAL SELF-MANAGEMENT

The basic units of territorial self-management are the local communities. They are established in urban and rural settlements, in parts of the settlements or jointly for several settlements. If broader interests are not concerned, citizens may regulate their affairs autonomously and directly at their place of residence. The local communities work out programmes which — taking into account the requirements of the citizens, households and communities — stipulate instructions concerning the housing sector, education, health service, sports, social welfare services and defence. The local communities are in charge of the administration and the maintenance of dwellings, roads, public lighting and other services of local concern.

The direct participation of the citizens in local decision-making is achieved by the electors' meeting. It elects the council of the local community, which carries out the citizens' resolutions. The administrative staff is not professionalised. Through their delegates in the Commune Assemblies, the citizens living in the local communities are able to ensure consideration of their interests in the communal process of decision-making.

On a higher plane is the commune, defined in the constitution as a self-managing and basic socio-political community, mainly responsible for the regulation of social matters. Within the system of self-management the commune forms the framework integrating the OALs, the work communities, the local communities and the communities of interest within their territories. It also exercises state power.

The communes have the task of creating conditions for the satisfaction of the material, cultural and social needs of the citizens. They co-ordinate the activities of the self-managing organisations and local communities in the fields of economics, education, culture, sport, health, social welfare, construction and public utilities. They should protect the human rights of the citizens and regulate their social and legal affairs, ensure public order and security, guarantee the cultural development of minorities, regulate the utilisation of land and protect the environment. The communes also set up units for territorial defence and raise funds for their equipment, training and maintenance because 'general people's defence' is an integral part of the right of the citizens to self-management. Commune expenditure is financed by the OALs, from the personal income of the citizens working in the social and private sector, by taxes (especially purchase tax) and by fees.

Local policy is decided by the Commune Assembly. It is

carried out by the Executive Council, whose members are elected or appointed by the Commune Assembly and are responsible to it, as well as by administrative organs, concerned with the detailed implementation of laws, decrees and decisions.

According to the conception of an extensive self-managed satisfaction of needs, social and welfare services are increasingly provided by self-managing communities of interest. This is the case in the fields of education, research, health, social protection (where their establishment is obligatory), housebuilding, transport, power and water supply, and so on. Communities of interest are founded by agreement between people who offer services (e.g. doctors and teachers) and their beneficiaries (e.g. citizens, OALs, local communities, communes, provinces and republics), financing them by paying contributions. Their delegates participate in the work of the commune, province and republic assemblies.

ADMINISTRATION OF JUSTICE

Justice is administered by the regular courts of the communes, provinces, republics and the federation, whose members are elected by the corresponding assemblies, by military courts and self-management courts. Supreme courts of the SFRY are the Federal Court and the Constitutional Court of Yugoslavia, whose judges are elected by the Assembly of the SFRY on the principle of parity representation of the republics and 'corresponding' representation of the provinces.

The Federal Court decides in the first instance, *inter alia*, on property disputes between republics and/or provinces and between the federation and a republic or a province; on the legality of finally-binding administrative acts of federal organs; on jurisdiction conflicts between courts of several republics and provinces, and between military and other courts.

The Constitutional Court decides on the conformity of federal law with the SFRY constitution and of republic or province laws with a federal law and with the SFRY constitution; on disputes over rights and duties between the federation and a republic or a province, between republics and/or provinces, and between communes from the territories of different republics; on jurisdictional disputes between the constitutional courts of the republics or of the provinces, between federal organs and organs of the republics or provinces, and so on. If the Constitutional Court finds that a federal, republic or province law is not in conformity with the SFRY constitution, or that a republic or province law conflicts with a federal law, the corresponding assemblies are obliged to bring about the conformity; otherwise, it declares such a law or single provisions to be invalid. The Constitutional Court of the SFRY may become active either on request or on its own initiative. Its jurisdiction as well as that of the constitutional courts of the republics and provinces does not, however, include decisions on violations of fundamental rights of the citizens. Citizens may lodge a complaint against administrative acts only with the responsible organ; a regular court decides on the legality or illegality of such an act.

The protection of self-management is entrusted to self-management courts (courts of associated labour, arbitration tribunals, conciliation courts, etc) and to social attorneys of self-management (a kind of ombudsman). Self-management courts are established by a self-management act or by an agreement of the parties, in which the composition, jurisdiction and proceedings are regulated. They decide on disputes arising from socio-economic and other self-management relations insofar as they do not fall within the jurisdiction of a regular court. The social attorneys of self-management may become active at the request of citizens, self-management organisations, state organs, or on their own initiative, instituting proceedings at the assemblies of the socio-political communities and in courts. Organs of self-management and state organs are obliged to supply necessary information to the social attorneys. The observance by the management of the rights of self-management in each enterprise is watched over by the self-management control of the workers.

FOREIGN POLICY

Yugoslav foreign policy is based on such guiding principles as the independence and equal rights of the states, the self-determination of the peoples, security and democratic international relations. From these are derived the conceptions of non-alignment and active peaceful coexistence. The conception of non-alignment involves the non-adherence to any political or military bloc and the rejection of any state's claim to leadership. It does not, however, imply neutralism in the sense of impartiality: Yugoslavia considers itself to be a socialist state, the LCY a Marxist-Leninist party – facts which result in common interests with the socialist countries and 'progressive governments' and 'liberation movements' in the Third World.

Yugoslavia's geographical situation and its ideological position as the determinants of its foreign policy makes the Soviet Union the most important partner and/or opponent. In June 1948 Yugoslavia was, through Soviet pressure, expelled from the Cominform because of its claim that the Communist Parties should be equal. Not until 1955 was the Soviet party and state leadership ready to recognise Yugoslavia's independence and equality and the principle of non-interference in domestic affairs and thus Yugoslavia's right to an original form of socialism. During the following two decades the Soviets repeatedly tried to undermine these principles underlying the mutual party and state relations, which had been confirmed in the Belgrade Declaration of June 1955 and the Moscow Declaration of June 1956. In November 1976, on repeated requests from Yugoslavs, the Soviet leaders reconfirmed them.

Following the Soviet intervention in Czechoslovakia of August 1968, Yugoslavia reactivated its relations with the People's Republic of China, which had been frozen for many years, on the basis of their common interest to oppose the 'hegemonism' of the Soviet Union. Tito's visit to Beijing in August and September 1977, and the return visit of the Chinese head of party and government in August 1978, definitely normalised the relationship between the two Communist Parties and socialist states. The rejection of Soviet hegemonial ambitions also makes Yugoslavia a close partner of Rumania. Relations with Bulgaria are burdened by the Macedonian question (Bulgaria's refusal to recognise the Macedonians as a nation); relations with Albania are strained because of Yugoslavia's post-war policy of subordinating this country, Albanian criticism of the Yugoslav model of socialism and Belgrade's policy towards the Kosovo-Albanians.

Within the Non-Aligned Movement, of which Tito was one of the founders, Yugoslavia strove to prevent this grouping of states from following the Cuban and Vietnamese initiative in considering the Soviet Union as its 'natural ally'. At the Summit Conferences of Colombo (1976) and Havana (1979) Tito succeeded in convincing the non-aligned countries of the necessity to co-operate constructively also with the capitalist industrial states, with which Yugoslavia maintains active relations according to its conviction that a balanced position between East and West best serves its national interest.

Following its policy of non-alignment, Yugoslavia is a member neither of the WTO nor of the CMEA, but is associated with the latter. In view of its high indebtedness to hard currency countries, Yugoslavia had intensified trade with the CMEA countries in recent years. But it is vital for Yugoslavia to increase its exports, including industrial goods, to Western countries, especially the EC, in order to reduce its dependence on exports to Eastern Europe.

NATIONAL DEFENCE

Following the tradition of the people's liberation war, national defence has become an integral part of self-management on the basis of a law adopted in 1969. The communes, provinces and republics are obliged to organise national defence on their territory and to direct the people's armed resistance. The acceptance or recognition of the occupation of the SFRY or of any of its parts, as well as capitulation, are declared to be unconstitutional acts.

The president of the SFRY Presidency is entrusted with the command of the armed forces, and is chairman of the Council of Defence. A law of April 1982 assigns to the LCY a key role in the organisation of national defence in extraordinary situations; for example, when responsible state organs are incapable of action.

The armed forces consist of the YPA and of units of territorial defence. The regular armed forces comprise 267,000 men: 200,000 in the army, 27,000 in the navy, and 40,000 in the air force. Additionally, there are 15,000 border troops. The Territorial Defence Forces are assessed at between 1 and 3 million.[8] They are organised on production and territorial principles; that is, they are maintained by the OALs and the communes, republics and provinces. In the case of a war the units of territorial defence are subordinate to the commanders of the units of the YPA with which they operate militarily, and the operations of both are to be co-ordinated.

The composition of the officer corps and promotion to senior commands in the YPA should proportionally represent the republics and provinces; in matters of command and military training, any one of the languages of Yugoslavia's nations may be used. The People's Army is considered to be a stronghold of Yugoslav patriotism and, as such, as the main force for safeguarding the country's unity.

NOTES

1. English text in William B. Simons (ed.), *The Constitutions of the Communist World* (Alphen aan den Rijn, The Netherlands, and Germantown, Md., 1980), pp. 428–577.
2. Richard F. Staar (ed.), *Yearbook on International Communist Affairs 1984: Parties and Revolutionary Movements* (Stanford, Cal., 1984), p. 403.
3. *Dvanaesti kongres Saveza komunista Jugoslavije: Referat, Resolucije, Statut SKJ, Završna reč* (Belgrade, 1982), pp. 54-5.
4. *Statistical Pocket Book of Yugoslavia 1984* (Belgrade, 1984), p. 30.
5. *Ibid.*, p. 23.
6. For this and the following demographic data see *Statistički godišnjak Jugoslavije 1982* (Belgrade, 1982), p. 437.
7. *Statistical Pocket Book*, op.cit., pp. 18-21.
8. The International Institute for Strategic Studies, London, *The Military Balance 1984–1985* (Oxford, 1984), p. 56.

FURTHER READING

Bertsch, Gary K., *Nation-Building in Yugoslavia: A Study of Political Integration and Attitudinal Consensus* (Beverly Hills: Sage Publications, 1971)

Burg, Stephen, *Conflict and Cohesion in Socialist Yugoslavia: Political Decision Making since 1966* (Princeton, NJ: Princeton University Press, 1982)

Carter, April; *Democratic Reform in Yugoslavia: The Changing Role of the Party* (Princeton, NJ: Princeton University Press, 1982)

Clissold, Stephen (ed.), *Yugoslavia and the Soviet Union 1939-1973: A Documentary Survey* (London and New York: Oxford University Press, 1975)

Comisso, Ellen T., *Workers' Control under Plan and Market: Implications of Yugoslav Self-Management* (New Haven, Conn.: Yale University Press, 1979)

Denitch, Bogdan D., *The Legitimation of a Revolution: The Yugoslav Case* (New Haven, Conn.: Yale University Press, 1976)

Drulović, Milojko, *Self-Management on Trial* (Nottingham: Spokesman Books, 1978)

Dunn, William and Josip Obradović (eds.), *Workers' Self-Management and Organizational Power in Yugoslavia* (Pittsburgh: University Center for International Studies, University of Pittsburgh, 1978)

Gruenwald, Oskar, *The Yugoslav Search for Man: Marxist Humanism in Contemporary Yugoslavia* (South Hadley, Mass.: J.F. Bergin Publishers, 1983)

Horvat, Branko, *An Essay on Yugoslav Society* (White Plains, NY: International Arts and Sciences Press, 1969)

——, Mihailo Marković and Rudi Supek (eds.), *Self-Governing Socialism*, 2 vols. (White Plains, NY: International Arts and Sciences Press, 1975)

Jambrek, Peter, *Development and Social Change in Yugoslavia: Crises and Perspectives of Building a Nation* (Farnborough, Hants: Saxon House, 1975)

Kardelj, Edvard, *Democracy and Socialism* (Belgrade: Yugoslav Review, 1978)

Ramet, Pedro, *Nationalism and Federalism in Yugoslavia, 1963–1983* (Bloomington, Ind.: Indiana University Press, 1984)

Rubinstein, Alvin Z., *Yugoslavia and the Nonaligned World* (Princeton, NJ: Princeton University Press, 1970)

Rusinow, Dennison I., *The Yugoslav Experiment, 1948–1974* (Berkeley, Cal.: University of California Press, 1977)

Shoup, Paul, *Communism and the Yugoslav National Question* (New York: Columbia University Press, 1968)

Stanković, Slobodan, *The End of the Tito Era: Yugoslavia'a Dilemmas* (Stanford, Cal.: Hoover Institution Press, 1981)

Ulam, Adam B., *Titoism and the Cominform* (Westport, Conn.: Greenwood Press, 1971)

Zukin, Sharon, *Beyond Marx and Tito: Theory and Practice in Yugoslav Socialism* (London and New York: Cambridge University Press, 1975)

Index of Names

Index of Subjects

Administrative acts, protection from:
Albania, 40; Bulgaria, 52; China, 76;
Czechoslovakia, 112; GDR, 130;
Hungary, 147-8; Mongolia, 181;
Poland, 198; Rumania, 212; Soviet
Union, 248; Vietnam, 267;
Yugoslavia, 295

Administrative structure: Albania, 38;
Bulgaria, 50; China, 71; Cuba, 92;
Czechoslovakia, 110-11; GDR, 128;
Hungary, 145; Korea (DPR), 158;
Laos, 171; Mongolia, 180; Poland,
196-7; Rumania, 210; Soviet Union,
223-4, 231-2, 242-4; Vietnam, 265;
Yugoslavia, 292-3

Albania and: China, 41; CMEA, 40-1;
CSCE, 42; Soviet Union, 40-1;
WTO, 40-1; Yugoslavia, 40-2

All-people's state, 5, 35, 44, 64, 137, 139-
40, 219

Anti-Sovietism, 120, 140

Armed forces
strength and composition of:
Albania, 42; Bulgaria, 53; China, 81;
Cuba, 97-8; Czechoslovakia, 114;
GDR, 135; Hungary, 149; Korea
(DPR), 162-3; Laos, 173-4;
Mongolia, 182; Poland, 201;
Rumania, 217; Soviet Union, 252-3;
Vietnam, 269-70; Yugoslavia, 298;
supreme command of: Albania, 11,
42; China, 62, 69, 82; Cuba, 85, 91;
Czechoslovakia, 108; GDR, 135;
Korea (DPR), 157; Poland, 196;
Rumania, 209; Soviet Union, 241;
Vietnam, 264; Yugoslavia, 297

Bloc parties, 18-19; Bulgaria, 44, 46, 48;
China, 64-5; Czechoslovakia, 100,

104; GDR, 120-1, 124, 126-7; Korea
(DPR), 155; Poland, 184, 189, 193;
Vietnam, 260-1;

Brezhnev Doctrine, 26, 113, 215, 249

Buddhism (Buddhists), *see* religious
communities

Bulgaria and: CMEA, 52; Soviet Union,
52; WTO, 53; Yugoslavia, 52-3

Castroits, 85-6, 88, 97

Central Military Commission (China),
62, 69, 82

Central People's Committee (Korea,
DPR), 156-7

Charter 77 (Czechoslovakia), 106

China and: Albania, 78; Japan, 78; Non-
Aligned Movement, 81; Rumania,
79; Soviet Union, 77-9; USA, 77-80;
Vietnam, 79; Yugoslavia, 79

Christian associations (Poland), 188-9

Chronicle of Current Events, 231

Chuch'e, 151-2, 154-5, 158, 161-2

Cominform, 40, 296

Comintern, 25-6, 45, 57, 176

Committe for Culture (Bulgaria), 47

Committees for the Defence of the
Revolution (Cuba), 89-90

Communism, building of, 1, 3, 5, 21, 23,
63, 88, 118, 152, 155, 219, 229, 247

Communist Parties, in federal states:
Czechoslovakia, 103-4; Soviet
Union, 226, 228, 234; Yugoslavia,
274-6;
and regional interests, 17-18, 276

Communist Party: leading role of, 7, 8,
13-14, 18-19, 22; Party of Labour
of Albania, 33-4; Bulgarian
Communist Party, 44; Communist
Party of China, 55-6, 61-2;

302

Communist Party of Cuba, 85;
Communist Party of
Czechoslovakia, 100, 102, 105;
Socialist Unity Party of Germany,
116, 118; Hungarian Socialist
Workers' Party, 137, 139, 141, 143;
Workers' Party of Korea, 151; Lao
People's Revolutionary Party, 165;
Mongolian People's Revolutionary
Party, 175; Polish United Workers'
Party, 184, 189; Rumanian
Communist Party, 203; Communist
Party of the Soviet Union, 219, 225,
226, 239; Communist Party of
Vietnam, 256-7; League of
Communists of Yugoslavia, 272, 277;
organisation of: Albania, 35;
Bulgaria, 46; China, 61; Cuba, 88;
Czechoslovakia, 103-4; GDR, 118-
19; Hungary, 139; Korea (DPR),
154; Laos, 168; Mongolia, 177;
Poland, 187; Rumania, 204; Soviet
Union, 222, 226-8; Vietnam, 259;
Yugoslavia, 274-5; recruitment and
membership of: 2; Albania, 35;
Bulgaria, 45; China, 61; Cuba, 87-8;
Czechoslovakia, 103; GDR, 118;
Hungary, 139; Korea (DPR), 154;
Laos, 168; Mongolia, 177; Poland,
186-7; Rumania, 205; Soviet Union,
229; Vietnam, 259; Yugoslavia, 274-
5; relationship with the CPSU:
Albania, 35; Bulgaria, 46; China, 63-
4; Cuba, 88; Czechoslovakia, 104;
GDR, 120; Hungary, 140; Korea
(DPR), 155; Laos, 169; Mongolia,
177; Poland, 187-8; Rumania, 206;
Vietnam, 260; Yugoslavia, 277-8;
supreme organs, 10-12: Albania, 35;
Bulgaria, 46; China, 61-2; Cuba, 88;
Czechoslovakia, 103; GDR, 119-20;
Hungary, 140; Korea (DPR), 154;
Laos, 168-9; Mongolia, 177; Poland,
187; Rumania, 205; Soviet Union,
222, 226-7; Vietnam, 259-60;
Yugoslavia, 275-6;
Communist world movement, 26, 35,
64, 104, 155, 177, 206, 277
Community of socialist states, *see*
socialist world system
Conference on Security and
Co-operation in Europe (CSCE),
see country entries

Constitutional Council (Hungary), 147
Constitutional courts: Czechoslovakia,
24, 111-12; Poland, 24, 199;
Yugoslavia, 24, 294-5
Constitutional and Judicial Commission
(Rumania), 212
Constitutionality of laws, supervision
of, 24-5: Albania, 37, 40; Bulgaria,
49; China, 68; Cuba, 90; GDR, 129;
Hungary, 147; Poland, 199;
Rumania, 212; Soviet Union, 247-8;
Yugoslavia, 294-5;
Constitutions, 5, 11, 25, 27: Albania, 33-
4; Bulgaria, 44-5; China, 55, 57-8,
65; Cuba, 85; Czechoslovakia, 100,
102; GDR, 116-18; Hungary, 137-8;
Korea (DPR), 151-3; Mongolia, 175-
8; Poland, 184, 190; Rumania, 203-4,
209; Soviet Union, 219, 232, 234;
Vietnam, 255, 257; Yugoslavia, 272,
244, 276, 285; functions of, 23-4
Control, 9, 10, 12-13, 33, 36-9, 47, 51-2,
90, 93, 95, 103, 109, 126-8, 131, 141,
154, 166, 176, 194-5, 211, 213, 230,
238, 242, 247, 261, 264, 267, 295; *see
also* dual subordination
Council of Mutual Economic Assistance
(CMEA), *see* country entries
Courts of law, composition and
functions of: Albania, 39; Bulgaria,
51; China, 75; Cuba, 94;
Czechoslovakia, 111; GDR, 130;
Hungary, 147; Korea (DPR), 158-9;
Mongolia, 180; Poland, 198-9;
Rumania, 211; Soviet Union, 245;
Vietnam, 266-7; Yugoslavia, 294-5
Croatian crisis, 276, 286
Cuba and: Angola, 97; CMEA, 95;
Ethiopia, 97; Latin America, 96-7;
Non-Aligned Movement, 97; Soviet
Union, 96, 98; USA, 96; WTO, 98
Cuban crisis, 98, 161, 249
Cultural Revolution (China), 41, 46, 57,
59, 60, 65-6, 71, 75, 78, 82, 162
Czechoslovakia and: CMEA, 113-14;
CSCE, 106; Federal Republic of
Germany, 114; Soviet Union, 112-
14; WTO, 103, 113-114

Decision-making, by consensus
(Yugoslavia), 273, 276, 286
Delegation and assembly system
(Yugoslavia), 287-9

Human and civil rights, protection and
limitation of, 24: China, 66-7, 75-76;
Cuba, 94-5; Czechoslovakia, 106;
GDR, 123, 129; Hungary, 142;
Mongolia, 181; Poland, 198-9; Soviet
Union, 229-30, 247; Vietnam, 267;
Yugoslavia, 295
Hungary and: capitalist countries, 149;
CMEA, 148; Rumania, 148-9; Soviet
Union, 148-9; WTO, 148-9

Intelligentsia, 55, 60, 66, 86, 116, 137,
139-40, 142, 153, 166, 175, 177, 188,
191, 205, 219, 229, 231, 256-7, 261,
276
Intervention in (invasion of):
Afghanistan, 79, 250-1;
Czechoslovakia, 26, 41, 78, 103, 113,
148, 200, 207, 214, 217, 249, 296;
Kampuchea, 79, 252, 268
Islam (Muslims), *see* religious
communities

Korea (DPR) and: China, 161-2;
CMEA, 159; Non-Aligned
Movement, 161, Republic of Korea,
160-1, 163; Soviet Union, 161-2;
WTO, 159
Kosovo (Kosovo-Albanians), 41, 284,
286

Laos and: China, 171-3; CMEA, 172;
Kampuchea, 169, 172; Soviet Union,
172; Thailand, 173; USA, 173;
Vietnam, 166, 169, 172-4
Law, conception and functions of, 22-4,
76
Legislature, composition of: Albania,
People's Assembly, 36; Bulgaria,
National Assembly, 48; China,
National People's Congress, 67;
Cuba, National Assembly of
People's Power, 90; Czechoslovakia,
Federal Assembly, 106; GDR,
People's Chamber, 16, 123-4;
Hungary, Parliament, 143; Korea
(DPR), Supreme People's
Assembly, 156; Laos, Supreme
People's Assembly, 170; Mongolia,
Great people's Khural, 178; Poland,
Sejm, 192-3; Rumania, Grand
National Assembly, 208; Soviet
Union, Supreme Soviet, 240-1;

Vietnam, National Assembly, 263;
Yugoslavia, Assembly of the SFRY,
287-90; constitutional powers of, 10,
23-4: Albania, 36-7; Bulgaria, 48-9;
China, 68-9; Cuba, 90-1;
Czechoslovakia, 106-7; GDR, 14,
124-5; Hungary, 144; Korea (DPR),
156; Laos, 170-1; Mongolia, 178-9;
Poland, 194-5; Rumania, 208; Soviet
Union, 240-1; Vietnam, 263;
Yugoslavia, 14-15, 290-1; permanent
organ of: Albania, Presidium, 37;
Bulgaria, Council of State, 49;
China, Standing Committee, 68-9;
Cuba, Council of State, 91;
Czechoslovakia, Presidium, 107;
GDR, Council of State, 126;
Hungary, Presidential Council, 144;
Korea (DPR), Standing Committee,
156; Mongolia, Presidium, 179;
Poland, Council of State, 195-6;
Rumania, Council of State, 209;
Soviet Union, Presidium, 241-2;
Vietnam, Council of State, 263-4
Legitimation (of communist rule), 8, 16
Local government: Albania, 38-9;
Bulgaria, 50-1; China, 71-3; Cuba,
92-3; Czechoslovakia, 110-11; GDR,
128-9; Hungary, 146; Korea (DPR),
158; Laos, 171; Mongolia, 180;
Poland, 197-8; Rumania, 210-11;
Soviet Union, 244-5; Vietnam, 265-
6; Yugoslavia, 292-4

Macedonian question, 52-3, 297
Mao Zedong Thought, 55, 63
Market mechanisms, 7, 21, 22, 56, 102,
280
Market socialism, 7, 21, 273
Martial law (Poland), 187, 189, 191, 195-
6, 201, 251
Marxism-Leninism, 1, 8, 33, 55, 86-7,
120, 249, 257
Marxist-Leninist Party, *see* Communist
Party
Mass line, 33, 62, 66, 75, 151, 154-5
Mass organisations, *see* social
organisations
Mediation committees (China), 72, 75
Military Council of National
Redemption (Poland), 196
Modernisation policy (China), 35, 56,
61-2, 65, 81